HOW TO RAISE A HEALTHY HAPPY CHILD

Turn Your Childrearing Experience
Into an Exciting Adventure Filled with
Wonder, Joy, Love, Laughter and Fun!

Janet Stegman

Printed in the United States of America

ISBN: 978-1-959483-28-1 (sc)
ISBN: 978-1-959483-55-7 (hc)
ISBN: 978-1-959483-56-4 (e)

Library of Congress Control Number: 2023906778

Books by Janet Stegman

History
2023.02.24

CONTENTS

ACCOLADES

"I love love LOVE it! YES – You were magic! YES – You did change children's lives! This is well written. It grabbed my attention with such wonderful, not 'advice' but 'living lessons' on how to create a great kid. These chapters should be handed out to all parents of elementary school children."

> – Kim Garber, Teacher and YMCA Camp Director, Long Beach, CA

"I love the positive energy this book gives out. It's very uplifting and a good read for not just parents but humans in general on how to treat children."

> – Carol Ann Garnett, Mother and BEST Cousin, Los Gatos, CA

"This book had a huge impact on me. The chapter 'High Fives' opened my eyes. I was having a conflict with my 17-year-old son. I took the suggestions in this book, and rather than focusing on what was bothering me about his behavior and his attitude, I started focusing on his positives. I complemented him on how he was improving so quickly in his Tae Kwon Do class and praised him for following a workout program all on his own. Shortly after that, I noticed he had cleaned up his diet. I told him how glad I was for the changes he had made. When a friend who hired my son to do some work told me what a great job he had done and how he had impressed her with something that showed tremendous integrity, I told him how proud I was of him for those things. As a result of what I learned from this book, my relationship with my son has improved tenfold. Thank you, Janet Stegman."

> – Gabriel Russo, Chiropractor and Energy Worker, Grass Valley, CA

"Janet Stegman, author of *How to Raise a Healthy Happy Child*, has an amazing flair for writing. This book contains the common sense advice parents need to help their child grow up right. With lots of interesting stories, Stegman explains in detail how to parent correctly. If you have children, or any interaction with children, this book is for you!"

– Elliot Kay, Grass Valley, CA

"It takes real talent to break 'brilliant' into 'simple', and Janet Stegman has done just that – to the benefit of generations of children to come!"

– Keem Targeet, Mariposa, CA

DEDICATION

I dedicate this book to my partners in crime at YMCA Camp Ta Ta Pochon: Kim Garber, the Three Chartreuse Buzzards – Janie Ballantyne, Judy Trapani, and me, and my brother, Matthew Stegman, the main characters who showed me how much fun and worthwhile working with kids can be – leading them, teaching them, singing for and with them, making them laugh, and showing them unconditional love. Camp Ta Ta Pochon was an expansive paradise full of love, laughter, fun, personal growth, and showing children that a belief in God and striving to be the best person you can be is the best way to live

I also dedicate this book to my book coach, Les ("Les the Book Coach") Kletke, for all the countless hours of interviews, encouragement, advice, accolades, comfort, crazy funny humor, laughter, brilliant ideas, and divine guidance. This book would not have been written had it not been for Les' unending dedication and support.

I also dedicate this book to all the kids – now thriving adults - both at summer camp and who performed in all the theatrical productions I ever produced and directed, and to their loving and devoted parents. What fantastic times those were!

Lastly, I dedicate this book to Sharee and Pete Vistaunet, my second set of parents, who touched my life more deeply than they will ever know with their unending love and support -- for their other daughter.

FOREWORD

I want people to pick up this book. I love it! Janet Stegman is so amazing. HOW TO RAISE A HEALTHY HAPPY CHILD is a must read for parents who do not want to spend millions of dollars on counseling for their child, either during childhood or when they become an adult! Raising children is an arduous and precarious task, but Janet Stegman has just offered the solution. So simple.

I met Janet when she was a counselor and I was the camp director at YMCA Camp Ta Ta Pochon in the beautiful mountains of Redlands, California. My fondest memories of Janet were when she and her brother, Matt, performed 'Lammy' after *every* meal. The campers stomping the floor and banging their fists on the tables screaming "Lammy! Lammy!" didn't give them much choice! And then there was 'Horace' at *every* campfire. The kids screaming "Horace! Horace!" could be heard at Camp La Verne, the next camp over.

Before I explain, I ask that you please don't tell any of my other employees throughout my 55 years of working with hundreds of leaders that I think Janet Stegman is by far the best. Let me just say that Janet had an innate quality to magically mentor the most challenging, emotionally damaged children at our YMCA camp. She was the go-to counselor who was always able to find a way to make peace with and calm down these children in turmoil.

But that was just the tip of the iceberg. In this book, Janet Stegman shares some of her hilarious antics that became traditions at our camp. But not only did she share the best parts of herself with our campers, she took this beautiful natural skill and brought it forward in her life and honed it. She began healing not just children, but emotionally damaged adults as well, who were struggling with addiction and depression.

Through self-education and healing herself, along with tons and tons of life experiences, trials and tribulations, she has become a wonderfully effective counselor to those struggling in life.

The combination of Janet's experience working with and mentoring children at our summer camp and that of counseling adults out of addiction and depression, she has come to understand the basis for all their struggles – UNHEALTHY PARENTING!

This book has the answers to save your child from YOU. It really is extraordinarily simple. If you truly want a healthy, happy child, read this book and LISTEN to Janet: She knows what she is talking about! Read and practice these techniques. Isn't it funny how it's always the simple things in life that hold the most value? It's not rocket science. Both you and your child, and their future as an adult, will the happier for it. As you read this book, you will find some wonderful stories and antidotes as well. Following the simple instructions detailed in this book will help you become a GREAT PARENT and get your child raised into a HEALTHY HAPPY ADULT!

Kim Garber, Director of YMCA Camp Ta Ta Pochon during the MOST fun times at camp!

DISCLAIMER

The content of this book is for informational purposes only and is not intended to diagnose, treat, cure, or prevent any condition or disease. You understand that this book is not intended as a substitute for consultation with a licensed practitioner. Please consult with your own physician or healthcare specialist regarding the suggestions and recommendations made in this book. The use of this book implies your acceptance of this disclaimer.

INTRODUCTION

After fifteen years of counseling people with addiction, depression, and the pain from their past that still haunts them, I have learned firsthand what parents both do and omit to do that cause their children to suffer from agonizing mental, emotional, and even physical afflictions. I also have learned what parents do and don't do that enable their children to grow up into happy, joyful, fulfilled adults. Having acquired this knowledge and the tools I use to help people heal and move on with their lives, I decided to write a book for parents in order that they may circumvent the craziness and misery that can accompany childrearing and know right from the start what mind-sets and methods will allow you to raise a fully-functional, healthy, happy, child.

In addition to working extensively with clients on a wide spectrum of disorders, clients with vivid, detailed childhood memories of the parenting methods and treatment that wounded them so badly, and helping them let go of those disorders, I spent many years working with children, first as a camp counselor at a YMCA summer camp, and later as a teacher, director, and producer of musical theatre with children. These experiences enabled me to pinpoint the precise attitudes and actions and that instantly turn children from feeling frustrated and acting out to feeling content and engaging in constructive behaviors leading them to live their best life.

As you begin to read this book, you will notice that I don't dwell on the negative. I don't advise about "discipline" or, God forbid, "punishment". That is because I firmly believe those parenting modalities masquerade as parenting tools but are really destructive to a child's happiness and end up destroying their sense of self, free spirit, and enjoyment of life. I have learned that discipline and punishment only serve to make a person live with the sense of feeling controlled, punished, and wrong, which is not a good place for anyone to lead from, ever in their life.

I advocate for and focus on parenting skills that embody love, compassion, fun, affection, and interest in and caring about the child's feelings. I have found that this positive approach raises a well-adjusted person that doesn't need discipline or punishment; conversations suffice. When your child is on your side and organically wants to participate in their own upbringing, they don't feel the need to rebel; they simply are focused on doing what they love to do, developing themselves into the kind of person they want to be, and finding the things in life that tickle them and make them feel alive.

I firmly believe that if you implement the parenting methods described in this book, you can avoid the unpleasant and difficult dramas parents often encounter, and your child will not have the need to seek therapy or recovery later in life. Besides, I need a vacation. Seriously though, it is true what they say: "An ounce of prevention is worth a pound of cure." Engage in the practices set forth in this book, and you won't have to worry about fixing your child later.

As you work to make the suggestions in this book your own – learn them know them, and live them – it will not be an adversarial 18 years; rather, it will be a joyous adventure, full of wonder, amazement, laughter, and fun. You will wish it would never end. And you will see your child raise up into their best self: a fully-functional, healthy, happy, treasure.

CHAPTER 1

∙∙

A FROZEN PIZZA – THE GREAT MYTH THAT CHILDREN NEED MOLDING

**parenting is hard and children
don't come with instructions**

When a baby comes out of the womb, attached to its ankle with a thin braided rope is a 45 page instruction manual with detailed instructions on how to raise it. On page 1 of the manual is a diagram of your baby with a minute-by-minute, blow-by-blow guide on how to feed your baby so it will be healthy, make sure your baby is safe from harm, teach your baby what to do not to get hurt, comfort your baby so it feels safe, loved, and taken care of, and teach your baby right from wrong without leaving lifetime scars. On page 2 of the manual is everything you need to know to parent your child when the baby becomes a toddler and then a child: how to talk to them so they know you love him like crazy but understand that you are in the one charge, when to tell them everything you know about a subject and when to let them learn for themselves; and how to be their parent without being their friend. That manual contains everything you need to know in order to raise your baby into a fully-functional healthy and happy adult.

No? There is no manual attached to its ankle by a thinly braided rope? Dang. Well then, how's a parent supposed to know how to parent their child? Simply raise them the same way their parents raised you? Well, that *could* work. Except AA meetings are standing room only and with a mere 7% success rate, and every day one in ten Americans age 12 and older takes an antidepressant drug. In Canada, 86 doses of antidepressants are consumed daily per 1,000 people. The prisons are full of violent criminals; and domestic violence, child abuse, and drug use are all too prevalent in today's world. I have one word to describe the reason for this: Parents have been using as their parenting guide their memories of the way their parents raised them. How's that working for us?

I am now going to step off my soap box, quit berating the parents of the past, and present you, in the next 200 pages or so, with an instruction manual containing all the information you will need in order to raise your baby into a fully-functional healthy and happy child who will grow into a fully-functional healthy and happy adult.

Now why on earth would you want advice from Janet Stegman, a non-doctor, non-psychologist, non-psychiatrist, non-parent on how to raise your child? I'll tell you why: because I have spent the last 15 years successfully counseling people with addiction, depression and other self-destructive behaviors such as uncontrollable raging and being stuck in toxic and abusive relationships. I have learned through sitting across from those pouring their hearts out to me about how bad off they are and, incidentally, how badly their parents treated them exactly what it was that their parents did or omitted to do that led them to a life of addiction, depression, and other types of mental disorders.

I have had to learn what causes addiction and the other disorders so that I can get an idea of what I need to go back and clear from my clients' childhoods that their parents – consciously or unconsciously, knowingly or unknowingly – inflicted on them. I have had to learn how parents damage their child by omitting to act in a kind, loving and supportive way. I have had to figure out in minute detail what it is that parents do to their child and don't give their child that causes that child to grow up having addiction, depression, and other self-destructive behaviors. That has enabled me to determine what needs healing from my clients' past in order that I can heal that person of those painful feelings and destructive behaviors. I am writing this book and sharing what I have learned, because I have had tremendous success in helping people heal of their pain from the past and get happy. I have watched client after client lose their addiction, let go of their depression, quit raging, come into happy relationships, get married, have success in their career, and reconcile with their ex. I know 100% what causes addiction, depression, and rage, and what, on the other hand, will instill contentment, confidence, self-esteem, and an ability to create a life filled with joy. Plus, I was a child, and I had parents who turned me into an addict, and I had to seek recovery and figure out what exactly they did and didn't do that caused me to become an addict so I could undo it. That's what started the whole ball rolling for my healing work. I healed myself, and then I saw how drawn I was to and how much I enjoyed helping others do the same! And because what I learned from healing myself was so effective in guiding others to heal, I wrote a book about it so that everyone who wants to can get healed. My book is entitled *Sandcastles: Tools for Letting Go of Addiction and the Pain of the Past* and is available all over the place! I am very proud of my book, and how it is changing lives. I have decided to write this book so that parents can know in the first place what to and not to do to not turn their kid into an addict, but rather to send them off into adulthood with a positive outlook on life and a healthy self-esteem so that they can concentrate on creating a life of their dreams and never have to even think about what's wrong with them that they just can't seem to get it together!

my extensive experience working with children

For many years, I taught musical theatre to and produced musical productions with children – to rave reviews and happy actors. I was a camp counselor at a YMCA camp every year from age 17 to age 26, receiving letters from my campers telling me they wished I was their mother. What I'm trying to say is I *get* kids. I *get* what makes kids feel safe and loved; I get what infuses them with self-confidence, self-love, and joy. So listen to me, darn it, I know what I'm talking about!

anyone can cook a frozen pizza:
kids are more like that than you think

The great myth that most of us grow up with is that children come into the world a chunk of modeling clay that their parents need to mold into the perfect person. But as I have lived and learned and worked extensively with children and adults, I have come to know that this is not the case – one hundred percent, absolutely not the case. The truth is, children come into the world with predetermined qualities and characteristics: a personality, likes and dislikes, skills and talents, interests, sexual orientation, challenges, and areas that they will need to work on in themselves. If you try to mold, control, and change your child, they will rebel, and you will quickly see that you are carrying out the world's greatest exercise in futility. It will have the opposite effect. You will not have the outcome you are looking for: a healthy and happy child able to walk on their own two feet. You will not get the version of your child that *you* decide *you* want and at the same time a child who is healthy, happy, and free – free to be who they feel healthy and happy being. A child who, at 18 years old, leaves the house with a wave good-bye, and a "Thanks, Mom, thanks, Dad, I'm going to go pursue my dream career, have wonderful, healthy relationships and children, and live life as a fully functional, healthy, happy adult. I love you, and I will stay close. You don't need to parent me anymore; I'm good! You've been great! High five!"

The truth is, when you have this baby, this child, in your arms, he or she simply needs a welcoming and a warm upbringing. Think of your baby as a frozen pizza: It's already got everything it needs to turn out wonderful! A frozen pizza comes already made. It's got the dough in the right shape and the right size; it's got the sauce, the cheese, and all the toppings that you like. All you have to do is put it in the oven and make sure you don't over-bake it.

A child comes in with everything. All they need is warmth, love, kindness, affection, food, water, shelter, clothing, education, encouragement, compliments, and praise. They need to be taught to be safe, but they need to be taught in ways that will expand them, not harm or contract them, and they need to be given enough freedom to grow and mature into their own version of themselves.

a recipe for addiction

When you try to mold your child into having the personality you want them to have, liking the things you want them to like, participating in the activities you want them to participate in, enjoying the things you want them to enjoy, and pursuing the talents you want them to cultivate, you are setting both you and your child up for disappointment. If you get angry with them, put them down, punish them, or criticize them when they don't adhere to your agenda, that right there is a slippery slope into conflict and possibly addiction and depression for your child. That is a recipe for your child to eventually become someone who is depressed, lives with self-destructive tendencies, is incapable of holding onto a relationship, puts on massive amounts of weight, and/or finds themselves fired from one job after another.

Working with addicts for fifteen years has taught me what causes addiction. I have listened to clients tell me about their childhood and how they were hit by their parents, spanked, neglected, and abandoned. They have told me about their parents raging at them. I have been able to help them clear these wounds through the energy healing work. Once a client clears all that, they change into a fully-functional, healthy, happy adult. But until a person knows what is causing their addiction and does the healing work, they're stuck with wounds that will never heal. Those wounds are caused by being criticized, humiliated, yelled at, made fun of, ridiculed, put down in front of other people, having their feelings invalidated with mean sarcasm, being judged for their looks, being neglected, being abandoned, and being hit. Parents damage their children by trying to control them and teaching them through punishment. They harm their children by omitting to advocate for them, praise them, find good things to say to others about them, and overlook their shortcomings and focus on their strengths.

A parent needs to discipline their child, obviously. Parents need to deal with their child's shortcomings. But there are ways to do those things that don't leave painful scars on their child that last a lifetime. You don't want to teach your child with fear or violence. Those two teaching modalities leave a painful mark on the child for life. I offer strategies for how to parent your child with love, kindness, emotional support, understanding, compassion, praise, more praise, affection, humor, games, and soft-discipline.

cherish their feelings every minute of every day

Children are non-stop emoters. They have feelings every minute of the day – every second of every day. Those feelings are precious and need to be understood, acknowledged, and cherished. Children need to know that their parents *want* to know what they are feeling, and they need to know that their parents *get* that their feelings are not wrong, they just are. Children need to be encouraged to allow their feelings to come up and praised when they express them in an honest and healthy manner. Children need to know that it is healthy to embrace whatever feelings they have and allow themselves to feel them. Parents need to let their child know that those feelings are not going to hurt them, and that if they feel their feelings and don't judge them, those feelings will dissipate, and the child can then move on to the next experience. With that foundation of validation, a child will learn how to nurture and process their feelings and feel heard. And *that* will do them a whole lot of good for an entire lifetime.

It is important – SO IMPORTANT – for parents to cherish their child's feelings and give their child credence for having their feelings. Children need to be treated with the kind of respect you would treat a new boss, the minister that comes to dinner at your house, and the doctor making the house call – that *exact* kind of respect, that *exact* kind of reverence, that *exact* kind of appreciation. And awe.

"I love how you can entertain yourself with simple things like building a sandcastle!"

Find positive things to say about your child to your child – all day long, every day. You say, "Whaaaaat? What if I can't think of anything positive to say about them, because they've been a monster all day!" Find *something, anything*. There's gotta be *something* you like about them or that they have done well today! "What a cute smile you have!"

"I *love* your hugs!" "I love how you can entertain yourself with simple things like building a sandcastle!"

a question, a listen, and a hug

I went to summer camp from the time I was 8 until I was 26. I started out as a camper and then became a CIT (Counselor-in-Training) and then a counselor. Well, somehow I became known as the miracle worker for troubled campers. I usually had the older girls, but when a counselor would have trouble with one of their campers, they would say, "Have Janet talk to them" – excuse me, it was: "Have Janet *work* with them." That was the way it was said. So one camper, James, was making life miserable for his counselor and the other kids in his cabin, always acting angry and never doing what he was asked to do. It was a nightmare for his counselor. He asked me, "Janet, would you please work with James?" I loved it, "Sure, no problem!"

Instead of going to Archery, James, at the behest of his counselor, met me at the mess hall for a talk. It was just he and I in the mess hall. The cook was in the kitchen busily cooking. James and I sat next to each other on the couch, looking at the fireplace – it wasn't lit because it was daytime, but it was ready for an indoor campfire in case it rained. I put my arm around James' shoulder, turned to him – I remember it like it was yesterday – and asked him, "What's going on?" It was so easy. I simply asked him, "What's going on? Why are you acting like this? Is there something bothering you?" I made it clear that I felt great love for him. He started telling me all about what was going on at home. It was hard. He started to cry. This was the most precious, adorable, little boy you will *ever* met in your life. He was 10 or 11. I got the feeling no one had ever sat down with him and asked him how he was feeling. When he finished talking, I said to him, "I'm so sorry you have to go through that. That must be really hard." He said, "Yes, it is." We talked some more, and then I said, "Do you want a hug?" And he said, "Yeah." I gave him a big hug. I said, "I'll tell you what. If you feel bad, or if you feel like, you know, misbehaving, why don't you come talk to me? I'm here for you. I love you. I'll always be here for you." He said, "Okay." We spent 45 minutes talking in that mess hall, in front of the unlit fire place, and then he went back to the camp activities with his cabin mates. That little boy did not act out ever again after that, and he had a ball at camp from then on, swimming and hiking and canoeing with his buddies. His counselor was ecstatic. I mean, before we talked, James had been ruining the whole experience for him, but after I worked with James, he never acted out again – not one more time. We'd look at each other at campfire, and he'd know I was telling him, "You know I'm here for you." Sometimes I'd go over and say, "How you doin'? "Good." "Good. Wonderful. High five." It was at that moment that I knew that I knew the secret.

Two weeks ago, I was talking to one of the directors of that camp that I am still good friends with, Kim Garber, one of the angels in my life. And you know, I'm an entertainer, a comedian, and a singer, so I'd be in charge of the campfires. I would MC the campfire. I was in charge of who was going to do what skits, and I'd perform in some hilarious skits. The entire cast of counselors was hilarious in those skits. My brother and I would put on hilarious skits. And then, after it got dark, I would pull out my guitar and accompany the quiet camp songs, "Today", "Where Have All the Flowers Gone?", "Country Road", "Leaving on a Jet Plane". Everybody would sing. It was a magical time. Kim said, "I remember you made campfire magical. With your skits and your music, it was so wonderful, the kids, it touched their lives." And she said, "I remember you working with the kids – you were amazing!" She remembers that to this day. So, I think God gave me a gift for how to reach children, and what you need to do to comfort them, heal them.

I bet that to this day James remembers that talk we had – or should I say our kind, caring, honest, and compassionate breakthrough? Like I said, I used to get all kinds of letters from kids after they got home, and they would all say, "I had such a great time at camp. I miss camp sooo much! I miss you sooo much! I wish you were my mom." I had a great time at camp too, and I love that I was able to share with them my love for fun, comedy sketches, hiking, music, nature, and camp songs that we never forgot. We all saw what contentment looked like, and we all knew we could create the same thing with our own families when we grew up.

CHAPTER 2

....

HIGH FIVES: PRAISE YOUR CHILD EIGHT TIMES A DAY FOR SOMETHING

**you are the center of their world;
your words of praise mean everything to them**

How does it feel when somebody gives you a compliment? When your boss or your client finds something you did that was helpful and praises you for it, do you feel lifted up? Does it make you feel good about yourself? Does it make you feel worthy? Do you feel like you matter? Do you feel accomplished and talented? I do. It's human nature to feel appreciated when you receive a compliment.

kids need compliments too

It is a common misconception that children instinctively know how wonderful they are – how adorable and brilliant and precious. After all, it's the truth: They are all those things; they should already know it! The truth is, they don't know it. They *are* it, yes. But they don't *know* it. They need the people they look up to the most – the people that comprise their world – to affirm that they are worthy: worthy of being loved, deserving of being happy, able to be successful, capable of reaching their dreams, and talented enough to reach their highest creative potential. Able to achieve whatever it is they want to achieve.

Going back to summer camp, when I was a counselor, the kids would say to me, "You're so funny," "We love your singing," "We want you to do 'Lammy'. "We want you to do 'Horace'." They went nuts when

I did the funny skits. My brother and I did this skit called "Lammy". It was a skit within a song. It went back and forth between the girls and the boys. Like this:

Girls:	What's your name, little boy?
Boys:	My name is Lammy.
Girls:	Lammy what, little boy?
Boys:	Lammy kiss ya.
Boys:	What's your name, little girl?
Girls:	My name is Ida.
Boys:	Ida what, little girl?
Girls:	Ida wanna.

I'd do that cute melodramatic walk and then turn away really fast, shake my head and walk away. All of the verses, I'd make something funny up. The kids ate it up.

Girls:	What's your name, little boy?
Boys:	My name is Lammy.
Girls:	Lammy what, little boy?
Boys:	Lammy kiss ya.
Boys:	What's your name, little girl?
Girls:	My name is Mabel.
Boys:	Mabel what little girl?
Girls:	Mabel later.
Girls:	What's your name, little boy?
Boys:	My name is Lammy.
Girls:	Lammy what, little boy?
Boys:	Lammy kiss ya.
Boys:	What's your name, little girl?
Girls:	My name is Ollie.
Boys:	Ollie what little girl?
Girls:	Ollie right!

And then the campers would yell, "Kiss her! Kiss her! Kiss her! Kiss her!" And my brother was so funny, he would grab me, dip me, put his hand over my mouth, and pretend to kiss me. They'd cheer and laugh. I think that was the whole reason they loved "Lammy"! Anyway it was a lot of fun.

It got to the point where if there was a gap between sketches on the campfire stage, or when the kids were finished eating their breakfast, someone would start it, and all of the sudden, the entire camp was erupting into the chant: "Lammy! Lammy! Lammy! Lammy!" – at the top of their lungs – feet stomping, fists pounding on the tables, until my brother and I had no choice but to pop out from wherever we were sitting, usually on opposite ends of the campfire circle or mess hall and perform "Lammy". It was the highlight of the camp for everyone. That camp was literally over-bursting with joy and laughter during "Lammy".

The other hit of the week was "Horace" (pronounced "Horath"). The kids would chant: "Horath! Horath! Horath!" And, of course, how could we say no? For "Horace", I'd sit on my brother's lap with my arms under his, behind him; he'd be the arms and I'd be the voice. We'd tell the story of Horace the Lion. Horace was a pet lion who, one by one, ate each member of the family – one each evening. Everyone felt so sad hearing this story, until the end, when lo and behold one by one, each family member had reappeared, until everyone was back! You know what happened? "Horath burped!"

Making kids laugh and facilitating them to have a good time has been the highlight of my life. I mean besides playing Peter Pan, of course. But you know what? Same thing! It is Heaven to feel *that* appreciated, *that* wanted, *that* validated, and *that* complimented for entertaining people and making them laugh!

When the kids complimented my brother and me and the other counselors and told us how much fun we made camp for them, it sent my self-esteem through the roof. Every time I went to camp, my self-esteem would soar back up through the roof. I rode on the overtones of the high vibrations of summer camp all year – summers filled with love and laughter and affection and fun and appreciation and comedy and music and awesome entertainment and praise – until camp the next year. Even when the kids at school were mean to me – and they were mean to me – I knew I always had camp. And I knew I was great, because camp taught me I was great. My camping experience showed me what a talented entertainer I was. Receiving all that praise for my comedy and singing and acting made me feel ecstatic and really good about myself. The praise and acknowledgment I received for sharing my theatrical talents and the appreciation I was shown for the hard work planning campfires, guiding hurting campers back onto the right track, and providing pretty and heartfelt music helped me become the successful and happy person I am today. Or should I say, the "fully-functional, healthy, and happy" person that I am today. I struggled for many years with the fully-functional, healthy, and happy part, but I believe that because I was told at camp how magical I was, and because I knew beyond a shadow of a doubt that my parents wanted and loved me, I was able to overcome my problems and become ... all together now ... a fully-functional, healthy, happy adult.

Let's be honest: I'm just a big kid. I can tell you unequivocally, without a doubt, that praise, accolades, compliments, gushing, words of appreciation, acknowledgment of accomplishments, love, and fun is how you instill in children an in-their-cells default belief in their greatness. Not only in a thinking way, but in a forever residing in every-bone-in-their-body way as well, so that the belief that their life is important, that their feelings matter, and that they are terrific and talented and worthy and a precious gift to society is imprinted on their psyche. In indelible ink. That belief becomes the permanent, all pervasive, set-in-stone, baseline belief they have about themselves. Forever. They will carry it around with them wherever they go. They will never even have to think about it: They will simply inhabit that mindset 24/7. And when challenges come, their belief in their greatness and competence will override the triggers those challenges could conceivably present, and your child will, from a fully-functional, healthy, happy place, be able to solve those challenges.

When you tell a child something – *anything* – good about themselves, with feeling and a smile, and you mean it, and you give them a high five, it sends their self-esteem through the roof. And their zest for life. Let's say they win a relay race at the church picnic, and they come over to where you are sitting, and you yell, "All right!" and you give them a big hug and a high five. That will send their self-esteem to the moon!

Children want desperately to please their parents. Even later in life, when they're all grown up, they still want to please their parents.

You may think, "Oh, I don't know if I can think of anything good to say," think think think. Find *something. Anything.* All day long. They never get tired of it. Let's say they make pudding and bring it to you for you to have lunch. You say, "Oh, this is delicious! Thank you so much for my pudding! I *love* this pudding! You're the *best* pudding maker! And a *wonderful* son!" That will make them feel terrific about themselves. It will reinforce their instinct to be giving and caring and generous. Something like, "I *love* your hugs! You give the *best* hugs!" or "You finished your homework already?! Wow!! You're fast!! Can I see it? Let's make sure you got all the answers right." And then you look through their homework and say either, "Wow! Every single answer is correct! Good job! High five!" or "Oh wow! There's only one answer you need to go back and re-read the worksheet and find the right answer for. Nice job!! Let me know when you find it." Children *crave* positive feedback. They *crave* for you to acknowledge their accomplishments. Even if the accomplishments are tiny.

If you're in a group of people, and you acknowledge something wonderful about your child – even if it's something little, and the whole group swoons, "Oooooh wow!!" that will shoot their self-esteem all the way to Mars! "Johnny got an A in Math!" "Woooow! All right Johnny!!" You know what? Johnny's going to get an A⁺ next time. Because it felt *so* good to be acknowledged and praised for his accomplishment. That is when children strive to do their best – and fill with happiness and enthusiasm while they are striving – when they are acknowledged for their accomplishments and praised for their successes. *That* is how you raise a successful and accomplished child.

I would like to suggest that you go and get yourself a journal. Each day, when you have a moment to yourself – yeah, like that ever happens – just kidding, I know you can make time for yourself, it's important: Like my mom used to say, "You are your baby, too." Once you have it, open it up, and make a list of all the things you love about your child. Write down all the things your child did well that day; all the things your child did right: the kindness, generosity, affection, creativity, commitment to physical fitness, eating healthful foods – *anything* you can think of, just write it down. Then read the list out loud to yourself. I guarantee there will come a moment when one of those accolades will be the perfect thing to say. You'll be amazed how easy it is to simply pull one of them out of your back pocket. "Oh, you give the *best* hugs!" "Look how clean your room is! High five! Did you have help or did you do that all by yourself? You did that all by yourself? Wew wew! I'm so proud of you!!" or "...You had the courage to reach out for help? Wew wew! I'm so proud of you!!" It doesn't matter how they did it; however they did it, they succeeded, and they thrive on the acknowledgment of that success. That is the nourishment children need to live a life filled with self-esteem and accomplishment.

Imagine how you feel when you are praised. Now imagine how a child feels when the person who is their whole world – their parent – praises them. When someone gives you a compliment for something you did, you feel worthy of the praise. Your efforts are recognized. You feel good, and it improves your self-worth. Because children have no filters, they are able to imbibe your praise, relish it, drink it in, and allow it to dwell deep within, forever. Like when I went to summer camp, and I was showered with all that love and appreciation. That praise and acknowledgment of my accomplishments buoyed me through my entire school year until the next summer, when I would go back to camp, and fill back up with self-love.

When you praise your child, it goes straight to their heart. Your child is then able to live in their heart. When there are smiles and laughter and hugs and high fives, the gift you give your child is that extreme – it's that good. The greatest gift you can give your child is praise and acknowledgment. It's not easy being a child: You don't know stuff till you learn it. They need to know you see the good things they do and that you will show your appreciation for them.

Praise is ESPECIALLY powerful when it's in a group setting, because it lets the whole world know that Johnny is "brilliant!" When you tell a child they are brilliant, they become brilliant, and they will work hard and strive to do their best. But when you praise a child to others, it skyrockets their self-esteem – you won't even be able to fathom their achievements because you have done that. Those habits to foster success start early in life, and you are laying the groundwork for an accomplished child and then adult. So I say, make it a priority to get into the habit of praising your child for all the little things they do that are a positive contribution to life.

Remind yourself what a good thing you are doing for your child by praising them for their accomplishments, no matter how small. Think back on how you felt when someone complimented you. That is how your child feels when you compliment them. You can praise your child all day long, and it will not be too much. Your child will tell you if you are going overboard with the praise. Like I said, children have no filter, and if encouraged to say their honest feelings, they will do that! They will tell you if you are going overboard with praise. They will tell you how much fun you are. They will tell you how happy they are. They will tell you how much they love you! The kids at camp let me know how much they loved it when we entertained them and made them laugh! They let us know how badly they wanted my brother and me to do "Lammy".

Laugh. Have fun. Find the positives and say them. High fives all around.

CHAPTER 3

· ·

A GINGERBREAD HOUSE

the long-lasting negative effects of criticism

A child is like a gingerbread house: beautiful, brightly colored, multi-faceted, brilliantly designed, original, unique, perfect. But when you criticize a child, you tear off a part of the gingerbread house: You rip off a window pane; you demo the chimney; you chip away at the paint, until after a childhood full of criticism, that gingerbread house becomes a dilapidated fixer-upper. Nothing is left but crumbs and a dollop of frosting. If you criticize your child, you will end up inheriting a dysfunctional dilapidated fixer-upper. The gingerbread house will have disappeared; it will be an unrecognizable ghost of what it once was. After a childhood filled with criticism, your child will become just like that gingerbread house – a ghost of what it once was; unrecognizable as a human being; completely and utterly dysfunctional.

In order to survive and enjoy a modicum of success and happiness, the child of criticism will turn to food, alcohol, drugs, or other self-destructive behavior in order to block out the pain of the scars left from being torn down and criticized.

the top counter-productive strategies:
criticism, shaming and punishment

Criticism is the number one strategy to use if you want to never get your child to do what you want, or what he wants. The most counterproductive action you can take as a parent is to criticize your child – for anything. You may think that in order to teach your child right from wrong, it is your duty to let them know when they have done something wrong. But if you teach your child that what they did was wrong by criticizing them or their actions or behavior, for the rest of their life they will dig their heels in and specifically not do what it is you want them to do and specifically do exactly what it is you don't want them to do. That child will carry a resentment towards you for that to the grave.

If you criticize a child, they will believe they are bad and wrong and worthless. The good news is there are ways of correcting without criticizing. Even if you think you need them to know absolutely that they can never do again the thing they just did, the truth is that criticism will have the opposite effect. Even if they do what you want in order to please you or get you to approve of them or get you to love them or get you to stop criticizing them, your criticism will leave a scar on them the size of Montana, and in the end, your child will go in the opposite direction. A person NEVER wants to do something they've been criticized for not doing. A person NEVER wants to not do something they have been punished for doing. Criticism and punishment may seem like a great way to control your child: let them know who's boss, teach them to be a good person. But I am telling you, after 15 years of helping people heal from addiction and depression, I know beyond a shadow of a doubt that criticism and shame are counter-productive and destructive to a child's healthy development. If a child went a whole lifetime without being criticized, that child would make it out alive. If they are given love, support, supervision, clothes for their back, good food, quality time together, no criticism, no shaming, and guidance over punishment, the sky's the limit for how happy and successful that child can be, and the sky's the limit for how happy and successful that child can be as an adult, too.

an alternative to criticism

As an alternative to criticism, why not let your child know that you are not happy with what they did and why: Discuss the behavior and not the person. There's nothing wrong with a good old fashioned time out in their room. Take out all television sets, cell phones, and video games. Leave wholesome books. Tell them they can come out when they are ready to act in a respectful manner.

criticism leaves scars on a child that never leave

With their criticism, my parents stripped away all of my self-esteem. Their criticizing me taught me I was worthless and didn't deserve to be happy. It taught me that I was incompetent and had no ability to accomplish anything worthwhile. It held me back from reaching my highest potential in every area.

If your child doesn't succeed at something the first time, don't criticize, scold, or talk down to them; instead, give them words of encouragement to boost their self-esteem. Criticizing a young child can leave physical, mental, and emotional scars. A child who has been criticized can develop low self-esteem, self-destructive habits, anger, and addiction. Instead of expressing anger in healthy ways, they may become violent or turn to drugs and alcohol to calm their anger, all of which lead to ill health.

criticism in full swing when my parents split up

The criticism started in full swing when my parents split up and my dad moved out; that's when it became open season with my mother. With my father, the criticism came more in the form of excessive control and draconian parenting. When I became an adult and went to college in the same town, however, the flood gates opened, and my father's criticism began and never stopped.

MOM'S CRITICISM

leave your 2¢ worth at the door

Let your child learn their lessons without always adding your 2¢: They'll learn, I promise. Kids are smart and have their own intelligence telling them: "Note to self: 'Self, don't do that again.'"

One time in the fifth grade, I cheated on a social studies test – it was on the state capitals. But the way I chose to cheat made it painfully obvious that I was cheating. It was like I was screaming, "You there!! Teacher!! Over here!! Hey! Look at me – I'M CHEATING!! Can't you see?! I'm *CHEEEEEATING*!?" I laid my giant social studies textbook, I'm talking like a 3" thick textbook, over my cheatsheet – a piece of paper with the name of the capital city next to each state – underneath the book. And I'd lift that heavy ass book up every time I didn't know the answer to a question. Like I was begging to get caught. Don't ask me why I didn't just memorize the darn capitals the night before. That would have been too easy. Well, I was put in the dummy math class, so right there they showed me that I was dumb. I was preoccupied by my parents' misery around their miserable marriage – they were in marriage counseling and ended up splitting up less than a year later. My self-esteem was in the toilet from being bullied, ostracized, and made fun of every second of every day by the kids at school; and I was unhappy with myself for not knowing the secret to getting the kids in my class to like me. I felt lost and like a social reject and had no one who understood and could lift me out of my funk. I think I was just not in my right mind to study for a social studies test. Ya think? So guess what? I got caught. No, really? Yeah, big surprise. The teacher stomped over to where I was sitting and in front of the whole class plastered a giant "F" across my paper.

I had already learned BIG TIME on every level that I never wanted to cheat on a test again. I felt ashamed, embarrassed, humiliated, and confused about why I had cheated. I had already decided I didn't want to experience *those* feelings again. When my mother came to pick me up from school later that day, I got in the car and immediately confessed. "I cheated on my capitals test. The teacher caught me and gave me an F." Instead of being concerned that I might be feeling awful about what I had done, my mother immediately leapt to the jugular. "What?! You cheated on your test?! I can't believe it. My own daughter. What have I done wrong?!" All the frickin' way home. 20,000 lbs. of guilt and shame on a little 10-year-old sensitive empath for the entire 20-minute car ride. Not one time did my mother ask, "What made you decide to cheat? Were you worried about getting a bad grade and your dad and me being disappointed in you for it? What was going on with you that caused you to not have the willingness or the where-with-all to learn the names of the capitals before the test? Do you need help studying? I can help you every night; I don't mind."

The ONLY thing my mother's severe disappointment, being mortified, and harsh criticism did for me was tear down what minute shred of self-esteem and self-respect I was still able to hold onto. There was no compassion or understanding. There was no love. Only disgust, contempt, anger, judgment, disappointment, disdain, and disapproval. I was never given the chance to learn from my mistake and love myself through it. I was not given the opportunity to keep my head above water; I was so swiftly and brutally pounded into the ground by my mother's shaming right out of the gate.

I had just made a mistake, that was all. I made the mistake of getting caught, is what it was. My mother should have said to me, "How stupid was that of you to get caught? Why didn't you cheat in a way that you wouldn't get caught? Let me teach you some proper cheating skills so that you never get caught." I'm kidding, of course. But you see my point. It was one test, I was 10, and it was my first time cheating. Oh, let's call the newspapers! What I am trying to say is, before you strip your child of every ounce of self-esteem, ask yourself, "Do I really need to scar my child for life over this? Was her mistake so bad that I can't forgive her and help her learn from it, through understanding, words of wisdom, and compassionate guidance?"

coming to my doorway to criticize

After my father moved out, my mother would come to my doorway at night after I had gone to bed and criticize all the things I had done wrong that day and all the ongoing things I was doing wrong. "You left a *mess* in the kitchen." "Why did you get a job working for someone else? I need you at home cleaning *our* house and doing *our* laundry. I'll pay you!" Did she ever stop and think that maybe the reason I got a job outside the house was to get away from her?! So now, later in my life, I have problems allowing myself to make good money at a job outside of my mother's house, because I feel I am bad for working outside of her house. Only she's gone now, so that's no longer possible. But the belief and punishment have remained a lifetime. And don't even get me started about cleaning my house and doing my laundry.

My mother also at our doorway conference would tell me all her problems and fears. Like I could do anything about them. I guess I saved her a lot of money on therapist fees.

a full-blown addict at 17

At 17, after a childhood wrought with criticism, punishment, and being made to play the venting receptacle, I emerged a full-blown addict. I was addicted to food – bingeing out of control, and relationships – with boys, and then men. It was serious – seriously out-of-control serious. Whether I was criticized as a child or as an adult by my parents, it was equally damaging and left scars that have lasted a lifetime. Their barrages of criticism were like whippings, leaving deep and painful scars that take a lifetime to heal.

childhood criticism causes a person to vibrate in "defective"

Having been criticized as a child, I did not have a healthy self-esteem. Even through my adult years, I could never allow criticism to bounce off me: I couldn't stop it from permeating every inch of my being, like honey in a honeycomb, absorbing, holding onto, and believing any criticism that came my way. I was a honeycomb filled with low self-esteem. I vibrated in "defective". No matter how old I got, every time someone would criticize me, it would re-injure me, again and again. It felt like someone was throwing salt in the wounds of my childhood that never had a chance to heal.

to a child of criticism, any hint of correction is magnified 100 times

Throughout my life, every time I would have an encounter with a person in which something they said or did hinted, *hinted* at even the slightest bit of criticism, it would go in me like a knife - "OOOOOOH" (picture me bent over holding my stomach). Seeing how hurt I was, they would say to me, "I didn't mean that in a critical way," "OHHHHHHH. It sure felt like you were criticizing. It hurts so bad." The hurt was magnified 100 times anytime anyone said anything the least bit critical or off-putting or was simply suggesting a way in which they felt I could better myself. I was sensitized to criticism.

I lived in fear of being criticized

My whole life, I have led from a place of, "I'm so afraid you're going to criticize me! Please don't criticize me! I can't handle it!" I would not complete things I started, because I was so afraid of being criticized or made fun of or put down about it. I would not make myself visible; I would not put myself out in the public eye; I would not do anything worldly successful. I led from "I'm so terrified of being criticized; I just want to hide over here behind this couch."

criticism does the opposite of what you intend

This needs to be in gold letters on your wall: Criticizing a child is the quintessential exercise in futility. Not only does it *not* get you what you want, which is a well-trained, healthy, happy child, it does the exact opposite and creates a self-loathing, contracted, fearful child and then adult, with little to no self-esteem, and a belief that they are worthless, useless, incompetent, and undeserving of any kind of happiness or success.

plan a or plan b

You can implement Plan A in parenting your child, or Plan B.

Plan A is: Criticize everything you don't like that your child does. Let them know every time they make a mistake what a bad mistake they made; train them with criticism, put-downs, and sarcasm; make sure you let them know everything they're doing wrong so they can learn.

Plan B is: Go under the assumption that your child is a blank slate learning what they need to learn to become a functional, successful, accomplished, self-loving, and self-respecting adult. Assume that everything they do they do with good intent and are using the best knowledge they have. You treat them with the utmost respect when teaching them.

acknowledge the positive
and make suggestions

If there is something you need to tell your boss about how the company could improve the company's coffee maker, you don't go into his office and say, "This design sucks. You're the most incompetent coffee maker designer that ever lived. You should get a job screwing caps on toothpaste tubes instead!" No! You go in and say, "This coffee maker has a beautiful design. I love the way the coffee pours out quickly and smells so wonderful as you're pouring it and tastes so good. I just have one suggestion: Maybe you could add a button where if you want to add a flavor, you can."

You will hear, "Ooh, good idea!"

You must treat your child with the same reverence and respect with which you treat your boss and the minister that comes to dinner and the doctor making a house call. You must teach with love and praise. You must tell your child what they did right. Everything you want to teach them, sandwich with seven compliments for every correction. "I love the way you helped me get Junior into the car seat before getting into the car yourself. You're such a good big sister! Oh, by the way, could you put your seatbelt on? Okay! Thanks! You're the best!"

There is always, *always* a way to say something, a way to get your point across to your child – or to another adult – with an attitude of appreciation and acknowledgment of their wisdom and a suggestion.

instead of criticism, try a gift

Instead of criticism, try a gift. "If you get in the car by a quarter to eight this morning, there will be an ice cream cone stop on the way home! Start thinking about what flavor you'd like." Or "I have a present for you because you were so kind to your brother. Here's a Superball."

parables are an earthly story
with a Heavenly meaning

Children love stories. The Bible is full of stories. Jesus taught with parables because people love listening to stories. Parables are imagination theatre and so were the best way for people to really imbibe his lessons. Teach what you want to teach using parables and stories.

and humor

Children *love* to laugh at funny stories: They will listen all day long to your funny stories. Funny faces, funny noises, funny characters – teach with humor and your child will *love* the lesson!

don't tell your child what bad things
are going to happen to them

Telling a child what bad things are going to happen to them teaches them that bad things are going to happen to them. And you know what happens when a person believes that bad things are going to happen to them? Right? It's not rocket science. You've heard of a "self-fulfilling prophecy". Well, it's more true than you know. "You're going to fall and break your neck if you climb on that roof." "You're going to get sick if you go outside in this cold." "You're going to catch pneumonia if you don't put on a coat." "You're going to flunk all your classes if you don't do your homework." "You" "You" "You" "This bad thing is going to happen to *you...*"

you'll be the death of me

My father had a client whose mother told him every time she was upset with him for his whole life, "You'll be the death of me." He was in his 50s when she died. After his mother died, he never left the house again. Because he believed he was the cause of her death.

Wouldn't it be better to say, "You're going to get all As if you keep finishing your homework every night and doing a good job!" "You're destined for greatness – I can tell you that right now! Just listening to you practice the piano tells me that! I loved *Fur Elise*! Play it again! I just love it!" "Wow! You beat me! I can't believe how fast you can run! You could be an Olympic runner!! You're amazing!" That teaches them they can achieve anything they put their mind to.

criticism teaches criticism

Before I began to study the art of healthy relationships – the art of how not to push people away, the art of how to expand people instead of contract them, the art of how to love someone so that they feel loved and not attacked, communication skills and the merits of "I" messages rather than "you" messages, and that finding fault serves no purpose – I was very critical in my relationships. And why was that? Because that was what I had learned from my parents. That was all I knew. Thank God I was able to open my mind to new ways of treating people! But I want to tell you that when you criticize your child, you are teaching them to criticize those around them everywhere they go.

how did it feel when
someone criticized you?

Do you remember when someone criticized you? Put you down? Found fault with you? Did it empower you or did it contract you? Did it hurt your feelings to the point where you couldn't learn the lesson that was there for you to learn? Did it make you feel bad about yourself? Did the hurt last an awfully long time? Well, for me the answer to all those questions is a resounding YES! Being criticized has never helped me see the error of my ways and to change. All it ever did was re-introduce the pain from the past, and I ended up feeling worthless. The times I benefited from being guided in the right direction were when I was guided in the right direction with sandwiches: suggestions embedded in love, compliments, and appreciation.

Even a "Did you learn anything from what happened at school today?"

"Yes, yes, I did."

"What did you learn?"

"I learned that I need to study and memorize the material so that I don't feel the need to cheat. I learned that even if I don't get a good grade, it's better than cheating and probably getting caught."

"Do you feel that you will learn more from studying the material, which you will remember for the rest of your life, than from cheating and getting a good grade based on a lie?"

"If I memorize my capitals, then all my life, I will remember that Tallahassee is the capital of Florida!"

"That's right!"

Or how about, "Is my depression and the fact that the kids are mean to you at school, oh, and your father and me fighting loudly every night in our bedroom causing you to not be able to concentrate on your homework? Is that what is causing you to leave your body and not have the ability to concentrate so you can study for tests and do your homework?"

I was *such* a good kid. I *so* wanted to please my parents. I never drank or smoked; I never did drugs. I got good grades, told the truth. I wasn't perfect; I cheated a couple more times in high school by asking my friend for the answer when I didn't know it. No one is perfect. We're all just trying to find our way in life. The last thing we need is to be shamed for our mistakes, or shall I say our lessons; the last thing we need is to be yelled at and punished for simply living and learning. Growing up is tough enough without the wrath of a disappointed parent in your face all the time.

Before you act, before you speak, imagine yourself walking a mile in your child's moccasins. And then take a joke from your joke book and tell it. Tell it twice. And then remember the time once before when you made a mistake and learned from it and tell the story. And then laugh about it together. Laughter and humility ARE the BEST medicine!

CHAPTER 4

....

THE IMPORTANCE OF TOUCH

**nothing says I love you
like a tender touch**

Do you ever feel sad about something, and then someone gives you a hug and you feel instantly better? Amazingly and miraculously peaceful inside? There is something magical about touch. Nothing says I love you like a hug, someone holding your hand, a loved one touching your face, or a few minutes of snuggling.

We all need touch; we all need affection. In years past, parents were warned against picking up and holding their baby when it cried for fear the baby would *always* want to be held when it was scared or crying. "Let the baby cry herself to sleep; otherwise, she will expect to be held every time she cries." Seriously? And? Where is the harm in that? Where is the love in that? By all means, parents, if your baby is crying, PICK IT UP AND HOLD IT! Rock him until he falls asleep. If that baby is not comforted when he cries, he will form a life-long belief that no one cares about his feelings, that he is all alone in life and isolated, and that life is a cold, dark, terrifying place. That is not a good place to start.

What I have observed in my counseling practice while working with clients with addiction and depression is that the common thread among them is a lack of affection – a lack of positive, loving, nurturing touch. Not only did they not get the positive compliments, praise, and attention they needed, but they also were deprived of the necessary loving touch. Hugging, cuddling, holding hands, piggy-backs, sitting on a parent's lap. Touch is not icing on the cake for a child; it is not an extra added benefit from their parents: It is a need like air, shelter, nutritious food, and clean water.

We've all heard about the horrible 1944 experiment in which half the babies in a hospital were held and half were not. The babies who were not held died, and the ones who were held lived. I am mortified that someone would design such a cruel, cold-hearted "experiment" knowing the grave consequences it might produce. St. Pauls VX Community (https://stpauls.vxcommunity.com/cms/learn) tells the tragic story:

> In the United States, 1944, an experiment was conducted on 40 newborn infants to determine whether individuals could thrive alone on basic physiological needs without affection. Twenty newborn infants were housed in a special facility where they had caregivers who would go in to feed them, bathe them and change their diapers, but they would do nothing else. The caregivers had been instructed not to look at or touch the babies more than what was necessary, never communicating with them. All their physical needs were attended to scrupulously and the environment was kept sterile, none of the babies becoming ill.

The experiment was halted after four months, by which time, at least half of the babies had died at that point. At least two more died even after being rescued and brought into a more natural familial environment. There was no physiological cause for the babies' deaths; they were all physically very healthy. Before each baby died, there was a period where they would stop verbalizing and trying to engage with their caregivers, START HEREgenerally stop moving, nor cry or even change expression; death would follow shortly. The babies who had "given up" before being rescued, died in the same manner, even though they had been removed from the experimental conditions.

The conclusion was that nurturing is actually a very vital need in humans. Whilst this was taking place, in a separate facility, the second group of twenty newborn infants were raised with all their basic physiological needs provided and the addition of affection from the caregivers. This time however, the outcome was as expected, no deaths encountered.

The book, *The Family Bed* by Tine Thevenin, advocates for allowing children to sleep in the family bed until they request to sleep in their own. I don't advocate one way or the other, but I do recommend parents read the book and come to their own decision.

Jane Sheppard, Certified Parenting Coach and Functional Medicine Health Coach, writes a fascinating article in her blog, "The Family Bed Defended", in which she explains how to keep the family bed safe for babies and children. She points out that children go all day having every need met, and then all of a sudden they are cast into a dark room to spend the night all alone. She writes:

> Maria Montessori said that "If you want to understand the needs of the child, observe and study the child." It isn't hard to realize that your child needs you at night as well as during the day. How confusing it is to a child to be hugged and kissed, have their needs and wants attended to during the day, only to be pushed away at night. Your child's cries, nightmares, and fears of the dark are reminders that they are not meant to be left alone. When a child is left to "cry it out" in his or her own bed the parent may assume that the child has learned to sleep alone. What the child has really learned is that their cries were not answered. Their needs not met. And what appears to be a well-adjusted child sleeping in her own bed may be a child that has learned not to ask for help.

touch is *the* most necessary showing of love to a child

Touch is *the* most nourishing showing of love and nurturing a child can receive. Physical nurturing is every bit as essential to a child's health as spiritual, emotional, and mental sustenance. Touch is everything to a child. Touch is a natural phenomenon – a natural, God-given phenomenon that when there's a loving intention in the touch, it improves your body chemistry and raises your spiritual vibration. Your inner state bursts into one of feeling loved, supported, wanted, nurtured, and hopeful. And happy!

You can use words to communicate how much you love someone, how much you support them, and how great you think they are until you're blue in the face. But a single touch will transmit those sentiments in the blink of an eye. A touch of a hand communicates that message in a heartbeat; it shoots it straight into the veins where it gets absorbed immediately into the heart. Kind words are very nice, but you still have to wait until your mind transmits them to your body: With a gentle caress on the shoulder, your heart instantly fills with joy.

affection learned

I did not come from an affectionate family. When I was a little girl, I had terrible, *terrible* stomach aches. I remember when I was five sitting on the carpet in the corner of the dining room writhing in pain from a stomach ache. When my mother walked by, I cried, "Mommy, my tummy hurts." She said, "I'm sorry, I wish there was something I could do." A day or two later, my dad had me up on his shoulders as he was taking me down the ramp to summer day camp, and I was screaming, "Daddy, my tummy hurts! My tummy hurts!" My dad turned around and took me to the doctor. The doctor then sent me to the hospital where they did a whole battery of tests and other, unspeakable, tests. Do you think anyone ever asked me what was going on at home? After 12 days in the hospital, they decided I had an ulcer and sent me home with a bottle of little white pills.

When I was a junior in high school, I met these two fellas in the marching band – the sweetest, most darling boys, two years younger than I was – and we all were just affectionate with each other. I'd sit on their laps in the band room and on the bus on the way to the football games. We'd walk around campus arm in arm, even though we were just friends. I think we kissed a little too. But I just thought, "Oh, this is just so nice! I like this!" That was my first introduction to affection, and I'll never forget it. I thought I was very strange, but now I understand that I was simply finally getting the affection I had been craving my whole life.

And then, of course, when I got to college, I found the world of dating and making out and all that stuff. Yes, you are correct, I did love it.

When I was 19, I went to Overeaters Anonymous, and all of a sudden, everybody hugged. I thought, "What is this hugging thing?" I mean, they hugged each other, often – hello hugs, good-bye hugs, I-understand-what-you're-going-through hugs. Soon it was we all hugged each other, and I got to learn more about how much I loved affection. It changed my life for the better enormously. In short order, I became a *very* affectionate person. I began to live in the world of nurturing touch – hugging, cuddling, making out (ooooooh!).

When I became a camp counselor, I would hold the little campers' hands on the way to the mess hall, put them on my lap during campfire, hug them good-night. They had *loved* it. Those are the ones who wrote to me from home, after camp was over, and said they wished I was their mother!

Later on when I was an adult, I told my therapist about my memory from when I was five when I told my mom how much my tummy hurt and she said, "I'm sorry, I wish there was something I could do." My therapist said, "There was something she could have done." "What?" I asked. My therapist replied, "She could have said, 'Come here and let me hold you.'" I can't be sure, but I think my stomach aches were caused in part by a lack of tender touch. I know my mom touched me when I was a baby, like when a mother holds her baby to carry her around and change her diaper and go out places – I've seen pictures. But there was no tender bonding cuddling, holding, or hugs in my family. One time when I was older, I asked my mother, "Why didn't you hug me and hold me more?" She said, "I didn't know you needed that." So you see, it wasn't that my mother was purposely depriving me of affection: She simply did not know that children needed constant affection and touch. She raised me with the same amount of affection she was raised with.

So I'm not blaming my mother: I am simply sharing what I have learned about how incredibly important loving touch is to a child's well-being.

And now, as you can imagine, I am super affectionate in my life: I mean, I'll hug strangers if they'll let me. I hug my dogs, I cuddle my dogs. I cuddle my kitty. And I LOVE it!! I really feel the difference between then and now; after having gone so many years without it, I see the huge change in my emotional state. When someone holds me, I notice the change in my body chemistry immediately. When someone hugs me, touches me, when I cuddle my pets, it immediately lifts my spirits. My endorphins go crazy! In a good way of course. I feel happy, I feel loved, I feel nurtured. I feel hopeful. I feel self-esteem through the roof! All the good things.

include touch in all aspects of parenting

I reiterate, for gosh sakes, PEOPLE, if your baby cries, pick it up and hold it. Who cares if it's 4:00 in the morning. You can't give a baby too much love. And to that out-of-touch mythological axiom that if you hold your baby when it cries, it will become spoiled and want to be held every time it cries, I say, "Yeah, AND? Is that so bad?" What if we were held every time we felt sad or scared? Would that be the end of the world?! I think not. I think it would be a little piece of Heaven.

touch all around

When a child is upset, invite them to come over and sit on your lap. Hold them until they feel comforted. You can always ask your child when they feel sad, "Do you want a hug?" Smile and pronounce, "Get up here on my lap, and let me tell you a story." "Do you want to snuggle and read a book together?" OFTEN. EVERY CHANCE YOU GET. Shower your child with affection. Hold them and say, "I love you so much! You're my girl!" – "You're my boy!" Kiss them on their cheek and forehead. If you do those things, you will see your child instantly uplifted. And here's a secret: They won't even know they're being "uplifted": Comfort, affection, and love will be their homeostasis – their modus operandi. They will expect those things in all their relationships. Yay!!

model the tender touch

Be tender and affectionate with those you love in front of your child. Let your child see that you give hugs to family and friends often. That will teach them that affection is a natural way of being with people you love and care about. That way, they will grow up to be naturally affectionate and will receive all the nurturing they need to lead an uplifted life. Know this: When you're affectionate with your child, you're giving them abundant, unconditional love; you're touching their life deeply.

Sometimes I'll give someone I know a long, heart-felt hug that says more than just "Okay, here's a hug." It's more like, "I really appreciate having you in my life; you're really special to me. I love you; you have touched my life deeply." With that type of enduring touch, our souls soar together – they meld into one. We both fill with light. I know it; I can feel it. When that long, nurturing hug ends, the person will say, "Wow!" Because it's rare to get a hug like that.

opening your heart to loving and being loved

Long, heart-felt hugs can be scary sometimes, because you're opening your heart to loving and being loved, and that can bring trepidation because perhaps there was a time when you opened your heart to love and got hurt. But if you are conscious of that and acknowledge it, you can come right back into the love. You can allow the love to penetrate *deep* into the cells of both the hugger and the huggee!

touch fills in the gaps

You know, nobody's going to be a perfect parent. That perfect parenting thing just ain't gonna happen. But if you give your little one lots of affection – touching, cuddling, hugging; if something's wrong, and you say, "Come here: Let me hold you," "Would you like a hug?" "Let me kiss your boo-boo," it will make up for any mistakes or omissions you might make as a parent. Assuming, of course, that you have integrity with your child, and if you mess up, you say you're sorry and make an effort to do better the next time. But when you have a parenting mishap, that loving touch will reach above and beyond the call of duty to fill in the gaps. When there is abundant affection forthcoming, your child will have no trouble forgiving you and moving on to play "I Spy" as you drive to the store.

touch: the language of love

Touch truly is the language of love. It costs nothing, hurts no one, takes no extra time, and benefits your child for a lifetime. If you fill your child's life with tender touch, heart-warming hugs, and snickering snuggles, you will give your child a gift that will last forever. You have the power to touch your child's life in a way that will make the difference between them feeling lonely, isolated, and afraid and feeling supported, wanted, and cherished. You got this!

Sending lots of hugs!!

CHAPTER 5

CONTROL FOR THE SAKE OF CONTROL

It is possible – recommended in fact, and more beneficial to all involved for a child to be raised with respect, deference, and compassion. Controlling your child purely for the sake of controlling your child – simply because you can – does not serve you or your child. Children can see right through control for the sake of control, and it makes them feel angry and powerless.

It is possible, recommended, and, in fact, beneficial to all involved in more ways than anyone can ever fathom that a child be raised with respect, deference, and compassion. A parent controlling a child purely for the sake of controlling the child and not for any good reason does not serve the parent or the child. Children can see right through control for the sake of control.

check yourself

There is a chapter in *Sandcastles* entitled "An Addiction to Control", which outlines how control can get so out of control that it literally becomes an addiction. Far too frequently, parents use their children as a foil to act out their addiction to control. I know because I was on the receiving end of that addiction to control, and it didn't do me any favors. The only thing it accomplished was to make me resent my father for it.

I ask that each parent reading this book periodically ask themselves: "Am I attempting to control my child for reasons other than their best interests?" If you are, shift your behavior to one of living consciously in each moment, and do your absolute best to never use your child as a foil for your need to control a person or a situation.

give your child a reasonable reason
for saying no and hope for the future

"Because I said so" is a non-answer. You want to work with your child to raise him, not rule over him. Yes, you need to make sure he obeys you – so that you can keep him safe and teach him. But you have no reason for making a decision you make other than because you said so: It will end up making your child feel disrespected and like you don't care about his feelings. When your child asks if they can do something, and the conversation goes like this: "No." "Why not?" "Because I said so." "But why not?" "I don't have to have a reason: I'm the mom and I said so," your child will feel like you do not care about his wants or feelings and that you do not cherish him. And that right there will create resentments in him that will come out inexplicably and often and that will last a lifetime. When you are showing that you care about and acknowledging your child's feelings and desires, you are working *with* them to raise them. Let your child participate in his own upbringing: Let him know why you are doing what you are doing, and you will be infinitely more pleased with his attitude towards you and your choices for him than if you draconianly respond, "Because I'm the mom, and I said so."

When you respectfully communicate to your child the reasoning behind your decisions with acknowledgment and care for their feelings, your child will feel they have a say in who they are becoming, and they will know that whatever decisions you make regarding them will be for their highest good and nothing else.

respect and compassion:
your child's needs first

Billie's request: "Mommy, can I go to Johnny's house to play?"
Mom's frequent response: "No."
Billie's reply *every time*: "Why not?"

Mom's too frequent response: "Because I said so."

Mom's correct response if the answer must be no: "No, not today, sweetheart: We have to leave for the chiropractor in half an hour. Would it be okay with Johnny's parents if you went over there to play later this afternoon?"

Correct response if there is no reason why he can't: "Sure. Can you call Johnny so I can speak with his mom and get all the logistics ironed out? And then I can walk you over there."

If you follow the spirit of the above scenario, your child will always know that you have his best interests in mind and truly care about his feelings and well-being when making decisions that affect him. When you always have your child's best interests in mind and are communicating to him the bases for your decisions in ways that he both can understand and will know the reasoning behind, you will get welcomed responses and behavior from him. When you treat Billie with respect, Billie will treat you with respect, and your relationship will vibrate in respect and love.

again, the minister and the house-call

Imagine the minister is having dinner with your family at your house. Rev. Pat says, "Would you pass the peas please?" And you answer, "No." ... *Awkward* ... right? She musters an *Alice in Wonderland* Mad Tea Party response, "Aaahm, why not?" "Because I said so!" Well, that's going to go over like a lead balloon! Why does that not go over well? Because it is a disrespectful and discounting response. You would say, "Absolutely! And would like me to pass the butter as well? How about another roll?" Then everybody's happy.

I can't stress enough the importance of treating your child with respect and showing that you care about his feelings in everything you do. Teach with love. Teach with compassion. Teach with respect. Teach with kindness. Not only will that teach Billie that his feelings are important, considered, and cherished at every moment, it will also model for him being a kind human being. Won't it be nicer to have a happy child and adult around than to have to deal with a crabby, resentful, child who creates chaos, conflict, and strife wherever he goes?

check yourself on the control

A suggestion for when you feel like controlling your child simply because you can: Remember how we talked about that journal for writing down all the good things your child did that day? Well that same journal can save your hide if ever you find yourself feeling frustrated and maybe not having the best attitude when interacting with your child. If you are feeling stressed or unappreciated or angry, take out your journal. Give Billie a coloring activity or have him do something he enjoys doing by himself, and buy yourself a few minutes. This will only take a little while.

Write down this question: "What's wrong?" And then let the pen take over. Write down all the things you are feeling upset about – no holds barred – no one ever as to read it. Just get whatever is irking you down on paper. It can be a sentence, it can be four paragraphs. It doesn't matter, just get it out. After you write your feelings down, take a minute to tap on the feelings that have been causing you to be short with your child. Tap yourself back to sanity and into a calm place. The most important thing for you to do when raising your child is to stay calm and keep your vibration high. You can do that with the journaling and the tapping.

I can hear it right now: "But I don't have *time* to journal and tap!" You don't have time not to. When you journal and tap, your vibration will remain high; your child will pick up on that, and then you will be raising him from a calm and high vibration, and you will not feel the need to be controlling. You will want to give him good reasons for your decisions and choices. You will want to go out of your way to allow him to do the things he wants to do. You might even enjoy doing some of those activities with your child, because you will be dealing with him from a reasonable and calm mind-set.

if the answer is "no" give your child hope

There will of course be times when you will have to say no to your child – for purposes of logistics, family activities, or safety measures. When you communicate to your child in a respectful manner the reasons why you are saying no and give her hope for the future, your child will understand and begin looking forward to the next time. You will have a win-win when you give your child a favorite alternative activity for the one she is not being allowed to do. "I can't take you skateboarding right now, because I'm in the middle of doing laundry, but would you like to play "Sorry" with me right now, and then we can go skateboarding tomorrow? I might even skate with you!" Win-win, happy child, happy child.

how my parent's control for the sake of control negatively impacted my life

My father loved taking me to fun places and showing me a good time, but when it came to everyday life, he was excessively and unreasonably controlling and did not seem to care very much about my feelings.

no car for you!

I don't remember very much of my childhood, but one memory do I have is from when I was 5. I so badly wanted the electric car I saw advertised on all my cartoons and t.v. shows over and over. The little boy on the commercial rode all through the house and all over the back patio on it – all by himself, driving the car *himself*! The little blue car was just my size; I would be the driver *all by myself*; and I could ride it all around *our* house and all through *our* back patio. I saved my allowance for five months for it. I was *so* excited to finally be getting my car and to be buying it *myself* with *my own* money! When I had the $24 all saved up, I said to my dad, "Okay, Daddy, I have my $24! Let's go get my car!" He said, "Oh, hell no, I'm not letting you get that car: It's a piece of crap." And that was it. That is the perfect example of control for the sake of control – not for the sake of keeping me safe or teaching me something valuable. It is a perfect example of a parent not carefully considering what would be in the best interests of their child. My father did not put himself in the shoes of a five-year-old who had been looking forward to buying something and saving her money for it.

What would it have hurt if my father had taken me to get the car? The worst that would have happened is he and I would have had a wonderful father-daughter bonding trip to the toy store, and I would have felt proud of myself for succeeding in saving my money for something I really wanted. To the naked eye, it may not look like criticism, but my father's message to me was clear: The things you are excited about are worthless; you have bad judgment; your wants and desires are meaningless; your father has no concern for your feelings or the messages he is sending you; don't even think about receiving accolades for saving money for something you want. So right there: I have bad judgment; the things I am excited about are pieces of crap; the person who is supposed to care about my feelings the most doesn't; get used to devastating disappointment. And last but not least, don't bother saving money because at the last second, you will not be allowed to get what you have saved up all that money for, and it will hurt like hell when it happens. Take that to all future relationships and attitudes towards money and your dreams, because that's life, baby.

let children start to make
decisions for themselves

When you let children start to make decisions for themselves (hint: like buying a $24 little blue electric car for which she has spent five months saving her allowance), it teaches her that she is capable of making wise decisions and choosing positive life paths for herself. She will also learn from being allowed to make her own decisions. Even if you, in all of your parental wisdom, see some of your daughter's decisions as mistakes, if you allow her to make her own decisions, as long as no one will be hurt, she will have permission to learn from her mistakes. And then you can discuss with her what she learned from the choice she made – good or bad – without harsh judgment – and praise her for learning from her "mistake". It's good for a child to learn that it's okay to learn from their mistakes – in fact, the *best* way to thing back on a "mistake".

a pretty blue party dress and a not good lesson

The other memory I have from my five-minute sizzle reel in my mind is from my eighth birthday party. I was all dressed up in my pretty blue dress (blue is apparently the color theme of Janet's childhood wounds) playing London Bridge.

We sang:

"...Ashes to ashes, we all fall down!"

My father asked, "Who wants to be the bridge next?"

I had so much fun playing the bridge the first time, I screamed, "I do! I do!"

He snapped, "No, you were already the bridge; give someone else a chance."

"But I want to be the bridge!" I pleaded.

My father yelled, "Go to your room!" I did.

Apparently I had committed the crime of the century by insisting I wanted to be the bridge a second time at my own birthday party. So even though to the naked eye, it might not seem like criticism, believe me, it was. The message was: "Your requests are unreasonable, and you deserve to be punished for asking a second time for something you want after I have said no." I spent the rest of my party watching from my bedroom window as my guests played on my backyard roller coaster and had a good time at my party. I have blocked out the rest of the day, but my father probably let me out of my room for the cake and ice cream and the "Happy Birthday" song. My mom made the most beautiful and delicious cakes and really went out of her way to make my birthday special.

My take on this is that a better parenting choice would have been to go with the philosophy that if giving a child what it is she is requesting is not going to hurt anyone, give her what she is requesting: It's the loving thing to do; it teaches her it's okay to ask for what she wants, even a second time, and even if someone has said no before. She will come to believe that she has a good chance of having her heart's desire. That is a much better lesson than pounding into your child that you're in charge, what you say goes, and they better not object when you are attempting to control them. Kids know when there is a good reason for your decision and when it is just a parent controlling them because they can.

Saying yes whenever possible teaches a child to never give up on their dreams, and then later in life when they want a promotion at work or they want to start their own business, they will not give up after one try. They will not think, "Oh, what's the use, I never get what I want anyway, so why even try?" No! They will have learned from you that: "It's okay to ask for what I want; I have a good chance of having my heart's desire, and I'm going to ask for it and then ask again!"

empower your child to ask for what they want

You want to empower your child. Empower her to ask for what she wants and know that she will eventually have it. Empower him to understand why he must do the things he must do, and empower him to accept no for an answer without being angry, hurt, or disappointed.

Give your child something to look forward to; show her you care about her feelings; help her to understand why you make the decisions you make, and praise her for being agreeable, understanding, and a pleasure to raise!

CHAPTER 6

....

TAPPING FOR PARENTS

If through the course of your parenting you have no outlet for your frustrations or means by which to help you deal with your own, personal, issues (as if you actually get a life of your own outside taking care of your family), you will end up feeling trapped in a life of quiet desperation – stuck and trapped with no escape route. But because this is your lucky day, I am here to offer you the gift of a proven method to keep you sane and even relaxed and contented as you take on the Herculean task of raising a child. It seems unfathomable to think that there is a system by which you can stay sane and relaxed and even enjoy this challenging time, I know. But I'm telling you: If you use this system whenever you start to feel hurt, upset, contracted, angry, or confused, you will feel immediate relief. Using this method you allow you to move through your roadblocks, grow your soul, and raise your vibration. The feelings of anxiety and frustration will cease to exist in you, and you will feel freed up to move on to the next adventure.

what the heck is "the tapping"?

Emotional Freedom Techniques ("EFT"), also known as "the tapping", combines ancient Chinese medicine with the verbal expression of what is ailing a person or animal to release negative thoughts, emotions and patterns through the body's energy meridians. Tapping is a way to release unwanted emotions such as fear, anger, overwhelm, confusion, jealousy, and any other unwanted feelings and habits through the energy channels of the body. I have been doing the tapping, for myself, with friends, and in my counseling practice, for the past twenty years – with *crazy* good results. I healed myself of addiction using the tapping, along with the journaling and the inner child work. I still use the tapping on a bi-weekly, sometimes daily, if not hourly, basis as a means to continue to heal my childhood wounds and cope with the challenges of everyday life. I promise it will work *wonders* for you when you are feeling upset or impatient with your child or confused on how to handle a situation.

The tapping will keep your parenting skills tip top and allow you to parent your child from a place of calm, reasonableness, logic, and love, with a centered presence. It is only human for a parent to become upset when their child is misbehaving. Or when something their child is doing or feeling is reminding them of their own childhood and bringing up painful feelings from that time: Children are mirrors for our own inner child. It can also weigh heavy on a parent when a situation arises that they don't know how to handle. It's times like these when parenting problems can easily arise. When a parent is thrown off their center, they are not at their best and thus are not acting from a loving and patient place. When a parent is not sure how to parent their child – not sure whether to discipline them or sit down with them and have a heart-to-heart talk, they get frustrated, because, well, that darn instruction manual is just nowhere to be found: It was inadvertently baked into the floor of the gingerbread house! So when parents don't know how to handle a situation, they end up feeling frustrated, confused, incompetent, ignorant, and impotent. Especially when the baby gets to be a child, or, God forbid, a teenager. I don't envy any parent trying to parent a teenager. But there is a way to be on your top parenting game for your child at every age, and if you can remember that you're never going to be a perfect parent no matter how hard you try, you can be kind and compassionate with yourself and stay calm, centered, and confident. That will make it a win-win for both parent and child. It's the attitude that you parent from, it's the care and love you put into your parenting, and it's the educating yourself on the most kind and loving ways to raise your child that put you on the top tier of your parenting skills.

The BEST strategy for optimal parenting is: Whatever you do, make sure you are in a calm, loving, and centered place when you make decisions for your child, when you choose your words, and when you guide your child. A thousand times over you will make the best decisions for your child's well being when you are coming from a calm and expanded place inside.

To keep it simple when you are feeling frustrated, confused, unsure how to proceed, or overwhelmed, or when, although you have your child's best interests and highest good in mind, you feel ill-equipped to parent, here is what you can do:

If you can spare the time, grab your journal and a pen and sit down with a cup of something warm and comforting. I prefer hot chocolate. Write all the thoughts going through your head, all the feelings you are experiencing, and anything that is bothering you. If you cannot spare the time right then, don't worry: There are punting measures you can use to ease your mind. But if you at all can, sit down with your journal and a pen, and start writing:

WHAT ARE THE THOUGHTS INHABITING YOUR BRAIN RIGHT NOW?

WHAT are you feeling?

WHAT is making you feel that way?

WHAT do you wish would happen?

WHO are you mad at, frustrated with, upset with?

WHO hurt your feelings?

WHO didn't care much about your feelings?

When you are finished writing down the EXACT sentences in your head that are screaming at you and bringing you down, write a one-word summary for each entry in the margin of your journal – for example, "disappointed", "angry", "ignored", "disrespected".

Here are some examples for your journaling:

"I feel *so* angry at my child for making his food and then going upstairs and leaving a mess for *me* to clean up." That's all you need. It can be a lot or a little. Any expressing of your thoughts and feelings is good. Just GET IT OUT. And then take a few minutes to tap on the feelings, like this: "Even though I feel *so* angry at my child for making his food and then going upstairs and leaving a mess for *me* to clean up,

I deeply and completely love, accept, and forgive myself." As you say that sentence, you will either draw circles over or tap on certain energy meridians as will be explained below, and this will clear the charge and the angst.

If you do that, you will feel calmer, and when you go up to deal with the situation, you can just say, "Hey, Billie, do you think you could clean up after yourself when you make food? That would just be really great." That way, you can handle the situation from a calm and centered place and will not have a huge charge on it, and you will automatically handle it in a matter-of-fact, here's-the-deal, there's-no-other-path-you-will-be-taking from-now-on kind of way.

Let's say it happens again. Uh, so frustrating. You may want to take away a privilege and explain to your child why. But if you tap before you do the deed, you will be able to do this from a centered, calm place where you feel expanded and confident. Your child will see that you still don't have a big charge on it, and they're not going to feel like, "Mommy hates me; Mommy's mad at me; Mommy doesn't approve of me." It's just, nope, here's the deal, you've got to learn this, and you need to treat me right. I love you, but you can't keep doing this. If you journal and/or tap before all of your parenting challenges, you can parent from a calm and loving place, rather than with a big charge; not with anger, not with rage. Eventually your child will figure out that they can't rile you up; they can't get your goat; and they can't control you. You'll also be much more pleasant to be around because you won't be carrying around all that animus, and that pleasantness will be contagious, leading your child to just calm down and be nice.

everything you always wanted
to know about tapping

When I was first introduced to the tapping, I thought it was a little silly. But because I was so desperate for help, and because I trusted the therapist I had been seeing for eleven years and had seen amazing results in myself as a result of my work with her, I suspended all judgment and gave it a try. After I saw how effortlessly and quickly my healing progressed, I was sold.

I will now illustrate how to do the tapping. I predict that this method for clearing out frustrations with your child, unwanted habits, hurt feelings and other painful emotions, and even your own childhood scars, will come to be your best friend. It will revolutionize your parenting skills to the point where you will come to truly enjoy and relish every precious moment of assisting your child in growing up.

get comfortable and sit or lie down in a private place

Go to a place where you have privacy and feel relaxed. Either sit or lie down in a comfortable position, and close your eyes. If you have written down your main emotions in the margin of your journal, have your journal readily available and open so that you can streamline the tapping right to the core emotions that are causing you the most upset.

Here is what you will be saying as you are tapping:

- "Even though I feel angry and taken advantage of by Billie for cooking and messing up the kitchen and not being considerate enough to clean up after himself, I deeply and completely love, accept, and forgive myself."

And then the next thing will be:

"Even though I'm furious with Billie for being *so* inconsiderate and thoughtless and unappreciative of me, and for taking me for granted and not caring about my feelings, because he left the kitchen a mess and left a filthy mess for *me* to clean up, I deeply and completely love, accept, and forgive myself."

- "Even though I am confused on how to handle this situation with the kitchen, I deeply and completely love, accept, and forgive myself."

– "Even though I feel overwhelmed and don't know how to parent my child about this, I deeply and completely love, accept, and forgive myself."

FIRST TIME THROUGH

1. Soft Spot on the Left Side of Your Chest

Find that soft spot on the left side of your chest where it's really tender when you push on it. Gently make circles the size of a quarter over that spot with one or two fingers, in a clockwise direction, and say, "Even though I feel angry at Billie for cooking and messing up the kitchen and leaving a mess for me to clean up, I deeply and completely love, accept, and forgive myself." You do that five times there.

2. Tender Spot Above Your Eyebrow

Gently tap with your index finger or your index and middle fingers together on the tender spot ½" above your eyebrow and say, "This anger at Billie for cooking and messing up the kitchen and leaving a mess for me to clean up," and continue tapping there until you feel the vibrations of that rage rush down and out of your body.

3. Temple or Side of Your Eye

Gently tap on the side of your eye, on the temple, and say, "This anger at Billie for cooking and messing up the kitchen and leaving a mess for me to clean up," until you feel the vibrations of the rage clear from that meridian.

4. Tender Spot Under Your Eye, on the Bottom of Your Eye-Socket

Gently tap on the tender spot under your eye, on the bottom of your eye-socket, and say, "This anger at Billie for cooking and messing up the kitchen and leaving a mess for me to clean up," until you feel the vibrations of the rage clear from that meridian.

5. Tender Spot on the Top of Your Head, Right in the Middle

Do the same for all remaining tapping points.

6. Under Your Nose

7. Under Your Bottom Lip

8. Middle of Your Chest

9. Tender Spot 4-6" Below Your Underarm on the Side of Your Body

10. Karate Chop: With the Palms of Your Hands Facing Up, Tap the Sides of Your Hands Together

11. Abdomen

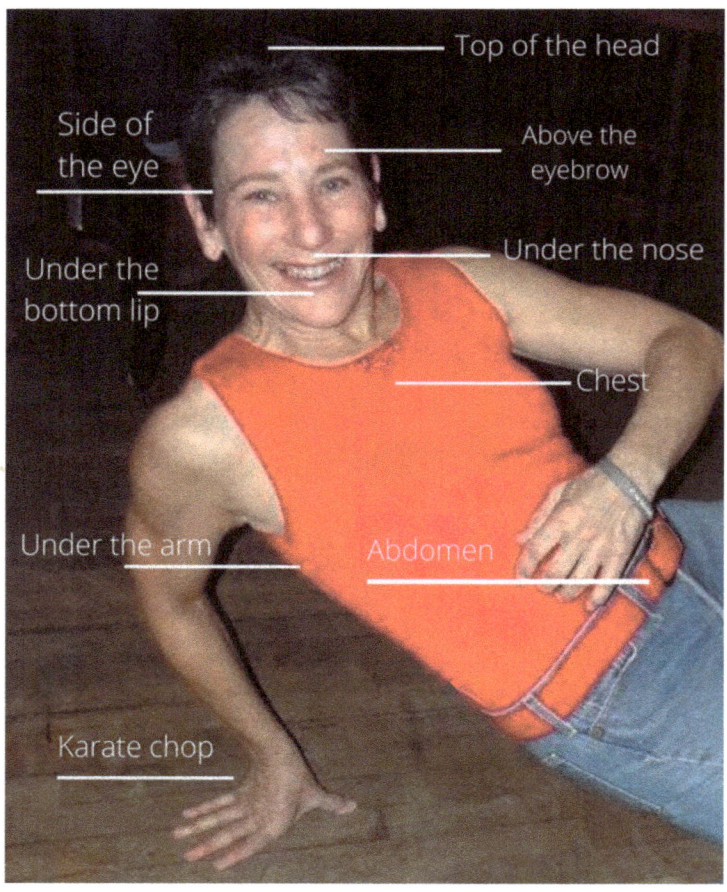

SECOND TIME THROUGH

Repeat 2-11

THIRD TIME THROUGH

Repeat 2-11, only this time say, "This *remaining* anger at Billie for cooking and messing up the kitchen and leaving a mess for me to clean up." And for all 10 spots you will say, "This remaining anger at Billie for cooking and messing up the kitchen and leaving a mess for me to clean up." Wait for the vibrations to clear from each tapping point before going on to the next point.

a little list

Below is a list of emotions that I use to clear childhood wounds in my healing sessions. Feel free to come up with your own: Whatever emotions ring true for you and bring up a feeling of "yeah, that's it!" The word you say that best describes the emotion you are feeling will be what you will use for the emotion you will be clearing when you tap. Here's the list:

Angry / Anger	Stuck
Sad / Sadness	Helpless / Helplessness
Afraid / Fear	Hopeless / Hopelessness
Enraged / Rage	Powerless / Powerlessness
Sad / Sadness	Impotent / Impotence
Terrified / Terror	Worthless / Worthlessness
Longing	Defective / Defectiveness
Grief / Excruciating grief	Trauma / Traumatized
Blinding terror	Conflicted
Paralyzing fear	Contracted
Jealous / Jealousy	

relate your current pattern of behavior
to something from your past

As we clear current negative emotions, we can go even deeper when we identify the original wound that is the precursor to the current emotion. For example, if you have ever felt anger at someone for not being considerate of your feelings or your time, say, as you make small circles on the left side of your chest, "Even though I feel angry at Billie for cooking and messing up the kitchen and leaving a mess for me to clean up, just like I felt towards my father as a little girl growing up, I deeply and completely love, accept, and forgive myself." And then, twice through on the rest of the tapping points, "This debilitating anger at Billie for cooking and messing up the kitchen and leaving a mess for me to clean up, just like I felt when towards my father as a little girl growing up," and once through on, "This *remaining* debilitating anger at Billie for cooking and messing up the kitchen and leaving a mess for me to clean up, just like I felt towards my father as a little girl growing up."

If you find yourself feeling jealous when you allow your child to go out and play with the neighborhood kids, and it occurs to you that *your* mother never let you play with the neighborhood kids, and that is why you are feeling jealous of your child, say, "Even though I feel excruciating grief and sadness that my mother never let me play with the neighborhood kids when I was a little boy, and I hate her for it, I deeply and completely love, accept, and forgive myself." Remember, you say it because it's the truth, and once you clear it, you won't feel that hatred any more; you will have released it, and then you will feel love for your mother. Say your true feelings when you tap because that is how you clear them. You don't ever have to tell anyone what you tapped on relating to them, because, really, they are only the catalyst for bringing up the painful emotions that have been lying dormant inside your psyche, waiting to be cleared for many years. I look at it like, "Wow, thank you for showing me this wound that has been screaming at me to be healed! Thank you, oh great teacher!" You can feel appreciation for the person you are tapping about, because they gave you the gift of being able to clear a childhood wound. The only purpose in saying and tapping on these emotions is to release them.

Continuing on with the rest of the tapping points: "This excruciating grief and sadness that my mother never let me play with the neighborhood kids, and this hatred of her for it." Twice through. And then once through on the same points with "This remaining excruciating grief and sadness that my mother never let me play with the neighborhood kids, and this hatred of her for it."

To recap:

Even though I feel debilitating anger at Billie for cooking and messing up the kitchen and leaving a mess for me to clean up, just like I felt towards my father as a little girl growing up, I deeply and completely love, accept, and forgive myself.	5X small gentle circles on soft spot left center of chest
This debilitating anger	2X thru on rest of tapping points
This *remaining* debilitating anger	1X thru on rest of tapping points

Sometimes it is necessary to tap more than once on the same painful feeling from a memory from your childhood or on a frustrating situation in order to clear it completely. Many times there are more layers of an emotion that need to be cleared for total peace around it: That's normal for energy work, and the more times you tap on these painful and frustrating emotions, the sooner you will feel better.

get ready to feel an amazing peace

After you tap for 45 minutes or so, get ready to feel exhausted and ready for a nap. But also get ready to feel an amazing calm, and your body pulsating in peace.

children are a mirror

Your child is a mirror of you when you were little, and so every way from Friday, parenting that child, looking at that child, being in the same room with that child, watching that child grow are going to bring up memories and wounds from your own childhood. You might feel a longing to have been given what you are giving to your child. You might feel anger towards your parents, because they didn't spend as much time with you as you are spending with your child. The painful memories and longings can run the gamut. But I guarantee parenting your child is going to bring up your childhood "stuff". I mean, it's just an option – I know you're busy raising your child – but if you want, and you have the time, sit down and write about how what you're going through is reminding you of your childhood and the painful feelings that are coming up for you. And then you can tap on the disappointments and hurts coming up for you, like, "Even though I feel excruciating grief that my parents hardly spent any time with me and I ended up being raised by my babysitter, I deeply and completely love, accept, and forgive myself."

When raising a child, you are going to be constantly reminded of your own wounds, but if you use those times as an opportunity to heal your heart, it will be a win-win for you.

help for the teenager years

Some children grow into challenging teenagers. Heaven help a parent who has one of the challenging ones: Parenting a teenager can be baffling and disconcerting. But if you practice the tapping from the time they are little, you will master the skill, and by practicing the tapping when your child is little, you will not only circumvent some of the crazy when they are little, you will be sufficiently accomplished at these skills when your child gets to be a teenager, and you will be able to transmute them for use with your teenager.

We hope raising our teenager will be effortless, fun, and joyous. Please, God. We hope this would never happen, but, you know, if, God forbid, they should stay out all night, and you don't know where they are, or they come home and they introduce you to their new boyfriend with a bunch of face tattoos and one ear and his nose pierced, you're going to need a way to stay calm. I mean, teenagers can do some pretty stupid things. I certainly did some stupid things when I was a teenager. Stupid, inconsiderate. Probably everybody does stupid things they're a teenager. It is a time to make mistakes and learn from them. So if you have the tapping skill down pat, when your child gets to be a teenager, and you feel thrown off by your teenager's teenage "mistakes", you will instinctively know to head straight for the easy chair and start tapping. That should help you come back to your center quickly enough.

I can't stress enough that if it happens that the frustration, the overwhelm, and the anger get blown up ten times in the teen years from what they were when your child was little, if you practice using the tools of journaling and tapping, those tools will become ingrained, and you will instinctively know when it's time to reach into your parenting tool box and use them.

Just to pound the subject deeper into the ground, let's take the possibility, hypothetically speaking, that your teenager has been gone all night, and you don't know where they are. That will undoubtedly bring up terror of losing a loved one, and all the accompanying abandonment issues you have ever felt in your whole life. It's terrifying when something like that happens. It's severely traumatizing. But even in a situation like that, you can tap and bring yourself back to, "It is what it is. I don't know where they are, but no amount of me feeling traumatized is going to solve anything; I'm just going to have to wait until they get home and then let them know that they can't stay out all night ever again without letting me know where they are." And if you have taught them skills for taking care of themselves out in the world, most likely they will be fine – they probably are just not thinking about your feelings.

I remember one time when I was a teenager – oh, my poor parents – I went out for two to four hours with each parent, and they didn't know where I was. Once it was late at night. When I got home there was a police officer standing in the living room taking a police report for a missing child. My *poor* mother. I complain about my mom, but I definitely was no angel. My senior year in high school, I was living with my father, and I went to visit a friend and didn't tell my father where he lived. Or when I would be home. Both times both parents were worried out of their minds. If I had it to do over again, knowing how much they loved me and worried about me, I would have considered their feelings and been forthcoming about my whereabouts. But I was young and stupid. I didn't know to put myself in their shoes and think about how they would feel when I just took off. I'm just saying it happens.

kids can tap too

You can teach your kids to tap too. Therapists and school counselors around the country are having tremendous success in using the tapping to help children cope with painful emotions and trouble concentrating in school. It helps kids calm down and come back to center so they can do their homework, concentrate during class, and stop acting out.

An article in ADDitude, an online magazine, describes the tremendous success their therapist has had with using tapping with children:

> Mandi Freger, a Licensed Professional Counselor and former board member for the Association for Comprehensive Energy Psychology, has used tapping and other forms of energy psychology with hundreds of adults and children over the past 20 years. She notes that clients typically come in for help with anxiety or mood disorders, and have classic ADHD symptoms, including difficulty with focus and concentration.
>
> "Many of them have anxiety over and resistance to getting work done. You can't separate it," she says. "Tapping helps them release tension in the body. It changes their thought energy, and retrains the brain."
>
> Freger has seen how tapping helps reduce hyperactivity. She recalls a young client jumping on her couch, shouting, "I have to jump! I have to jump!" After a few

rounds of tapping, the child was able to sit quietly and say, "I don't have to jump anymore."

For more instruction and information on the tapping, see website, *https://www.thetappingsolution.com.*

from rage to love in 25 minutes

I can personally attest the efficacy of the tapping from my own experiences with the tapping. One night during the years I took care of my severely handicapped and frequently depressed mother, I was driving home from work, and – I don't remember the exact circumstance – I was feeling enraged at her for things she had said that felt to me like she did not care about my feelings. I was severely dreading going home and doing whatever she needed me to do and spending the evening with her. I was so filled with rage, my car was glowing red. And then somehow the thought came into my head, "I need to tap." So for the next 25 minutes, for the rest of the drive home, I tapped on my rage and feelings of hate for my mother for not caring about my feelings (sometimes ya just gotta let it all out). 25 minutes later, I pulled into the driveway, got out of the car, walked into the house, went downstairs, and threw my arms around my mother. "Hi, Mom! How are you?" She LOVED it! But here's the thing: It was genuine. I tell you, I felt only love for my mother and was genuinely happy to see her and give her a hug. I was blown away. All I could think of was, oh my gosh, 25 minutes ago, I was filled with hate for my mother and dreading coming home, and all that is gone now, and I am bursting with love for her. At that moment, I was 100% sold on the tapping.

you can tap with your child

Try tapping with your child. If he or she is upset, say, "You seem kind of upset. Are you feeling upset about something?"
"Yes."
"What's wrong?" They'll tell you.
Then ask them, "Do you want to tap?"
"Sure."

And then sit down with them and share a 15-minute feeling better session. It will be a win-win for both of you! You can even devote one night of the week to tapping as a family. I can see it now: "Cookies and punch are on the table for Healing Wednesday!"

"Come one come all – It's Feelings Friday!"

You can't imagine the phenomenal results you will see when you utilize the wonder tool of tapping – by yourself in your easy chair, you and your child being there for each other, or tapping together as a family, it's all helpful. You will be amazed at the instantaneous and miraculous results!

Tap on my precious ones!

CHAPTER 7

COTTAGE CHEESE AND PEACHES

a soft shell

When you're a child of criticism, you don't grow up to have a strong, secure sense of self or a high, healthy self-esteem. Your "tough skin" tortoise shell never had a chance to harden, and you end up constantly getting hurt and offended by what others say and do. You frequently feel hurt, offended, rejected, ostracized, attacked, put down, unappreciated, slighted, bullied, insecure, less-than, disliked, unpopular, made wrong, and left out. A person who grows up with praise, compliments, and accolades, on the other hand, develops a strong, secure sense of self and a high, healthy self-esteem – a rock hard tortoise shell that sends put-downs and insults bouncing off of them. A child of praise, appreciation, and respect will have neither the time nor the propensity to think about what a person meant when they said something critical or harsh about them: they are too busy having a life and enjoying it: Every cell of their being knows that what other people think of them is none of their business and does not affect them in the least. They spend their time laughing, playing, and creating their dreams. People who were treated with courtesy and kindness during their childhood years are able to use insightful reasoning to disseminate between words expressing qualities that warrant attention and correction, and uncalled-for put-downs or words that are said merely to hurt. Those people are able to disseminate between a lesson presenting itself to be learned and meaningless criticism, because they are not sentisitized to criticism. They are not writhing in pain from the criticism of their childhood or guarding their criticism bucket that is full to the brim with painful memories of criticism making sure no more comes in.

their bucket is full

For those raised with criticism, words of correction or suggestions for a better quality life will always feel like criticism. All manner of correction *feels* like criticism, and the thought of letting any more in makes them feel panicked and manic. They can't hear it; they can't grow from it; they get defensive and hurl insults back. They can't handle it. They get badly hurt and feel offended, rejected, ostracized, attacked, put down, unappreciated, slighted, bullied, insecure, less-than, disliked, unpopular, made wrong, and left out. They will use whatever they have in their arsenal to make the other person look wrong so they don't appear wrong.

Whether parents criticize their child during their childhood or begin criticizing them in adulthood, the damage is equally devastating. Criticizing anyone – your young child, your adult child, your friend, the person in front of you at the grocery store – can leave lasting scars.

first-hand knowledge:
adulthood and open season

When I reached adulthood, I was no longer obligated to obey my father, and I became my own person. I did the things I enjoyed doing. I didn't run anything by him first; I didn't get his permission to do anything. I lived the life I wanted to live; I was the person I wanted to be. My father had a predetermined image of what Janet should look like, and when I didn't match up with his preferred version of me, which was really his preferred version of me *for him* – if I deviated from what he liked and believed – he felt he had the right to criticize me and put me down. And me not knowing I had a choice in the matter, I let him criticize me anytime he wanted. He took advantage of my not knowing any different and criticized me and criticized me and criticized me.

criticism of my body

The first thing my father criticized me for as an adult was my body: He felt I was too fat. When I was seventeen and in my first year of college, I moved into the dorms. Life happened, and within a few months, I had gained twenty pounds. Big deal. As far as I'm concerned, gaining twenty pounds is not the crime of the century or the end of the world. Unless you're my father's daughter, then he'll let you know just how heinous a crime you have committed in gaining twenty pounds. One Saturday afternoon after the big gain, I went to visit my father at his apartment. When I walked into the bedroom, I saw he had a friend in there taking a nap. A few minutes after his friend woke up from her nap, my father informed me that she didn't recognize me when I walked into the bedroom because I had gained so much weight. Boy, thank God *somebody* had the courage to tell me; otherwise, I would never have known that my clothes didn't fit, that I was lugging around a heavier body, and that I looked fatter when I looked at myself in the mirror.

Sharon and my father sat me down at the kitchen table to have a talk. Sharon proclaimed: "You've got to lose this weight." My father chimed in: "Yes, you've *got* to lose this weight. Men are only attracted to slender women." Sharon let me know in no uncertain terms: "You must put a carton of cottage cheese and a can of peaches in the refrigerator and eat only from those every day until you've lost the weight." It was a seriously long lecture about my body and the only type of body men are attracted to. Not mine, apparently. If I had known any of the words "control freak", "out of line" or "officious", I would have looked my dad right in the eye and announced: "Women are only attracted to men who are not out-of-line, officious, control freaks. Your obsession with every ounce of fat on my mother's body and pounding into her that she 'be slender', even if it meant Mom eating a bowl of soup a day and fainting and destroying your marriage, and now you're going to let it destroy your relationship with me, too? Do you not learn from your mistakes?" And then with a gleeful condescension towards both of them clarified: "In case you are not privy to the definition of 'officious', it means 'objectionably aggressive in offering one's unrequested and unwanted services, help, or advice.' I will weigh what I choose to weigh, and I don't ever want to hear what you think about *my* beautiful body! So back the f*** off and never bring up the subject of my body again!" It only took me forty-five years to come up with that brilliant tortoise shell quip that would have nicely fended off their life-scarring accost to my spirit. Ooh, I feel a third book coming on...

At the tender age of seventeen, and with my diminished and precarious self-esteem, my dad and Sharon's criticism of my body systematically robbed me of any inkling I might have had that I was at all attractive. How about just keeping your mouth shut? Why not just don't say anything? Did my father think I didn't notice that none of my clothes fit? Did he think I didn't ever look in the mirror? Seriously? I was seventeen years old. I think that's old enough to notice when you've gained weight. Besides, my body size was none of his business. Who cared if I was twenty pounds heavier than the last time he had seen me; I wasn't hurting anybody. How was I hurting him by gaining twenty pounds? I could never understand why he was so obsessed with the shape of my body and why he felt such a pressing need to pound me into the ground over a little bit of extra fat on my body.

From that moment on, I believed I was unattractive whenever I had one ounce of fat on my body more than . . . I really had no idea what amount of fat on my body was acceptable, because my father did not give me explicit instructions on just how thin I had to be, what his definition of "slender" was, or how perfect my body had to be in order to maintain medium attractiveness. By criticizing my body with the evil little bit of extra fat on it, he let me know just how worthless I was on account of my unacceptable and unattractive body. And the two of them ganging up on me about it was devastating to me. A daughter wants her daddy to have her back; protect her from bullying; love everything about her; think she's beautiful.

not exactly appropriate parenting

My father would tell me how to act in order to be attractive to boys, and then men. He told me I was mistaken if I thought hanging around with my best friend in college would improve my social life, because "boys" would think I was gay and would not ask me out. The truth was,

I had never been happier or had more dates. With boys. The two strong messages I got from my father were: "Your worth is dependent upon whether or not you are asked out by boys, and you won't be asked out by boys if you are at all fat or socialize with your best friend. You're wrong for happily hanging out with your best friend because you might not be asked out by boys, and you're wrong for being twenty pounds 'overweight', because it makes you unattractive, and you might not be asked out by boys because of it." I guess he really wanted to impress upon me how dire being asked out by boys was to my worth as a human being, and that if that wasn't happening, I was pretty much worthless.

The end result of all of my father's judgment, control, and criticism was:

(1) A lifetime obsession with every ounce of fat on my body, because that was the sole determining factor for my value.

(2) The belief that I was unattractive, because I had a little bit of fat on my body. I mean, let's face it, girls and women have to have some fat on their body in order to be healthy; I've always strived to be healthy, so in order to be healthy, I had to live with being ugly (or so I thought).

(3) The belief that if boys aren't asking me out, I'm worthless, so when I'm not being asked out by boys, or men, I'm worthless.

When a father harps on these principles every time he sees his daughter, she ends up believing them, and those beliefs become seared into a daughter's psyche and last a lifetime. They never heal. Until there's conscious recovery. And books that teach how to do it.

so fortunate to have been presented with the healing work

I am much better now, having done many years of healing work. But why should a person have to spend a single second feeling like a failure for *anything*? Why not walk around feeling like we are *wonderful, a gift to life*, attractive, and beautiful *at any weight*? Why waste a minute feeling lowly about anything? And the way to raise a child who feels wonderful and beautiful and attractive and a gift to life – one who turns into an adult who feels all those things as well is: Tell them they are. With feeling!

I did not know I could
Just say no to criticism

That wasn't the end of it: As I said, my father criticized me for socializing with my best friend claiming it would damage my social life because people would think I was gay. (A) I had a booming dating life, and (B) who cared?! I was happy!! He criticized my boyfriend's looks. He criticized anything he felt like criticizing, with no regard for how it might affect me. And, like I said, I didn't know I could say, "Hey, quit criticizing me. Quit telling me my body is unattractive and quit ordering me to be the size *you* think I need to be in order to be loveable. Just quit telling me what I have to do and who I have to be. If you don't stop criticizing me, I won't talk to you anymore."

dodged that bullet

I tell you stories from my own childhood, and adulthood, so that you can dodge the bullet of damaging your child's self-esteem. If you encourage your child to love their body no matter the size, see them as their spirit and not their body and at the same time encourage them to eat a healthy diet and get plenty of exercise, and leave the rest to them, your child will come out with a win-win healthy body-image. If there is a serious problem regarding their health, ask them if they want to see an EFT Practitioner to help them generate a desire to exercise and eat a healthful diet. Ask once, in a loving and non-judgmental, non-critical manner, such as, "You know I love you and want you to be healthy and happy. What would you think about going to see a person who can help you get through any hard time you might be having with your eating and with exercising." If they say, "No, I'm good," leave it alone and revisit the subject at a later date – a time when it feels right. When you get a strong feeling inside that it is the right time to bring up the subject again and that they will take it in the loving and considerate way that you intend it to be. If they say, "Yeah, I want some help," get on the horn and call the nearest EFT Practitioner that you feel comfortable with who will do the same kind of energy healing work that I do: non-invasive, nurturing, compassionate, and healing counseling. With lots of non-judgmental listening and caring.

criticism on top of criticism

My father used to come up to me and, all of a sudden, out of the blue, set on me with a barrage of criticism. I worked for him as a legal secretary. I'd be working for him at his office, and he'd come over to me and say, "All your healthcare practitioners are quacks. Your therapist, your nutritionist, your chiropractor: all quacks; Charlatans. All those nutritional supplements you take – they're all snake oil." He'd go on and on about how all the supplements I took, that were keeping me healthy, were a waste of money. Not one time did he ask me whether those healers or the supplements I was taking were helping me. He hammered me with criticism over having differing beliefs from him. He used to tell me oh, he was so worried, he couldn't sleep at night thinking about how my natural supplements might be hurting me. Which didn't make sense, because I was amazingly healthy! I had healed myself of one illness after another. He would not listen to reason, only blame me for keeping him up at night with my . . . glowing health?! It still boggles my mind why he felt the need to let into me over nothing wrong.

When I would object to his barrage of criticism, he would say, "You're overly sensitive." His response to my objecting to his criticism was more criticism. Why am I not surprised? Abusive people always fire criticism back at you when you object to their abuse. Once your child grows up, make sure you are letting them live the life they are happy living. If they come to you for advice, give it to them. But if there's nothing wrong and they're just living a life that's different from yours, let them have their autonomy and just enjoy your relationship with them.

what are two poor slobs doing
going to Disneyland dancing?

Many recovering addicts do not have the where-with-all to make a lot of money. Many live hand-to-mouth making just enough money to pay the bills. It is *very* common among addicts. My father was an alcoholic who lived hand to mouth. But he did not hesitate to rip me up one side and down the other when my boyfriend and I would go down to Disneyland, an hour away from where I lived, to dance. I am a swing dancer, and I used to love going swing dancing on Saturday nights at the Carnation Plaza at Disneyland. It was my absolute heart's desire. Every week my father would say to me, "What are two poor *slobs* doing going to *Disneyland* dancing!? Can't you find someplace closer? You're going to run the wheels off your car, and then you won't have anything to drive!"

I had borrowed some money from my dad and thought nothing of never paying it back (typical addict behavior; you live and learn). That was wrong of me. But you don't see what you do until you see what you are doing. Rather than saying, "I'm really upset that you borrowed money from me and aren't paying it back, but you will spend money going to Disneyland dancing," which would have been honest; maybe I would have seen the error of my ways, apologized, and started making good-faith payments. But simply hearing that I was a poor slob and wrong to be going to Disneyland dancing, even though it made me SO happy, did not help me learn anything or grow in integrity. It didn't even help me make more money. All it did was reinforce my inability to make decent money, get out of debt, and save money. It reinforced my belief that I was a poor slob and wrong to be giving myself my heart's desire. That's *all* my father's criticism did. There was no redeeming quality to my father's criticism. All it did was hurt me.

If I had it to do over again, would I have done things differently? Of course! But being criticized one's whole life puts a person at the disadvantage of seeing the world as a cold, hard, unrelenting place and seeing themselves as a loser and a failure. Criticism is a lose-lose. A win-win would be to tell a person all the things you love about them and encourage them to love themselves, and if you have a problem with them, communicate the problem with "I" messages and requests. Those types of messages will have a much better chance of bringing about positive change in a person.

a very happy ending

In the end, I was able to re-raise myself, starting with the 12-Step program of Overeaters Anonymous for my eating disorder, and then reading self-help books on childhood trauma inflicted by parents and how to recover from it, like the book *How to Talk So Kids Will Listen and Listen So Kids Will Talk* by Adele Faber and Elaine Mazlish, *The Emotional Incest Syndrome: What to do When a Parent's Love Rules Your Life* by Patricia Love, and *Silently Seduced: When Parents Make Their Children Partners - Understanding Covert Incest* by Kenneth M. Adams. I was very fortunate to have therapists who taught me to be kind to myself and listen to my inner voice and love myself even when I made mistakes.

when you're on the battlefield
and someone's shooting at you,
you don't see the ones who aren't

My parents always complimented me for my singing and dancing and comedy – all my performing. If I got good grades. Little things. There were lots of compliments. But there was also too much criticism. When you're on the battlefield and someone's shooting at you, you don't see the ones who aren't. The criticism annihilated my self-confidence – not my performing self-confidence, somehow I was always able to perform brilliantly, but my day-to-day-living self-confidence. I did not have the level of self-confidence necessary to get called back for a professional musical. I did not have the self-confidence to pursue any career to a high level. I have had successes, but when I have wanted to take them to the next level, like with my singing, my dancing, my acting, my comedy, my directing, and my healing, I have always stopped myself short of abundant worldly success. Like I have to hide behind the couch to keep myself safe from criticism or put-downs. I would not take the risk of being visible, of putting myself out into the public eye, for fear I would be teased, criticized, ostracized, or rejected. The reason for that is because the criticism I received as a child reduced me to creating a life of bare minimum survival. But thank God, the love and laughter and dancing and music and pets I have had throughout my life have allowed me to have lots of fun. LOTS of fun. I mean, my life path has not been a bad one, but I have always known what I was capable of.

The criticism I endured from my parents crippled any possibility of me ever creating for myself a wildly successful career and financial abundance. Yes, it is true, I am not finished yet. I am a work in progress. Who knows? Maybe by the time you are reading this book, I will be a worldly successful household name famous bestselling author!

let your child dodge that bullet

Why not give your child a fighting chance to reach his or her highest personal, professional, creative, financial, and relationship potential, right out of the gate, and grow from there? It can't hurt; you got nothin' to lose.

re-raising myself and undoing the damage
done by my parents' criticism

I have had to learn to compliment myself and love myself unconditionally, both of which I have done. But why not raise your child in such a way that they skip the having to re-raise themselves part and go straight to the expanded, non-addicted, happy life part right from the start? Do not pass Go; do not collect $200. Just go achieve and be happy – no muss, no fuss. I have helped *many* people heal of addiction and other problems caused by the criticism, control, and punishment hoisted upon them by their parents. Raising a child is not an easy task. But if parents know right at the beginning what to do to raise their child into a healthy, happy, non-addicted person – including leaving out the judgment and the criticism and the control, it will be an excellent experience filled with joy and amazement.

a better way

Criticizing and finding fault in your child – young or old – serves *absolutely no* purpose: There is a much better way to deal with your child that does not leave damaging marks on them for life:

- Ask for what you want.
- Be clear about behavior you will not put up with because it is hurting you and/or feels disrespectful.
- Understand that everyone is right where they need to be, and judgment of them does not help them, or you. Judgment has no basis in truth or understanding, and besides, no one is "flawed" – we are all simply work in progress.

getting clear on the truth

A system for parenting from an expanded, kind and loving place:

- Take out your journal and write down what is upsetting you about your child. Write as much as you want, no holds barred – you will be the only one who will read it – unless you *want* to read it to someone else. After you have written down what you are upset about – the things about which you are finding fault in your child, write down the following questions:

1. "How does this affect me?"
2. "What is the reason I am wanting to tell my child I am upset with this thing they are doing?"
3. "How is this hurting me?"
4. "How can I communicate my needs and/or feelings without finding fault, judging, or making my child wrong?"

- Run your issue through the following filter:

1. "Is what they are doing reminding me too much of me?"
2. "Am I being controlling for the sake of being controlling – for no good reason?"

3. "Am I afraid that what I am upset about in my child is going to reflect badly on me and then I will look like a bad mother to others?"

If any of the above filters is true, refer to Chapter 4: Tapping for Parents. Example: "Even though I can't stand the way my son dresses and am afraid my family and friends will think I am a bad mother because they will think I approve of his choice of apparel, I deeply and completely love, accept, and forgive myself."

it's not fair

Oftentimes a parent will find themselves saying no to their child or trying to curtail their child's interest in or enjoyment of something because they were not allowed to enjoy that certain thing as a child. "It's not fair!!" is the inner dialogue. "I couldn't do that: It's not fair that she gets to!!" It's a type of jealousy, like it would be too painful to watch their child enjoying something they were not allowed to enjoy. This can include any manner of things: affection, love, kind words, encouragement, gentle and kind discipline, having nice things. The list can go on. As a parent, it is important to look deep within and question if you are stopping your child from doing something they want to do so that you won't have to face the pain of remembering how much it hurt you when you were not allowed to do that certain thing for no good reason. I get it; it's painful, and it can be *very* unconscious. If you think you *might* be coming from the place of this childhood wound when dealing with your child, refer to the journaling and tapping portion above. You cannot avoid having your child wounds brought up when raising your child, and you can choose whether to raise your child from the point of view of your childhood wounds or welcome that fodder for your own soul's growth, heal your past hurts, and become a super-parent who raises a fully-functional, healthy, happy, child. The choice is yours.

we take full responsibility

Essentially what you are doing by running your childrearing motives through the "could this be my issue" filter is taking full responsibility for any insecurities or unhealed wounds you might have that could be clouding your judgment in deciding how to proceed in the ensuing communication with your child. By making your child's highest good your highest priority, your child will not feel criticized when you communicate using reasonable "I" messages. For example: "When you dress in those types of clothes, I feel uncomfortable. But I know it is your right to dress however you choose. Therefore, I will be telling everyone I know you ran away from your band of gypsies and I am merely giving you safe haven." I'm kidding, of course. But you get the idea. If you lay a huge charge on how they are expressing themselves and let them know you do not approve of what they are doing, they will either rebel and *never* be able to move on from that choice, or they will obey you and lose their autonomy as they will be living only to please you. Less is more. Pick your battles. If what they are doing is not hurting anyone, let them do their thing, and love them at whatever stage they are at. Your unconditional love and acceptance will set them free to become the person they are truly happy being.

don't hesitate to advocate for yourself

Yes, it is important to give your child leeway to learn their own lessons and become the person they are truly happy being. But it is not okay for them to walk all over you or hurt you in the process. You have every right, every obligation really, to let your child know when they are doing something you feel is disrespectful or is purposely hurtful to you and that you will not tolerate it. When your words are coming from honesty, respect, and self-love, your sharing them will be an excellent learning experience for your child. When a parent shares their honest feelings, from their heart, their child will not feel judged; rather, they will feel communicated with honestly about something they are doing that is hurting another person and that they are not allowed to do. If your child is acting in a hurtful manner towards you or another person, you need to let them know that what they are doing is unacceptable and you will not tolerate it. Whatever you have to share, say it from your heart, without blame and without judgment. Just say your honest feelings about how what they are doing makes you feel and what you want from them. It will not hurt your child to be instructed with a tone of voice that says, "I mean it." They need to mind you, and they need to know that you will not tolerate bad behavior. There is no criticism in a stern tone that is instructing them to behave appropriately and on what they need to do to stay safe.

ask for what you want

Ask for what you want: "Would you be so kind as to refrain from wearing perfume when you are around me? I'm sorry to have to ask you to do that, but breathing perfume gives me a headache."

There are always ways to ask for what you want. You can abate being subjected to disrespectful or unpleasant treatment and create a healthy relationship with your child by using non-critical, non-hurtful, non-judgmental communication.

We are all children. To have childlike feelings and desires is to be human. You will be amazed at how much you will learn about yourself and grow by watching your thoughts and motives in your interactions with your child. Love yourself and embrace the opportunities for soul growth you are being given by accepting the gift of being a parent.

CHAPTER 8

SANDWICHES

teach with love

Just like with adults, no child is or will ever be perfect. Children have fragile feelings, a vulnerable sense of self, and tenuous self-esteem. Parents must do their best to teach their child right from wrong and how to stay safe and not hurt themselves or others in a way that shows them great love and respect. Even better, great love, respect, kindness, and fun. Parents must show their children the kind and respectful ways in which to treat others, correct them when they do things that will not serve them later in life, and demonstrate through their attitudes and actions how to be a good person. In fact, parents must live a life of great love and respect so as to set an example for their children in the ways of a life lived in great love and respect. Children learn by watching, and they are convinced that the way their parents do things is the right way to do things.

Wise stories and child-friendly explanations will do wonders for your child rearing experience. Never stop using your hilarious sense of humor whenever possible!

**teach with great love, understanding,
patience, and compassion**

Your child will learn the fastest, retain the most, and feel the happiest when they are taught without being made to feel wrong, or bad about themselves, or like a failure or a loser. You will have the best results with your child if they are not made to feel that you disapprove of them, don't love them, or don't like them. It is vital to your child's mental health that they be taught with great love, understanding, patience, and compassion. Parents need to overlook their child's "faults". I put "faults" in quotes because children don't have any faults. "Faults" is a term adults use when gossiping about other adults; children are perfect in their innocence and processes of learning. You must suspend every possible unfavorable judgment you might have about your child – the type of judgment that causes an adult to close their heart to a person they have decided they don't like or are angry with; someone they might have a long-term aversion to for some reason.

It is vital that you train your child from a place void of judgment and filled with only unconditional love, tolerance, understanding, and an open heart. Remember what it was like to be a kid? You don't know anything. You do stupid things all the time. You do things that hurt you; you do things that hurt others – oh my gosh, I don't even want to think about all the people I hurt when I was young.

There are two things to remember: (1) Children will learn from their mistakes, IF THEY ARE NOT JUDGED, PUT DOWN, OR PUNISHED FOR MAKING THEM. Judgment, put-downs, and punishment put a whole 'nother layer of muck and mire BETWEEN THE CHILD AND THE LESSON THEY ARE NEEDING TO LEARN. You want to make sure that when you are teaching your child, you are keeping it positive. Do you think you can praise them too much? No way. You cannot praise your child too much.

If you need to "criticize" your child – I won't call it criticize, I will call it "correct", "guide" and "teach", then it needs to be done using sandwiches. Correction sandwiches. 'Using sandwiches' means you don't walk into your son's room and say, "My God, you're a slob! Clean up this room right now: It's a filthy mess!" Telling your son he's a slob will not motivate him to clean his room. The way to get your son to clean his room, or do anything else you want him to do, is by, before saying anything about his room, first, think of three things your son has done recently that are worthy of a compliment. You get him feeling good about himself by communicating how proud you are of him for his good deeds. Now that you've got him feeling good about himself for his good deeds, and his vibration is high, right in the middle of the third compliment, ask, "Hey, can you do me a favor? Can you clean your room? If you want I can help you. We can do it together. We can sing while we clean. And guess what? I have a present for you if it's super clean when we're done." Your request has ceased to be a criticism and is now a compliment and a request. If you ask your child for what you want, tell her what it is you are looking for from her, you are giving her the opportunity to give you what you want and get an accolade and a reward for it.

have a discussion

Let's say your child has been outside playing with the neighborhood kids, and you notice that one of the children is being left out of the playing and it is hurting their feelings. The best way to handle this is to, right when you realize what is going on, find a bunch of things your child is doing *right* with their friends, siblings, and parents in relation to caring about their feelings and well-being. Then you say, "I have a question for you. It seems like Agnes' feelings are being hurt. Is there something you can think of that might be hurting her feelings?" Then you open up a discussion and let your child try to figure out what's going on. Then sandwich in there somewhere a suggestion that you'd love it if she would include Agnes in the playing and how good that would make Agnes feel.

proof that sandwiches work

Here is how I know that sandwiching works. For more than 8 years, I taught musical theatre to children. I taught a three or four hour class every Saturday during which I taught every aspect of musical theatre, including singing, dancing, acting, improvisation, audition technique, dialects, and performance, and I put on two major musical productions per year. The kids learned proper singing technique, including deep, tension-free breathing, how to project their voice using their 'stage voice', and to always enunciate their words. I taught them acting; however, truthfully, you don't have to teach kids how to act: They already know how. It's in the hard wiring. It's why they are so good at games like 'Let's Pretend'. You simply need to coach and direct children and then praise them. I have always said that if you tell a child they're brilliant, they will always be brilliant. And if you tell a child they're brilliant while they're performing brilliantly, they will always perform brilliantly.

The way I came to know how to teach all those theatrical skills and direct all those shows was, starting at age 5, I took dancing lessons, was always in orchestra or band, took private singing lessons and audition workshops, and performed in plays and recitals. I taught myself how to teach musical theatre by using as a frame of reference what inspired me to learn and have a great time when I was a student of musical theatre. When you teach musical theatre to kids, you are really just *reminding* them how to sing, dance, and act, because they already have it in them. You give them permission, you demonstrate, and voilá! Wind them up and watch them shine. Theatre is fantastic for children: It instills in them confidence, self-esteem, and courage to perform, stand in front of a group and speak, and express themselves in every type of situation.

I directed and produced *Into the Woods*, a complex Stephen Sondheim musical that played on Broadway for many years and then went on a national tour. I had trained and directed in musical productions the same kids for three years in the Santa Cruz Children's Theatre Company, and then I changed the name to The Santa Cruz Youth Ensemble when we presented *Into the Woods* because most of the kids had become teenagers by then. All the productions we put on were magnificent. Our final production, *Into the Woods*, was a Broadway caliber, magical, other worldly spectacular production. I mean, there was no acting involved: The kids *became* the characters. The singing was phenomenal. It was a theatrical masterpiece if I do say so myself. You can watch it on YouTube: "*Into the Woods* directed by Janet Stegman", parts 1 and 2. Well, after the run was over, a fellow came up to me at a gas station while I was pumping my gas and said, "Didn't you direct *Into the Woods* with the Santa Cruz Youth Ensemble?" I said, "Yes, yes I did." And he said, "Well I saw it. I also saw the National Touring Company production of *Into the Woods*. And I want to tell you, yours was better." That is how I know that teaching with sandwiches works. It is the most effective technique for inspiring children to reach their absolute highest best in all areas.

Here's how you do it: You sandwich. All the time. Sandwich, sandwich, sandwich. Ham sandwich, egg salad sandwich, tuna sandwich. Let's say the kids do a scene, and I need to make an improvement. I stop the scene and say, "Okay, hang on, cut! Jackson, I love the way you're projecting your voice. I can hear every word, and your diction is perfect. And I love how connected you are to your story. Now, I want you to cheat out, meaning turn halfway to the other actor and halfway to the audience so that when you're saying your lines, we can see your face and see you talking. And we can also hear you better. Let me see you do it." They try it. "Okay, good job! You got it! I love it!" They run the scene again and they do *exactly* as I have asked, and they're even *more* brilliant. You hide the critiques or notes in between a whole *bunch* of compliments. Instead of saying, "Don't do it that way, that's terrible!" I say, "Good. Nice work. Now I want you to try something for me." Or I might say, "I love what you did. I want you to try something a little different now, and let's see how that works." Or, "Cheat out! Beautiful! Brilliant acting! I really believe you are the character." Whatever it is I ask them to do, they do, and they are happy doing it. When I see them performing or backstage with each other or before the show or after the show, they are having the *time* of their *lives. So* happy. To this day I get messages from my students from 30 years ago saying, "Those were some of the best times of my life. I made some of my best friends in Kids on Broadway." (The shows were called *Kids on Broadway, Kids on Broadway II, Kids on Broadway III,* and so forth. We did revues of Broadway and movie musicals, so that each student could have a lead role and I could afford to put on major musical productions, because I didn't have to pay for any rights. Well, I had very little money back then. My scrappy strategy turned out to be a win-win!

I had a rule – a hard and fast rule: No bullying. Absolutely no bullying. I didn't use that word though: I would say, "In this company, we don't put each other down, and we don't criticize each other. We build each other up, and we support each other."

One time, I took the entire company on a field trip to the community college to audition for the musical *Oliver!* Every single one of my students went on stage, all by themselves, and auditioned, and I did, too. We all stood in the wings cheering on the one auditioning as each student, one by one, went out and sang their audition piece. Before one of us would go out on stage, we would all tell them, "You're going to be great!" "Knock 'em dead!" and when they'd come back afterwards, we all got a high five and an "All right! Nice job!" It was so easy. Everyone enjoyed their auditioning experience, when normally something like that would be so daunting that you'd almost rather just stay home.

I found just how far to the stars kids can soar for an audition or in a performance or a class or at a skill when they are taught with praise, acknowledgment, and encouragement, and their corrections are hidden inside a sandwich.

Not only did my students put on brilliant theatre, they carried that brilliance with them when they grew up. One of my students who studied with me from 9 years old through high school grew up and became a successful, top tier magician in Las Vegas. He wrote me a note a few years ago that said, "Janet, you generously worked with me and ultimately changed the trajectory of my life for the better. It's something I will never be able to repay because it goes far beyond value. Thank you."

One of my students went on to form her own theatre company in Nashville, Tennessee, and write, produce, and direct her own original musicals. A few years ago, she was nominated for a Tony Award for excellence in teaching theatre. When I wrote to congratulate her, she wrote me a note back that said, "Some of the best memories and best friends of my life I have because of you. Thank you…"

Another one of my students, a very shy one, played leading roles, and her theatre skills really blossomed through the years. With my encouragement, she went on to become a high school theatre teacher, to rave reviews from her students. After she grew up and was working at the high school, her father stopped me in the hallway of the community center where we had performed all of our *Kids on Broadway* shows. He said to me, "I never properly thanked you for everything you taught Amanda and how much confidence and self-esteem you instilled in her. I don't think she would have had the confidence to become a theatre teacher without your training and encouragement."

Three of my students went on to become professional singers and recording artists. I heard from the mother of one of my students when she was a senior in high school. She said, "We want you to come see Georgie in *My Fair Lady*: She plays the lead role, Eliza Doolittle. You taught her so much." And when I went to see her, she was thrilled to see me. I have driven from one end of California to the other to see my students with leads in musicals, such as the Artful Dodger in *Oliver!*, Tevya in *Fiddler on the Roof,* and Dorothy and The Scarecrow in *The Wizard of Oz.* I sat in the audience bowled over with amazement, crying. It is a wonderful feeling to know how deeply you have touched the lives of the children you have taught – through your love and praise. And that it has lasted a lifetime.

I don't tell these stories to blow my horn (although that's fun too); rather, I tell them to illustrate that if you teach with love, fun, praise, acknowledgment, and sandwiches, there will be unfathomable rewards afterwards.

Upon reviewing the situation, I have come up with the most winning delivery system for teaching your child:

1. Make your child laugh

Children *love* being made to laugh. Try making them laugh while you are telling them what you need to tell them. Find a good joke book and tell them a joke. Insert their guidance in between jokes.

2. Teach with stories

Tell your child stories that teach what you want them to learn – made up stories, tales, parables, and real-life stories. Somebody you knew did this, and this is what happened, or "I'll tell you a story about *my* childhood!"

3. Teach your child by reading books to them

Find a children's book that encapsulates the lesson you are trying to teach and read it to them. Children *love* it when you read to them! Everybody, *absolutely everybody* loves to be read to. Being read to is very nurturing. When someone reads to a person, it evokes rich feelings in them. It's SO important to introduce your child to books. Go to the book store and get some children's books that teach children how to be kind and loving, how to take care of themselves, and how to be safe. You can go together to the library and let your child pick out a couple of books to check out. Start them early on their quest for knowledge, wisdom, and history. It will help them become knowledgeable and autonomous teenagers and adults.

Have your child snuggle right in with you and read to them. Make it a quality time sharing a story bonding experience for the two of you. Encourage their grandparents to do the same. These moments will become the biggest moments in your child's life; oh, these times will be precious! Let your child think their bedroom bookshelf is a never-ending storehouse of stories and knowledge.

recommended reading

One excellent series of children's books is *The Berenstain Bears* by Stan and Jan Berenstain. There's *The New Bicycle* and *The Birthday Party* to name a couple. There are different books for different lessons like making new friends and going to a new school, and they will be excellent for your child.

Another series is anything, *absolutely anything,* by Dr. Seuss. My favorite is, of course, *Green Eggs and Ham.* You'll never stop laughing if you read *Green Eggs and Ham* with your child. Take turns reading stanzas. Then read it faster.

One good book is the very clever *Up Goes Mr. Downs* by Jerry Smath. It's about a guy that floats away with balloons. Another is the great rodeo book, *White Dynamite and Curly Kidd,* by Bill Martin Jr. and John Archambault.

4. Teach kids through play

Children love it when you make funny faces: It makes them laugh. Kids *love* to be made to laugh. They love it when you do characters – oh my gosh, do they ever love that! They love it when you play "I can't find the ball!" and "Where's the ball?!" (The ball is right there, but you act like you can't find it.) Kids love "Where'd you go? I can't find you!" "Jehnnnnnny! Where aaaahre you?!" Like when you're changing their shirt. Oh they love that. You can do that even when you're not changing their shirt; they'll get it. Children love it when you play and play and play with them. They get to laugh and laugh and laugh. You get a child laughing, and you can tell them anything. You simply sandwich everything with something you love about them. "I love you *so* much; I'm so lucky to have you!! C'mon, let's go home and clean your room. And then go out for hot fudge sundaes!" And then you give them a big hug. "Jenny! I can't find you! Where did you go?! Jehnnnnnny!" The best method for teaching kids is through play.

Have fun making funny faces at your child, laughing with them, playing games, and snuggling and reading books. This time with feeling!

CHAPTER 9

··

SPARE THE ROD, SPARE THE ADDICTION

Why is it that at 17 years and 364 days, hitting your child is considered "discipline", and at 17 years and 365 days – the *very* next day – it's a crime and a tort, and you can go to jail and be sued for assault and battery? Think about being hit. It doesn't feel very good, does it? Do you know why? Because it's violating your right not to be hit; it's abusive, traumatizing, anger-provoking, disrespectful, contemptuous, and damaging to the spirit. It can cause enough rage to catapult a person deep into a raging addiction. I know, I know, why don't I tell you what I really think?

Addiction, depression, and crime are at catastrophic levels here in the United States. So how's that spanking thing working for us? "Spanking" is just the word used to rationalize and downplay a parent committing violence upon their child, ostensibly for purposes of "discipline". There is no difference between the way a child feels when an adult "spanks" them and the way an adult feels when a mean bully hits them.

Just because a person is a child doesn't mean they don't have the same feelings as an adult when they are hit. I can't understand what makes a parent think their child will feel any differently about being hit than they would feel if they were hit. Being hit makes a person – OF ANY AGE – feel angry, resentful, hateful, rageful, and revengeful. Zakly!! A child feels all the same feelings when they get hit that a parent feels when they get hit. If you hit your child, they will feel all the grief, rage, and powerlessness that you feel when you are hit – all the way to the AA meeting.

I hear people justifying "spanking" their child saying, "The boy down the block is out of control, destroying the neighbors' property; he's a bad kid. Because his parents never spanked him; he's spoiled." After hearing this, I shudder and say, "Did you ever stop and think that maybe it isn't because his parents didn't spank him; rather, it's because they didn't *love* him." I am so tired of these armchair psychiatrists proclaiming that you have to hit your kid to keep them from becoming spoiled. Or rotten. Just once, I'd like to hear one of those armchair psychiatrists proclaim, "That rotten kid. His parents clearly didn't give him enough love, affection, or attention."

If you think about it, no matter how badly we as adults mess up – break the law, breach our contracts, speed, use illegal drugs, drink too much, no amount of beatings will ever teach us any kind of lesson. And we know that. The only thing a beating will do for us, no matter the reason, is fill us with blind rage, hatred, resentment, and a desire to commit untold acts of violence. Violence is merely rage taken to the annihilating level – the level of out-of-control, abusive, evil, and sick. A person who commits physical violence upon another is hateful, cruel, narcissistic, sadistic, and a psychopath. But what turns them into an abuser, and what causes them to become violent? Having it done to them:

> "My father hit me, so, then, that's just the way it is. If my dad beat me, that must be the right way to express my anger."

Abuse begets abuse:

> "Not only that, but because my dad did hit me, I'm excruciatingly hateful and enraged all the time, and all I want to do is lash out and express that rage and hatred. Not only that, but because I was abused, and it just felt wrong, I hate myself for not stopping it and not knowing I had the power to stop it. I can't STAND feeling my feelings because when I feel my feelings, all I feel is

rage and hate. I need a distraction that will also serve as an activity pregnant with self-punishment."

It's not fair:

"It's not fair that I was hit by my father, but my son doesn't get hit by me. To make it fair and so I won't have to feel my jealousy, I am going to hit my kid when he makes me mad."

Now we have an angry, hateful, cruel, vengeful, narcissistic addict who hates his father for abusing him and himself for allowing himself to be abused; hence, your out-of-control, conscienceless, abusive alcoholic/addict.

don't hit your kid

So don't hit your kid. I don't care how many times they run out into the street: find another deterrent. The physical violence of a spanking or a slap on the hand is the lazy way of controlling a young child, through hurtful violence and the terror of future violence upon them. The benefit to the parent of coercing their child into obeying them with a spanking does not outweigh the devastating long-lasting effects of having been violated.

only bullies hit children

A person who hits a child – a smaller, weaker, defenseless one – is a bully. Committing physical violence upon a person who is smaller, weaker, and defenseless is the very definition of a bully. Why is it okay to bully someone just because they're your child?

A child's young age does not negate the rage, trauma, and hatred they feel when they are hit. Children feel the same feelings adults feel when they are hit – no matter whether the hitter believes the child "deserves" it. Even when the hitter can't think of a better way to get the child to "do the right thing".

It will not make a child feel any less abused simply because the adult that hit them thought they needed to be hit in order to teach them to keep themselves safe. Put yourself in the shoes of a young child being hit. Does being hit make you a better person? Does it teach you *anything*? Nope, not a chance.

If all we do to "teach" our children to be a good boy or girl and not go into the street is hit them when they start to go into the street, all that will result will be an adult who is controlled by their terror of being hit. Causing a child to live in fear of being punished may keep him out of the street when he's 2, but it will make him depressed or a drug addict, alcoholic, compulsive overeater, or recluse when he's older. At the very least, he will be riddled with terror and turn to something to calm his anxiety.

It is not healthy for a child to be hit, just as it is not healthy for an adult to be hit. Don't hit your child. For any reason. If ever there was a time to heed Jesus' pleas to "Do unto others as you would have them do unto you," and the Law of Moses, "Whatever is hurtful to you, do not do to any other person," it is when you are raising your child. Choose compassion, empathy, and intelligence in raising your child. Always.

Some methods for getting your child back on track that don't include physical violence:

1. Look your child square in the eye and command a stern "No". They'll get the message. The upset energy coming from you will tell them everything they need to know.

2. Don't let them go outside unsupervised.

3. Put up a gate.

4. Praise them, then praise them some more, then praise them some more.

5. Give them presents for no reason.

6. Shower them with rewards for doing the right thing.

7. Laud them with compliments anytime they deserve them, even in the slightest.

8. Hugs all around.

9. Bribe them with promises of ice cream and trips to the park with you and then give them more compliments and more hugs.

children need praise, not spankings

How do you feel when someone praises you? Elated? Even better when that person is your parent? When you feel the need to discipline your child, first think of five things your child has done right, and praise them for those five things. Then correct them for what it is you are wanting to discipline them for by asking in words what it is you would like from them the next time, and explain why you are wanting them to do the thing differently the next time. Praise them every day. Every hour. A child cannot receive too much praise, and the praise that sandwiches your corrections will make them much more open to your patient and loving guidance.

Children don't need to be hit: they need to have their feelings cared about. They need to be talked to in a respectful manner. They need to be acknowledged and treated like they are important. They need good food, good water, and to be kept warm in the winter and cool in the summer. They need to know their needs are important to their parents. And they need to know their parents love them.

a "swat" is just a "hit" downplayed
to give parents permission to hit

I had a conversation with a friend of mine who has a 10-year-old son. Now, my friend is the salt of the earth, one of the kindest and smartest people you will ever meet. Her husband too. This will show the belief systems of good people just trying to do the right thing. My friend was telling me about when her son was a baby and was doing something she didn't want him to be doing. She said, "I just swatted him, and blah blah blah he never did it again." I'm sitting there thinking,

"Do I say something; do I not say something?" And I said, "Oh, I'm writing that chapter, "Don't Hit Your Kid" (the working title), because, why is it if you hit your kid at 17 years 364 days, it's 'discipline', but if you hit them one day later, at 17 years 365 days – the very next day, it's a crime and a tort, and you can go to jail for it and be sued civilly." And she just kept repeating "Oh, it was just a swat. It was just a swat. He turned out fine."

Well, of course, there are gradations. If you swat your kid once, or twice, or three times, that doesn't necessarily mean that oh now they're going to turn out to be a drug addict. Children have a certain amount of resilience before they get to their boiling point. But in the end, we don't really know the toll "swatting" takes on a child – you can't flat out say you know beyond a shadow of a doubt that it didn't affect them in a negative way, because a child is not a gumball machine: You can't put a penny in the slot and then immediately see what comes out right then and there.

Hitting a child is an invasion of their space, their person, and their self-respect. Look at it from your perspective. Imagine some stranger coming up and hitting you, straight out of the blue. Not only will it hurt you physically – you'll say, "Ouch!" – but you will feel spiritually invaded as well, and that your body has been trespassed upon. You will feel violated on all levels: mental, physical, spiritual, and emotional. And you will have this innate, knee-jerk feeling that, "Hey! You don't have a right to do that! Hey! It's my God-given right to be left alone and *not* be accosted by another. I mean, accidents happen. Someone could accidentally bump you or step on your foot, but you don't have that same visceral reaction that you have when someone purposely hurts you. It's just an oh, maybe it hurt a little, but you understand that it was just an accident and the person had no ill-intention. They say, "Oh, I'm sorry," and you say, "That's okay." And even if it hurt a little, you move on and forget all about it. But when somebody purposely invades your person and violates your right to be left in peace and quiet enjoyment of your body, it scars you. You may never get over it. Maybe you will, if you have a recourse. But a child does not magically have an "Oh thank you; I've learned such a great lesson now that you've hit me" feeling just because they are a child or just because they are your child. Their feelings of anger and of being violated are every bit as strong, and valid, as your feelings are when the same thing has happened to you. But a child's feelings of anger and resentment are never acknowledged or considered or viewed as valid when their parent is "disciplining" them with violence, and to make matters worse, the child has no recourse from being hit, so they're just kind of stuck with their anger and left feeling all alone and hurt that their feelings are not cared about or considered.

a child has no recourse against
violence upon their body

If an adult gets smacked – even with a hand on the butt – they can hit back, they can call the police and have the person arrested for assault and battery, they can get a lawyer and sue them civilly. An adult has some recourse to enable them to feel avenged. But a child (a) doesn't know about any of the above recourses, and (b) doesn't have the tools or the means to pursue a recourse, or the permission. They have no recourse against their body, their person, and their spirit being violated with violence by a person who claims they have the right to hit them simply because that child came out of them or because they provided the sperm for that child or because they adopted the child. I mean, parents don't "make" the baby; they don't make the child. They have sex, and then God, or whatever the creative force is that has the ability to make a baby, makes the baby. So that child comes out of the family baby-grower, and then that mother and father are responsible for nurturing, loving, and caring for that child – for keeping it safe and teaching it what it needs to learn to grow into a healthy, happy adult. But those parents do not have the right to commit violence upon that child. That child has a God-given right to be left alone and in peace; to be protected from harm. An adult hitting a child is the ultimate example of the stronger taking advantage of the weaker – the stronger one hits the weaker one because it's an easy way to control them: through terror and pain. And because they can.

Every single one of my clients who was a victim of child abuse has some sort of painful disorder: addiction, depression, rage, compulsive control. Call me fanatical, but I call hitting another person, or an animal, "abuse". If a boyfriend hits his girlfriend, it's abuse. If a husband hits his wife, it's abuse. If a wife hits her husband with the frying pan, it's abuse. You can call it "discipline"; you can call it whatever you want. I call it abuse. Because the violation is on a spiritual level – a vibrational level. If a person crosses that line and invades somebody's person with their violence, it's abuse and will scar them for life. *Especially* a child, who doesn't have the means to seek recourse in the courts or to hit the person back. I guarantee if a child or teenager hits a parent back, that parent is going to hit back harder and more times. If the child or teenager hits the parent back, the parent will call the police and have the child taken away to Juvenile Hall, and then the child will be in prison. So children and teenagers have no recourse. You can say, "Well, you're just wrong. My parents spanked me. It's necessary to spank a child in order to keep them safe. "You have to teach them!" "You gotta teach them, you know, to stay safe!" "You know, if they run into the street, you gotta hit them so they know it's not okay to run into the street." "You gotta hit them so they know they did wrong. So you can raise them into a good, respectable human being." No, that is incorrect. It's not the hitting that teaches them: it's that they know that Mom's not happy with them. They say, "Oh, I guess that thing I just did didn't make Mama happy." And then the logic chip in their brain tells them, "I guess that's not a good thing to do, because, welp, I wanna keep Mama happy. When Mama's happy, everybody's happy! She's fun to be around, she gives me hugs, she gives me treats, she gives me compliments, she gives me ice cream! And *everybody*'s happy." The transmitter of Mama's message is the look on her face, the message in her eyes. It's her vibrational energy when she's upset with Little Bobby that lets Little Bobby know he did wrong. No life lessons or feelings of love ever get transmitted through the use of violence – violence only instills fear and anger and hatred.

The clients and people I have known who were routinely abused as children have all suffered from debilitating rage, manifesting itself in substance abuse; physical violence; unprovoked, out-of-control raging; an obsessive need for control, narcissism, an inability to attract a healthy, loving relationship, and an inability to stay in a healthy, loving, committed relationship. They carry around this Hulk-like rage, and they either (1) show it in one of the above-mentioned ways, or (2) keep it controlled by the use of mood-altering substances. One client had a father who was big on spanking her younger brother whenever he "disobeyed". When her brother disobeyed, her father would lay him across his lap and spank him and spank him and spank him. And when her brother would laugh, probably to hide his feelings of shame, embarrassment, and rage, the dad would say, "Oh yeah?! You think that's funny!? I'll give you something to laugh about!" And then he would hit her brother more and harder. As she and her siblings watched on in horror, their spirits were tortured watching their brother being Draconianly abused by their father. To this day my client can't get that vision out of her head, and it still hurts whenever she thinks about it. That brother grew up to have some difficult life challenges.

When I was a child, I was such a good kid that my parents rarely had to discipline me. They spanked me when I was little, but not to excess. My mother especially did not spank often. I have blocked out most of my childhood, but one thing I do remember is when I was a teenager and I did something my father didn't like, and he came up to me and spanked me on the butt. I remember that moment to this day like a video playing in my head. I was 14 years old, old enough to feel like I wanted to be treated with the kind of respect an adult would be treated with and not be hit on my rear end. Well, my father didn't like something I had done; I don't remember – maybe I wasn't "obeying" him. What I do remember is him reaching down and extending his arm and hitting me on my behind – hard enough that it moved me forward. To this day I feel angry about that. I feel violated. I feel like, "Hey! You did *not* have the right to hit me! It just felt SO wrong! My whole body vibrated in "That was completely inappropriate and wrong. That violated every spiritual law. That violated every law of love. Don't ever do that to me again!" That was how I felt inside. I didn't say any of that, but that was how I felt. I think I said, "Hey, what're you doing?" Or maybe I just thought it. What I didn't say was, "Are you *kidding* me?! You just committed a battery on me! Don't you *EVER* do that to me again, or I will leave and never come back!!" Same thing happened with my mother: Same awful feelings.

My dad didn't hit me very often, because I was an obedient and good-natured child. I really loved me and loved life, and I had no reason to act out. All my parents had to do was hand me the clarinet, hand me the baton, have Mrs. Turrentine drive me to dance class. Wind me up and watch me raise myself!

But if *I* felt such outrageous anger and hate from my spankings, and still feel it today when I think about it, then I *know* that if you hit your child on a consistent basis, it will do zero ZERO good for your child. The ONLY thing it will do is enable you to control your child through force and fear and make them feel so afraid of you that they will allow you to control them. *All* it will do is scar them for life and cause them to live in fear and walk the straight and narrow out of fear of being hit. Like a dog who turns over onto its back, paws up in surrender, like, "I give up! I give up! Please don't hurt me!"

Let's review what hitting a child does:
– It makes them live in fear – forever.
– It makes them submit to being controlled out of fear of being hurt, being violated, and being hit.
– It scars them for life and can lead to addiction, depression, and the inability to sustain a healthy, happy, committed relationship.

fear of being close

Hitting your child will cause them to be too scared to let themselves get close to another. You see, you as parents are their original relationship. They will always draw on their feelings from the original relationship and project them onto all of their future relationships. If they attempt to enter into a romantic relationship, they will vibrate in fear within the confines of that relationship, thus never allowing themselves to get close to another human being. They will constantly be in and out of relationships – in and out of marriages and divorces. Even if they do get married and stay married, they will nonetheless forever be afraid to open their heart to love. It will be a marriage-in-name-only. They will not be able to bond with another person, and they will feign normalcy through the use of distractions and substances so as to save face. I know that from my 15 years of counseling people, my own experience, and my own intuition.

there is no violence in respect

For 15 years, I have been helping people heal from addiction, depression, anger, and low self-esteem, to name a few. My job has been to undo the damage that either loving but unknowing or downright monster parents have foisted upon them in an effort to either succeed at or, for some, merely survive their daunting parenting responsibilities. I have heard horror stories you can't imagine, and I have heard stories from which I have had to dig deep to find the causes of the woundings. I would say that if I know anything, it is that I know how adults need to treat children so they come up loving and believing in themselves, vibrating in high and healthy self-esteem, and organically making healthy and intelligent decisions for themselves.

a child doesn't need to be hit:
what they need is...

A child doesn't need to be hit. What they *do* need is for their parents to treat them with respect – the same respect an employee expects from their employer. Children are sponges, and you parents are their God. They haven't figured out yet that half of what adults say and do is stupid. Imagine yourself at an interview for a job you really want. THAT is how you talk to your child. No matter WHAT you have to say to your child, you can say it in a respectful, kind, and compassionate manner. There is no place for violence in respectful, kind, and compassionate.

a hurtful way to solve a problem with a
teenager and the loving, constructive way

NOT RESPECTFUL, KIND OR COMPASSIONATE: "The school called. Apparently you were late for school again this morning. If you're late again, I'm taking you out of wrestling." Neither shaming nor punishment will serve a child.

A RESPECTFUL, KIND, AND COMPASSIONATE WAY TO HANDLE THE SAME SITUATION: "I heard you won the practice match today. All right! Congratulations! What move do you think won the match for you?" After some creative positive feedback, you move on to the more challenging, "By the way, your school called and said you were late for school again this morning. What's going on for you in the mornings that's keeping you from getting to school on time?" And then you LET THEM TALK. You look into their eyes with love and respect and LET THEM TELL YOU WHAT THE PROBLEM IS. You will get to the bottom of the blockage, and, with respect, kindness, and compassion, you can help them solve it. That will teach them so many things on so many levels: (1) constructive communication skills; (2) sandwiching; (3) asking questions of a loved one rather than lobbing knee-jerk criticisms at them to find out what the problem is and then together figuring out how to solve it; (4) ways to resolve conflicts *without* blame, anger, or finding fault; (4) problem solving through love and understanding. Voilà!

By approaching a problem with an attitude of love, respect, and compassion, and by asking questions rather than barking out criticisms and orders, and knowing everything is resolvable with a calm and caring tone, you can attract so many flies with all that honey! There's no hitting necessary when you're all sitting in a honey pot together eating honey.

some clever strategies for teaching
that are both loving AND effective

When I took my dog to production training, they told us that if we hit our dog, it would only confuse him and make him neurotic. They said, "Dogs don't understand violence. Rather, they understand the anger in their owner's face and body. That lets them know Mama is not happy with what they have just done. It's not the hitting that teaches them; it is the energy in your body, your emotions emanating from you in that moment."

Children pick up on Mama's feelings as well. They are incredibly sensitive and intuitive regarding when Mama is happy with what they are doing and when Mama is not happy with what they are doing. And they always want to please Mama. So know that if you want to teach your child right from wrong and keep him or her safe, it's the emotion in your face and body that communicates to them that what they are doing is not okay. It is your energy that does the teaching. If you hit them, they will be confused, like the dog, because, "Why is Mama trying to teach me how to not get hurt by hurting me?" It does not compute. If Mama wants them to learn and be safe, then why is she hurting them herself? So remember that if you want to teach your child without permanently injuring them, communicate with them using your centered, serious voice, your attitude of seriousness, and your all knowing wisdom. Don't rage, don't be 'angry'. Anything you can say to your child in a rage you can say to them in a calm and centered manner. There is a difference between talking to your child in anger and talking to them in a stern tone, like you mean it. But when there's no physical violence involved, only a deliberate seriousness, they will get the message.

My friend Debra, who raised three beautiful children into healthy, happy adults – two girls and a boy. Each one is thriving in their career and in a long term loving relationship. The entire family loves each other like crazy – Mom, Dad, sisters, brother, spouses. In fact, they all just flew to Mexico for a week-long family reunion. Every single family member showed up for it, and everyone had a ball.

Debra told me one story and one strategy that she used that proved to be a win-win in her child rearing. Her two-year-old son kept running out into the street. She wanted to impress upon him how dangerous that was, but she didn't want to spank him, because she knew that would hurt him. So she got an inflatable ball and had her little boy sit on the back of the couch and look out the living room window onto the street. She said, "Sit here for a minute; I want you to see something." This was brilliant. Just as the trash truck was about to drive by the house, she threw the ball out into the street. The driver didn't even see it, but the truck destroyed the ball. Just flattened it like a pancake. Debra said to her son, "Do you see what just happened to that ball? That is what could happen to you if you run out into the street. So don't do that any more, 'kay?" At that moment, her son 'got it', and he never ran out into the street again. She knew how smart her little boy was, and she knew that seeing that ball smashed flat by the truck would leave a lasting impression on him. And it did. My friend understood how smart kids are, and she understood that communicating with her kids in an intelligent way, with proof, would teach them exactly what they needed to learn.

The other thing Debra did was, whenever she talked to her children, she would kneel down in front of them so she could be at their level. She didn't want to talk down to them; she wanted to always look them in the eye and speak to them at their level. To this day, Debra and her husband have happy and loving relationships with all of their children. Just sayin'.

a formula for a successful
18 years with no spankings

Hugs, jokes, games, patient talks explaining why you don't want them going into the street without holding your hand, a stern and insistent tone of voice when necessary, problem solving together, putting yourself in your child's position for feelings checks, reading books together while snuggling.

May your faces be covered with honey! Always!

CHAPTER 10

CARING MORE ABOUT YOUR CHILD'S FEELINGS THAN YOUR OWN

When you hold your precious little baby in your arms, are you not overcome with the desire to, in each moment – each tenth of a moment – make sure that tiny baby's needs are met: That it feels comforted, is given the right amount of food and water, stays warm and comfortable and not too hot or too cold, has clean and good-smelling clothes on? You want to play games with your baby to keep them in good spirits and laughing. And you want to do all this at the sacrifice of your own time, needs, and desires. You don't even have to work at it. Do you know what you are doing? You are caring more about your child's feelings than you are about your own.

But then somehow, as your baby grows into a toddler and then a child, things get complicated, and suddenly it's not so easy to make their needs being met your number one priority. Now you have to juggle keeping them safe, teaching them to stay safe, teaching them to be kind and considerate, and what to do about having a roommate who doesn't always clean up after themselves, says hurtful things, and doesn't do the things they're supposed to do. Now what? Aw heck, this is getting hard. You start not knowing when to take care of your child's needs and when to take care of your own, when to let them learn for themselves and when to step in, and when to preserve your sanity when they are acting out. "Whew! Where's my dang instruction book when I need it?!" It's still baked into the floor of that dang gingerbread house!! You're at your wit's end; you just want Junior to hurry up and get grown so you can have some peace! This is when your best strategy is to simply stay calm and pick your battles.

stay calm and pick your battles

Before you address an issue with your child, ask yourself whether it is really that important, or whether you can let it slide for now and simply say, "I see you're having kind of a hard time right now. Would you like a hug?" And I would venture a guess that your child will say, "'kay," and in the moments of that hug, all the worries of the world will vanish for parent and child. That will be the perfect time to ask your child, "What's going on? What's upsetting you?" and then let them talk. And cry. Crying is wonderful for getting out the pain. There is nothing better than crying and being held by someone who loves you. You can tell your child that you have felt that way before; that life is sometimes hard and you understand their feelings. Then you can say, "Is there something I can do that will make you feel better – make this less painful for you?" And then you will easily be able to help your child come up with a solution and at the same time feel supported and comforted. You can always shore it up with some words of encouragement like, "You got this!"

can I get a "you got this!"

When I was in my 30s, I put on two evenings of a show called *An Evening with Janet Stegman.* I sang, I danced, I did stand-up comedy, I told stories. The first night went great. The second night, I lost my voice before the show. I was backstage crying, trying to muster the courage to go on stage and do something, *anything,* and figuring out what I could put in place of all the singing that was in my show.

I had asked my mother to sell tickets from the ticket booth in the front of the theater. I was 20 minutes late starting, because I was, well, crying, because I had no singing voice. When she came backstage to see what was happening, she saw me crying. She could have said, "What's wrong? Oh come here, do you need a hug? Listen, you are a talented entertainer. You go out there and just have fun with whatever brilliant substitutes for your songs you do, and then so will we! You got this! Go get them! I love you, you'll be fine. You don't have to be perfect. Just go have fun, okay? Whatever you do will be great! I'm going to go sell those tickets now." But she didn't say that. Looking directly at the tears falling from my eyes from my panic, she demanded angrily, "Well, *is there going to be a show or not*?! I've got people wanting to buy tickets! They want to know if there's going to be a show!" That was it. That was the sum total of my mother's comfort. She was more worried about what people were thinking about her not knowing whether there was going to be a show than she was about my having to put on a singing show with no singing voice. Seriously?! People! Stuff happens, and all that really matters is loving and supporting each other through whatever we are going through. It's not how a parent might look to others. It is not about what people will think about the parent. It is not about what the neighbors will think. It's about, "What is my child feeling, how can I comfort my child, and what will make her feel encouraged to keep going and not give up?" "What can I say to make her feel complimented?" "What can I praise her for?" "Let me find *something, anything* to raise her spirits and give her the courage to pick herself up by her bootstraps and keep on going."

the only way you can fail is by giving up

The only way you can fail is by giving up. No one, absolutely no one, is perfect. If you can remember that and also that the *most* important thing to consider are your child's feelings – putting yourself in his position and thinking how you would feel if you were in that situation, asking yourself what would make you feel better if that were you. Children are *so* human! They just don't know how to do stuff. They don't know how to deal with pain. They don't know how to deal with rejection. They don't know how to keep on going when they fail. They don't know how to keep trying when they displease you. Compliments, praise, understanding, compassion, constructive advice, love, hugs, comfort, "It's okay. No one's perfect. I love you and it's okay if you're not perfect." Those kinds of things.

green eggs and ham

"Green Eggs and Ham! I'll recite *Green Eggs and Ham*! in place of my songs!" I did, and it was hilarious!! The audience *loved* it!! One of the students from my theatre company and her mother were in the audience, and they absolutely *loved Green Eggs and Ham*. The mom told me they went home after my show, made hot chocolate, and sat in front of the fireplace drinking hot chocolate and talking about all the things they loved about my show.

My parents took my boyfriend, who was also my accompanist and co-star, out to eat dinner after the show. I could really have used some praise right about then, so I asked, "Did you *love Green Eggs and Ham*? "We didn't really like *Green Eggs and Ham,"* and then they started talking about politics and the law. Where's my hot chocolate and fireside chat about all the things I did great with no singing voice?! Where's my "That was such a great show!!" "Here's all the things we loved about your show!" "We're so proud of you! Both last night and tonight! You came through, and the folks seemed to really love *Green Eggs and Ham*! How resourceful were you to think of reciting a Dr. Seuss book at the last minute! I definitely saw people smiling and laughing. What else? Your swing dancing was terrific. Your comedy was funny; I especially liked the one about the..."

Parents need to revel in showering their child with compliments and praise. And sandwich the...guidance...if you *must* share a suggestion for how they might do something differently. But gush on about the positive. You just can't gush too much!

caring for their feelings, compassion, understanding, and patience

Caring for your child's feelings, compassion, understanding, patience, tolerance, humor, help, love, and support, even when they make mistakes, do wrong, or mess up. Children will learn their own lessons, if they are left alone to do so. They will *not* learn their lessons if they are being berated for making the mistakes they need to make in order to learn those lessons. All we do is learn lessons. Even as adults.

What adult among us has never made a mistake? The hope is that we learn from our mistakes. Sometimes we have to make the same mistake twice or three times until we see the lesson our mistake is trying to teach us. That's called being human. No one is perfect – not even one of us. Okay one. But he was perfect because he didn't judge himself, and he didn't judge others. Everyone was perfect in his eyes. And that is the way to help your child reach a healthy, happy adulthood – with a solid sense of self and a high level of self-esteem. When it is your intent that your child exude self-confidence and self-love with every step, through all the successes and during every lesson being learned, they will. Love does not demand perfection. Love does not expect perfection. Love does not get angry when perfection is not achieved. Love loves unconditionally. Love *finds* good things to say about a person to that person. Love realizes that when a person is down, kicking them is not only counter-productive and does not serve any purpose whatsoever, it paralyzes the person from being able to pick themselves back up, brush themselves off, and keep going. When a child is down, treat them with love and understanding. Give them words of praise, love, appreciation, and compassion. I've been there: I've made some terrible mistakes. "It's okay, we all make mistakes. What did you learn from this? Anything? Anything?" And laugh. Find the humor, find the funny. Teach your child to learn from their mistakes and go on. Don't let them dwell on the mistakes. Dwell on the lesson, the funny, and understanding, and the compassion. Mistakes are no big deal; they are a part of life. Love yourself, love your child, love your lessons. And always remember: We all make mistakes.

a plan of action

When everyone is safe, take a step back and see yourself in the eye of the storm with this hurricane going on all around you. Keep your sense of humor and realize what's important, and most of all, know that this too shall pass. Then re-read Chapter 7: Sandwiches. Read it ten times so it becomes ingrained in your psyche and you automatically choose a positive strategy.

control disguised as punishment disguised as discipline

I was 6 years old sitting in my first grade class. The teacher led the class in a song. Then she asked, "Did you guys like that song?" All the kids yelled in unison, "Yes," except me; I yelled, "No!" Then the teacher led us through a second song. She asked, "Did you like that?" Everyone else yelled, "Yes"; my lone voice yelled, "No." Then the teacher said, "Janet, did you really not like that song? "No," I admitted. "Then why did you say "No"? I said, "I was just kidding." The teacher decided I needed to be punished for that and ordered me to "Go and sit on the bench outside the classroom and think about what you just did." I was five. I don't know why I yelled "No". Maybe I needed some attention – *albeit* negative, but probably I just needed someone who was not depressed to give me some attention and put their arms around me. Maybe I didn't like the song. I think I didn't really care, I was just needing some love. But seriously?! You're going to punish me for that? I was five.

I went outside and sat all alone on the bench outside the classroom and cried for the rest of music class, which seemed like an eternity. Then the teacher sent a student out to tell me I could come back in. Gee, thanks. Thanks for that. What if that teacher had just moved on and let it be okay for a student to say they didn't like a song? Let it be okay for a five year old to say no when you ask them if they liked a song. Or if it upsets you, give them the benefit of the doubt and think maybe they are needing some love and attention. Did she ask me if my mom was clinically depressed? No. Why not give a five year old the benefit of the doubt and give them praise and attention at recess or after school, or God forbid during class, "Janet, are you okay? Is there something making you feel sad? Do you feel it's your fault that your mom is clinically depressed? Do you feel helpless to lift your mom out of her clinical depression?" Not one time did that teacher set me down and ask what was going on at home. No care for my feelings, no love. Just punish, punish, punish. What that teacher taught me was that it's not okay to stand out or disagree with the group. She taught me that if I do stand out or disagree with the group, I will be punished.

Later that year, the teacher, out of the blue for no reason at all, moved me from my spot in the front row to the back row and did not tell me why. I felt I had been ripped from my people in the front row and sent to the back row where I didn't know anybody. I was six. Anyway, the teacher had given the class a writing assignment right before she moved me. Well, after she moved me, I was so upset and felt so unjustly moved – I didn't understand why she had moved me – and I just put my pencil and paper down on the corner of the desk, laid my head down, and cried and cried and cried. To this day, I remember how upsetting that was to me. That is one of the scenes on my five minute sizzle reel of the memories I have from my childhood. Do you think that teacher ever came over and asked me why I was crying, or cared anything for my feelings? She did not. Would it have been so hard for her to come over and ask, "What's wrong, Janet? Why are you crying?" And I could have told her, "Because you moved me away from all of my friends in the front row. I don't know anybody in this row." And she could have explained in a caring way something like, "I moved you because I needed Charlie to sit closer to the front so I could make sure he was paying attention and learning. You didn't do anything wrong. How about if I make Kate in the seat next to you your special friend? Kate, this is Janet, Janet, this is Kate. Kate, can you play with Janet at recess?" All I wanted was for someone – anyone – to say to me, "Why are you crying, Janet?" and care about my feelings.

caring more about your child's feelings than your own rocks!

The benefits of caring more about your child's feelings than your own are enormous: First of all, your child will be calm and happy. Second of all, your child will be calm and happy. Third of all, your child will be calm and happy. In addition, your child will know she is loved, that her feelings are cared about, that she is worthy of having loving relationships, that she is comfortable with loving relationships, that there are loving relationships to be had for the rest of her life. No one ever died from too much love, too much kindness, or too much quality time together talking about their feelings and what the two of you can do to make her feel cherished and cared about.

good, long hugs and then
more good, long hugs

Nothing says "I love you, my precious child. Everything is going to be all right," more than a good, long hug. Even better, a good, long, bonding 20 second hug. In addition to making you feel good for the rest of the day, a good, long bonding hug causes hormones and neurotransmitters to be released in your brain to lift your mood and strengthen your immune system. I always feel like a good, long hug restores my energy to my center and generates feelings of peace and calm in my body.

Stuff happens. People do what they do, and we don't always know why. But one thing is for certain: If you care more about your child's feelings than your own, life will be easier and more enjoyable for parents and child. And who knows? Maybe someday that child will care more about your feelings than their own when you are older and really need that. It will be a lovely sight to see that your child feels that caring more about your feelings than their own is a good way to live. And then you will know what an AMAZING parent you were!

CHAPTER 11

IF YOU TELL THEM THEY
ARE THEY WILL BE

*"If you think you can do a thing or think you can't do a
thing, you're right."*

–Henry Ford

Everything you tell your child will stick with them for the rest of their
life. They will never lose the feeling they had when they heard what you
said to them. Children are profoundly impressionable and absorptive –
soft to the core, like the inside of a ripe peach. They hang on to and
retain every word you say – good or bad – forever. You're God to them.
When they're young, they think you know everything: You are the sole
proprietor and dispenser of the truth. My mother loved to tell the story
of the time I asked her a question when I was 5 and she said, "What
makes you so sure I know the answer to that?" I replied, "Because you
know everything, huh Mommy?" But I meant it; I really thought my
parents knew everything and that everything they told me was true. It
is the natural state of a child to believe everything their parents say.
To a child, their parents are the ultimate fountain of information; the
quintessential bastion of truth. What their parents say is the way it is.

And to add to the pressure . . . Children believe that everything
you do is the right thing to do. Your child will copy you, because they
are convinced your way is the right way. When they're young and
impressionable and soft inside, your words and acts are gospel. Your

words and attitudes towards your child are what determine whether your child can or whether they can't.

Let's start with the bad. If you say to your child, "You're always late!" "You never finish anything!" "You never clean up after yourself!" "You're always hitting your sister!" "You're crazy!" "You don't know what you're talking about!" "You talk too fast." "You're not listening!" "You use bad grammar." "If you don't start listening to me, you're never going to amount to anything." "You never listen!" You could spend a day listing all the things parents say to their kids letting them know how badly they mess up. Translation: "You'll never amount to anything. You'll never be successful at whatever it is I am putting you down for." It may seem trivial, but the message will be received loud and clear.

a "you" message will ingrain
in your child the "you" message

Every time you use a "you" message to communicate with your child – you don't do this, you never do that – you are ingraining in them the belief that they can't, they don't, they won't, which they will take with them to the grave. All the things you determine are true about them and communicate to them about them from their beliefs about themselves until the day they die – unless they seek extensive healing work. So you want to be very careful never to use negative "you" messages, because what you say to them about them is exactly what you are teaching them that they are. You have to be very careful when you are upset with your child or are trying to correct them or don't like something they are doing or are angry with them never to use a "you" message, and instead to use an empowering message.

When it comes to communicating the positive to your child, I have found that, while "you" messages – "You're brilliant," "You're a smart girl!" "You're beautiful," "You're *such* a talented boy!" – will not cause any harm, a child would rather hear you compliment what they did: "Your mother told me you got an A on your Math test: Nice job!!" "That was an amazing catch!" Even when a parent gives a positive evaluation of their child, it would be better to give a positive evaluation of what they did. No one likes to be told what they are, because it means someone is "evaluating" them rather than simply enjoying their existence, acknowledging their accomplishments, and loving having them as their child. The most effective way to instill self-esteem and self-confidence in your child is with positive "I" messages like, "I laughed so hard at your play today; I never laughed so hard in my life!" Your child will bask in the knowledge that they touched your life in a positive way more than they will bask in the knowledge that you think they're funny. In a way, positive "I" messages are a judgment. Kids don't really want to know what others think of them; rather, they want to know how they touched your life in a positive way. "When I look at your painting, I feel light and joyful, like I'm up flying with the butterflies!" "I loved watching you pitch – I couldn't believe how you threw every single pitch *directly* over home base – amazing!!" "My heart fills with joy when I see you helping your sister learn to walk. So gentle!" "I laughed until I cried hearing you told those jokes at your birthday party!" I mean, yeah, of course, you will naturally want to tell them, "You're amazing," and "You're awesome!", "You're my love!" I'm not saying stop using positive "you" messages – maybe just mix them up with positive messages of how your child makes you feel when they do the great things that they do.

You can also say things like, "That was pretty darn smart of you to put that puzzle together all by yourself!" "Well, I think you're a genius! I can't believe you came up with that creative design for your Mr. Potato Head all by yourself!" or "I'm blown away that you whipped up a dinner for the whole family at 11 years old! And it was *delicious*!"

if you tell them their work is excellent, it will be

In my children's theatre classes and productions, whenever I told a student what they just did was excellent, they kept up the excellent work. When I said, "That was brilliant – keep doing that!" they did. And honest to God, the productions I directed and produced, after teaching the kids their musical theatre skills, were brilliant – Broadway caliber. I am not kidding; I am not just saying that. If you go online and watch *Into the Woods directed by Janet Stegman* or *The Pirates of Penzance*

Directed by Janet Stegman, you will see what I'm talking about. The main thing I did was constantly tell them what they did right and well – that their performance was brilliant, that I loved what they were doing, and that they made me laugh. They could see me out in the audience during rehearsals laughing at their comedic scenes. While they were singing, I would gush, "That's beautiful! Gorgeous vibrato!" or "Love it! That is a beautiful tone!" "You guys are brilliant! Really amazing!!" I know my positive feedback and profuse gushing worked, because many of them went on to have successful theatrical and musical careers. Some are recording artists, one started her own theatre company and was nominated for a Tony Award for excellence in teaching theatre, one is a professional magician in Las Vegas, one is a Christian recording artist. So I know to a T that if you tell children their work is brilliant, that they are a joy to watch, that their audiences are loving their performance, that they are touching the lives of their audience so much that each person in the audience is a different person when they leave than they were when they got there, they will command their absolute best everything. That is where they will forever live in their mind. That is the message they will remember. And that is what they will ultimately believe about themselves – consciously and unconsciously.

nix on the name-calling

The same goes for the negative. My father used to tell me constantly, "You're such a know-it-all". I'd tell him something, and if he didn't agree, instead of just saying, "Well, I don't agree with you," he would say, "You're such a know-it-all!" He said that all the time. "You don't know what you're talking about." "You're crazy". "You're nuts!" "Know-it-all!" The things he said about me to me have stayed with me my whole life. They made me feel disrespected for my knowledge and beliefs about a subject. They made me feel I was almost always wrong about what I believed or knew. Even if my father had a different version of the truth, he could have just said he didn't see it that way, or he didn't agree. He could even – God forbid – have said, "Well, what makes you think that? Where did you hear that?" And then we could have compared notes and sources. He could have given me credence for doing my own research and educating myself about the various subjects. He could even have, God forbid, said to me, "Show me the article you read about that: I'd like to read it – I can always learn new things!" But noooo. His constant name-calling continually eroded my self-esteem, belief in my own intelligence, and feeling proud of myself for reading and learning.

When my father told me I was "nuts", it felt awful. It is not helpful for a parent to tell their child they are mentally ill. Well that's what "You're nuts" essentially means. When I was an adult and he didn't like the fact that my boyfriend and I were going to Disneyland dancing, he would say, "What are two poor *slobs* doing going to Disneyland dancing?" because it was an hour away, and I didn't make very much money.

My dad would too often say to me, "You're so gullible" because a few times I trusted people I shouldn't have. He would tell me, "You're overly committed," because I played the clarinet in the high school band, took dance and baton lessons, and had sewing projects going. Whenever I would tell him I was upset that he had put me down or said insensitive or critical things to me, he would say, "You're overly sensitive." He'd say, "You live beyond your means." He was right, I did. I had money problems – because I had such low self-esteem from him constantly putting me down! I already talked about his proclamation to me while I was at his office working for him that, "You don't really want to be an entertainer, you just sit around on your ass and don't go to auditions." My father's proclamations of my flaws did not enrich my life at all, in any way, ever. Every time my father would tell me I was this bad thing or that bad thing, both as a child and as an adult, it ripped a window sill off my gingerbread house. Whatever my father told me about me, I believed. Forever.

mom said I had no skills
and I believed her - forever

If you tell a child they have no skills, not only will they not learn new skills, they will forever believe they have no skills – of any kind.

When I was 23, my eating order got so bad I had no choice but to drop out of college. I absolutely could not function: There was no way I could go to class, study, and take exams. I was in the throes of a hellish food and overeating addiction. Right after I dropped out of college, I went to visit my mother. She was livid. She said, "You have no skills; how are you going to support yourself?" That was how she showed her great understanding, comfort, and compassion. In one foul swoop, my mother invalidated every skill I had ever acquired with her proclamation that I 'had no skills'. I defended myself: "Well, I'm a legal secretary. I can always do that to support myself." She said, "Yeah, you work for your *father*. Big deal." I had been working for my dad as a legal secretary since I was 13. I literally was a well trained legal secretary. Since I was too dysfunctional to pursue my performing arts career, I went on to become a top notch, highly paid legal secretary. That's not something to be ashamed of, and that's certainly not something a mother should be shaming her daughter for. I suppose she could have sat me down and said, "What's the problem with this eating disorder? What can I do to help you get better?" My mother would never acknowledge or even talk to me about my eating disorder. She would say, "There were times I overate. I still finished college. Overeating, so what?! Bingeing?! Bingeing's nothing! When you have a college degree, that'll be something!"

After my mother told me I had no skills, I forever believed that I 'had no skills' – of any kind. Those awful words rang in my mind's ear and formed the bedrock for my belief about myself for my whole life. I felt I had no skills, at anything, like I was incompetent at all the things I had learned to do and all the things I did to help others. My underlying belief about myself was that I 'had no skills'. Truthfully, nothing could have been further from the truth. I was really good at lots of things! Not only was my mother's proclamation about my skill set uncalled for, it was untrue. I had amazing theatrical skills – singing, dancing, acting. I mean, she could have said words of comfort, words of encouragement, and words of wisdom to make me feel supported and hopeful – something like, "Well, you're a beautiful singer and a fantastic dancer and actress. Let's get you healed up and then get you to Julliard. I'm sorry you're having so much trouble with this eating thing.

Don't worry: Everything's going to be okay. I'm here for you." I guess she was worried she was going to have to support me for the rest of my life on account of me being so dysfunctional. But instead of trying to understand that I was having a *really* hard time of life and encouraging me to believe in myself, explaining to me that everyone goes through some hard times in their life, and assuring me everything was going to be okay, she just tore me down about everything.

how I know it's true

My whole life has been a training ground for using understanding and positive feedback to help people feel better and believe in themselves. I was shown that as a young camper at summer camp, and then I saw how well it worked for me as a camp counselor. I saw that by not criticizing or punishing my campers, but rather listening to them talk about feelings and talking to them about how they felt, by conveying understanding and compassion, by encouraging kids to get themselves on a better track and telling them good things about themselves that they maybe didn't know, I had a tremendous impact on their lives, and they went on to feel encouraged and fulfilled as adults.

When I taught musical theatre, I knew from my own training how effective positive feedback was – as much as I complain, my parents acknowledged and supported my theatrical endeavors by giving me dancing lessons, voice lessons, and clarinet workshops. And then when I got older, I immersed myself in classical, pop, and musical theatre voice lessons, dance classes, musical theatre workshops, comedy improv and stand-up comedy training and performing. When my teachers told me how beautiful my singing was, complimented my acting, loved my dancing, it fueled my tenacity and strengthened my ability to reach for and grasp my highest achievements. It filled me with pride knowing I had reached my highest theatrical potential.

So when I began teaching musical theatre to children, I said to myself, "Ah-ha! I know what helped me come to perform brilliantly on stage and lift thousands of people up with my entertainment skills! I'm going to use those same positives with my students and catapult them to *their* brilliance. Which is what I did, and which is what happened.

clients responded wonderfully to acknowledgment of their strong points

When I began my counseling practice, I saw that pointing out my clients' strengths and positive attributes worked wonders for helping them get well. In the beginning sessions, they would tell me all the horrible things they thought about themselves, and after I reflected back to them the wonderful qualities I saw in them, they would raise their head, have a sparkle in their eye, and say, "Yeah? Huh!" One of my most effective tools in my counseling practice is helping clients see the good in themselves –- all the love they give to their family, all their achievements, all their talents.

a moment to reflect on how yay and nay messages affected you

To really understand how deeply what you tell your child affects them, take out your journal and write down all the times you remember somebody telling you good things about yourself, both from your childhood and as an adult, and then write down all the times you remember someone telling you you're-this-or-you're-that, you're-a-this-or-a-that negative messages, and how it made you feel. Let that sink in with regard to how what you tell your child will teach them whether they can or they can't – for the rest of their life. The messages you convey to your child with your words are the beliefs they will take with them to the grave. Your yay and nay messages are the sense of self you will bestow on your child. They are the beliefs that will form your child's self-image – the version of themselves that will be imprinted on their psyche forever. The words you use with your child will be the beliefs they have about themselves for their entire life. If not consciously, then unconsciously.

the wise indian chief and the young brave

There was once an Indian Chief who was known by the tribe to be a great sage. One time a young Brave came to his tee pee and called to him. When the Chief came outside, the Brave was holding something hidden between his hands. "Oh, wise Chief, known by all to be the supreme oracle of the land," the young Brave began, "I hold in my hands a baby bird. If you really are the all-knowing wise man you claim to be, tell me, is the bird in my hands dead or alive?" The Chief took a moment to ponder the question, and then he answered, "My precious, precious child, the answer to that question is in your hands. If I say the bird is alive, you will crush it and then open your hands to reveal a dead bird. If I say the bird is dead, you will open your hands and let the bird fly free."

If you tell your child they are a lazy loser, they will be. If you communicate to your child that they are brilliant and loving and can do anything they put their mind to, they will be and will be able to. When you say, oh, my kids are this, my kids that, well, yeah, they are, because you told them they were.

You parents hold in your hands your child's self-esteem, self-image, beliefs about themselves, and heights to which they will allow themselves to reach. If you communicate to your child that they are a creative genius, if you show your child you think they are beautiful, if you impress on your child that you find them to be perfect just as they are, if you tell your child you love them unconditionally and nothing will ever cause you to stop loving them, if you let your child know they are smart and can do anything they put their mind to, THEY WILL BE THAT; THEY WILL FEEL SAFE AND SECURE AND LOVED AND CHERISHED, AND THEY WILL BE ABLE TO DO ANYTHING THEY PUT THEIR MINDS TO!

Some really great books on how to talk to your children for a favorable outcome are:

» *Stop Arguing with Your Kids: How to Win the Battle of Wills by Making Your Children Feel Heard* by Michael P. Nichols

» *How to Talk So Kids Will Listen & Listen So Kids Will Talk* by Adele Faber & Elaine Mazlish

» *How to Talk so Little Kids Will Listen: A Survival Guide to Life with Children Ages 2-7* by Joanna Faber & Julie King

» *The Power of Positive Talk: Words to Help Every Child Succeed* by Jon Merritt & Douglas Bloch

» *Parent Effectiveness Training: The Proven Program for Raising Responsible Children* by Thomas Gordon

Messages pregnant with understanding, compassion, love, and kindness will give a huge boost to your child's self-esteem and help them to believe they have the ability to achieve greatness and live in peace and happiness. You are the arbiter and designer of your child's belief in themselves. Go and design beautiful messages, and you will forever be happy with your BEAUTIFUL CHILD!

CHAPTER 12

QUALITY TIME WITHOUT THE GIRLFRIEND

stuff

Kids like stuff. But they don't really want stuff. They want a little stuff. But what they really want is you. They want your undivided, pleasant attention. They want you to want to be there spending time with them doing fun, interesting, and challenging things. They want to do things *with* you. They love putting puzzles together, baking a cake, going on a walk, shopping at the toy store for toys and books, going to the library and the bookstore, making crafts, playing ball, dancing, and singing. With you.

I know I complain about my parents criticizing me and my father being excessively controlling and inappropriate with me. But the one thing they did do for me was the most important thing a parent can do for a child: They showed me how much they loved me. The reason it was so easy for me to reach out for help for my addictions was that I knew in the deepest part of me that I was loved, that I was worthy of being healed. The way my parents showed me they unequivocally crazy loved me was by spending quality time with me doing fun, interesting, and challenging things. They came to all my dance recitals and plays; and then when I was older, they came to see every musical I ever directed and all the musicals I starred in.

My mother used to take me to the movies, to plays, out to dinner, on road trips, shopping for clothes, to visit friends and family. I liked having stuff, but I wasn't driven to harangue my parents into getting me expensive toys or clothing, because they gave me their time and their love.

My father would take my brother and me to Disneyland, on vacations, to the lake, up the coast, to the beach, out to fancy dinners.

My father and I used to love to get out and dance Swing whenever there was a band at the restaurant we were dining at. My parents taught me The Jitterbug when I was 7, and whenever we were at a restaurant or a wedding, my dad would flip me around and do all the aerials. As I got bigger and my dad got older, we didn't do all the aerials any more, but we continued dancing swing together until he died at the age of 92 . My dad *loved* swing dancing. It brought him tremendous joy. I guess the apple doesn't fall far from the tree!

When my eating disorder reared its ugly head at the ripe old age of 17, I tried a few "solutions" – Weight Watchers, sticking to diets - oh that went well; making bets (even better); Schick for the Control of Weight. When I realized none of the solutions aimed at merely controlling my addictive behavior were going to work, and that Overeaters Anonymous offered a way to hold my addiction at bay from the root, I did not hesitate to reach out for help: to go to meetings, get a sponsor, and work the steps. It felt very natural to me to immediately reach out for help for my addiction. I never even entertained the thought of simply wallowing in my misery and not doing anything about it. I never had the desire to walk away and go back to bingeing. Why? Because I loved myself so much that I wanted – with all my heart – 100% of me – to be healthy and happy. I had zero blocks to doing whatever it was going to take to heal my childhood wounds and become healthy, happy, and non-addicted. I know how I healed myself of addiction, and now I can help others do the same.

not perfect

No parent is perfect. No parent can parent perfectly. We all make mistakes. We don't have all the information. We have our own wounds. We get overwhelmed and frustrated. It's natural and human to get overwhelmed and frustrated. It is a complete and total misnomer to even think about parenting your child with perfect parenting skills and no mistakes.

thank God for "I'm sorry"

Thank GOD for "I'm sorry." Children are very forgiving of parenting mistakes or of a parent unintentionally hurting their feelings, when that parent is truly sorry and says so, and means it.

My mother always told the story of how my father once said to my brother, "I want you to apologize to your grandmother, and I want you to mean it!" My mother would tell that story, and then she'd say, "Edwin, you can force him to say he's sorry, but you can't force him to mean it."

If you're not sorry, don't say you're sorry. But if you know you messed up, and you can't bring yourself to say you're sorry, spend a little time exploring why you can't bring yourself to say you're sorry. Refer to Chapter 5 under the heading "check yourself on the control" and write down in your journal what you did that hurt your child's feelings or what parenting choice you made that you wish you made differently. Ask the question, "Why did I do that?" And then answer honestly what you were feeling and what motive you had that was not in your child's best interest. Ask yourself, "What is it inside me that is hurting or angry or afraid that is negatively affecting my parenting choices?" Don't be hard on yourself for whatever you discover: Love yourself through it and come up with some way to give yourself whatever it is that *you* need in order to heal that hurting little one inside you, and give it some time. Then look at the situation from your child's point of view, and see if you still don't want to say sorry. Maybe you will; maybe you won't. But you will have made tremendous progress in some aspects of your parenting skills. And you never know – you might look back at one of your parenting choices and say, "Wow! I made a better choice this time! Look at me go!"

find fun things to do together

Going back to your journal, make a list of activities you would enjoy doing with your child. When you have a free hour or afternoon, read the list to your child and let the child choose which of those things they would like to do. Then go have a blast together doing whatever you do, and know that what you are doing is the greatest gift you can give your child and the greatest way to teach them to love themselves enough so that later in life when challenges come up, they will think so highly of themselves that they will have no trouble doing whatever it takes to get themselves out of a tough spot.

leave the girlfriend at home

Just because you have a girlfriend or a boyfriend doesn't negate your child's need for quality one-on-one time with you. After my parents got divorced, there was a period of time during which my dad got this sexy girlfriend, and when I'd come over for the weekend, there she'd be, tagging along on everything, honing in on my quality time with my dad. I felt like a third wheel – like a voyeur, watching them on their date.

When I was 15, I got my learner's permit, and they'd have me drive them around while they sat in the back making out and exchanging mints. TMI I know. Imagine watching that in the rear view mirror at 15. And it's your dad. And then she'd stay the night and they'd fight and break dishes in the sink. Having her there did not in any way enhance my quality time with my father.

Every situation is a snowflake, for sure. But please *please* make it a priority to set aside time during the week or on the weekend for an outing or other enjoyable activity with your child for quality, one-on-one time together. Without the girlfriend or the boyfriend. Leaving your troubles at the door and immersing yourselves in the glorious moments you are having together.

Quality one-on-one alone time doing fun, interesting, and challenging things is VITALLY important for helping your child feel valued, special, appreciated, and loved.

give your child a fish, she eats for a day
teach your child to fish, he eats for a lifetime

By making it a priority to spend quality one-on-one time with your child doing fun, interesting, and challenging things, you aren't giving your child a fish (an expensive toy), you are teaching him how to fish (that he is loved and worthy of happiness), so now she can eat for a lifetime (reach out for help when she needs it).

What you are teaching your child by spending quality time with them is that they are loved, they are enjoyable to be with, they have great worth, and they are so loved and valued that they deserve to have an unbridled willingness to admit a weakness and reach out for help and do whatever is necessary to get themselves through their rough spots, traumas, and life's losses. You are also teaching them that it is possible to have a life full of fun, interesting, and challenging activities with people they love. What more can a child ask for than a parent who teaches her these things? I believe nothing, my win-win parent!

CHAPTER 13

NEGATIVE ATTENTION IS BETTER THAN NO ATTENTION AT ALL

belief system set personality trait formed

If a child is craving attention, and there is no positive attention to be had, they will seek negative attention. They feel, "I can get attention from Mommy and Daddy no problem – it's just going to have to be negative attention. But, hey, it's attention." And the next thing you know their new belief system that drives their life is "Doing good things gets Mommy and Daddy to ignore me. But doing bad things buys me lots and lots of attention. Note to self: Get my attention needs met by doing bad things." Belief system set, personality trait formed.

If you want to avoid imprinting on your child the personality trait of doing bad things for the purpose of receiving attention, what do you do? Rewind, reset, repair: If your child is craving attention: GIVE IT TO THEM – NO QUESTIONS ASKED.

If you have the thought that your child is doing something "just to get attention", or that they need too much attention, let go of that judgment and give them the attention they are needing. Positive attention. Loving attention. Praise, quality time together, asking them about themselves and letting them talk. Nobody ever formed an addiction from having too much love or attention.

What to do about your "being bothered" by the child "needing too much attention"? Realize it is a judgment coming from somewhere deep within your psyche caused by some unhealed childhood wound.

Take responsibility for having that trigger, and understand that your discomfort is you looking in the mirror at your own wounds.

then what?

Get out your journal, and get a pen. On the first line write: "Why does it bother me that Johnnie needs so much attention?" And then write this: "When do I remember wanting love and attention and feeling deprived because I did not get them?" Compose your own questions to yourself; tailor the questions to your own childhood memories. If you can't think of any, give it some time. You're smart–just be with it for a while: let it percolate in your psyche for a few hours or days; it'll come to you. Then come back to your journal.

Your protest: "I don't have time to write in my journal." The truth: You don't have time not to. Make it a priority, like social media or talking on the phone.

So how do you give positive attention when negative attention is sought? You look behind the negative behavior and find out what your child is really needing. When a baby cries, you don't get angry with that baby for crying: you pick it up and hold it; you see if it is hungry; you try different things until that baby is calm and happy. A child and an adult are just bigger babies. We ask for what we want in different ways, but we still need the same things: affection, attention, our feelings cared about, our needs fulfilled, delicious desserts!

No child ever died from getting too much love and affection or too much positive attention. When a child is satiated with love and affection and positive attention, they will move on to something else: an autonomous activity like making a craft or playing fetch with the dog. A positive activity. They got what they needed; next!

stop the untrue gossip in its tracks

You will hear parents, aunts, uncles, siblings, babysitters say, "Oh, don't mind him, he's just looking for some attention," or "She's just trying to get attention." People. PEOPLE. It's like a child asking for a glass of water because he's thirsty, and his family members say, "Just ignore him, he's just looking for some water." That child is not wrong for asking for water. That child is not less worthy because she's thirsty. That child should not be the butt of the family gossip, being put down, criticized, and made wrong, because he's asking for a glass of water. It's the same exact thing when a child is needing attention. It's not a crime to need love from and quality time with a loved one. It's human to need attention. It's healthy to ask for attention when you need it. Have you ever asked your spouse or boyfriend or girlfriend for a hug? How dare you need some extra attention! I'm kidding. My point is that, if a child is showing you through their actions, behavior, or mood that they are needing attention, give it to them. With panache. From an open heart. Graciously, generously, overflowing with love. Ask them: "Is somebody needing a hug?" "I guess so." "Is somebody needing a fun outing with their father?" "Sure." "Where would you like to go? Do you want ice cream before or after the park? Well, maybe we should wait till after if I'm going to push you on the merry-go-round."

see me feel me touch me heal me

Everyone needs to be seen by their family and friends – mainly by their parents. To be seen–acknowledged for their contributions: their creative contributions, their acts of kindness, their sense of humor, doing their homework, getting good grades, making everyone laugh, showing up for dinner. Did you ever walk by a friend or acquaintance in the hallway at school, and they didn't say hi. You don't know whether they are ignoring you or just didn't notice they had passed you. Either way, it hurts. You start to question whether you did something to offend, or whether that person has decided they don't like you.

I worked with a woman who had five brothers and sisters. With six kids to take care of, her parents became preoccupied by the necessity of putting food on the table, making sure everyone had clothes on their back and a roof over their head, but they failed to realize the importance of showing each child that they saw their love, light, and comedic abilities and acknowledging their greatness: their kindness, intelligence, creativity, sense of humor. It made her sad, and she carried that sadness well into adulthood, until we were able to clear it in a healing session.

it hurts to be ignored

It hurts to be ignored: you start to wonder whether you are worthy of being seen, if your life matters to anyone. Now imagine those feelings magnified 10 times. Adults can have a chat with themselves "Joan was probably deep in thought and just didn't see me. Worst case scenario, if Joan has decided she doesn't want to talk to me, it's too bad, but I'll be okay: it's not meant to be." A child does not have the philosophical wisdom or strong shell to fend off feelings of hurt and rejection. Long story short, when parents and family members don't acknowledge that they see all the wonderful things about their child, that child will end up feeling invisible and unworthy of being seen. And as an adult, that could lead to the inability to put themselves out there if their career path takes them in that direction. Not to mention that we want to avoid at all costs a lifetime of sadness that could set into your child's psyche from not being seen, not being acknowledged, and not being recognized for their love and light.

children bounce back quickly

Children bounce back incredibly quickly when they are given what they need through a delivery system bursting with love and caring for their feelings.

trouble on Broadway

One day, when I was directing and producing musical theatre with children, I had a bewy bewy bad day. First, I ate too much food earlier in the day–the kiss of death because it gave me a headache and a stomach ache the rest of the day (don't ask me, it was 25 years ago). And then can you believe it I got into a car accident on the way to rehearsal–a dress rehearsal for one of our Kids on Broadway productions. Needless to say, I leaned that quintessential lesson that all actors and directors need to learn, know, and live: Leave your problems at the door. Well, on this one afternoon, I omitted to do that. I'm embarrassed to admit it, but I did.

On this awful afternoon that I still haven't forgiven myself for, my little 7 year old student, Vinnie, a sensitive and brilliantly talented singer and actor, accidentally knocked over a set piece for the Phantom of the Opera segment. (Can you believe it I had 9 and 11 year olds singing Phantom songs–quite magnificently I might add.) Vinnie had inadvertently brushed it with his arm while walking to his place on stage. Oh, the crime of the century. Well you would have thought it was by the way I jumped down his throat like nobody's business, oh I was so mad at him. This poor little darling 7-year-old on the receiving end of the teacher/director's wrath just for knocking down some cheap, crappy piece of furniture. Well, guess what? The next day, Vinnie's mother called to inform me that Vinnie was not feeling well and wouldn't be coming to the rehearsal that night. I knew immediately what had happened. It hit me like a shovel in my gut what I had done. I said, "Would it be okay if I spoke with Vinnie for a moment?" Luckily she said, "Sure." When Vinnie came to the phone, I said, "Vinnie, I am SO sorry for jumping down your throat last night when you accidentally knocked that set piece down. It was wrong of me, it was awful of me, and I am SO sorry. I had a horrible day yesterday: I had a headache and a stomach ache all day, and I got into a car accident on the way to rehearsal. But none those things were your fault, and I had no right to treat you like that. I feel just awful about it. Anyway, I wanted to let you know how sorry I am, and I hope you feel better." Vinnie listened patiently the whole time and then said, "I forgive you." "Thank you. Vinnie? You're a wonderful student and I love teaching and directing you in the shows." "Thanks." "Bye." "Bye."

Welp, what do you know, a few minutes after rehearsal started that night, who came running in ready to rehearse his scenes? Vinnie. All rearing to go. I looked at his mother and she said, "He felt better and wanted to come." My heart burst.

At the next rehearsal, I sat everyone down and made a public apology to Vinnie in front of all his castmates. I felt it was important to apologize to Vinnie publicly as well as privately. I explained the same things to the cast as I had explained to Vinnie and told them that, with all that said, there was still no excuse for treating a student that way. I think Vinnie felt his feelings were cared about. And he was brilliant in the show, of course, as were all my actors.

always a valid reason

There is always a valid reason why a child is needing something from you: love, attention, an apology. They are never "being selfish" or "doing it for attention." If you dig a little deeper, you will find the hurt they are wanting you to heal–some feelings they are wanting you to comfort. Always ALWAYS give them the benefit of the doubt. Always. Always assume your child has a valid reason for wanting attention– from you, from the neighborhood kids, from the teacher, from their classmates, from anyone in their energy field. It is a healthy human need to want attention – to want to be loved, to want to be validated, to want to be recognized, to want hugs and praise and conversation and quality time with loved ones.

give it to them like emergency first aid

If you feel like you should ignore your child's pleas for attention and withhold necessary nurturing because you think your child is "acting out to get attention," don't. Give it to them. Like an effulgent fountain. Like emergency first aid. Give them an attention transfusion. ASAP. I guarantee you will not regret it. Because when you see that child happy and independent and drawing you a picture, with a smile on their face because you gave them the love and nurturing they asked for–every time, you will know you did the right thing. We drop all judgment, cancel all criticism and delete all preconceived notions of why a child is "needing attention". The truth is it doesn't matter why. They know why. If not consciously, then unconsciously. All you need to know is they are asking for your attention. It's not the worst thing in the world to want attention, and it's a good indicator that, in order to grow into a healthy, happy, non-addicted child and adult, they will be needing a little extra love and attention. It's not their fault; they are not wrong for it. They are simply being human. Just like me, just like you, just like all the precious little sensitive diamonds that are our children.

correct response

The next time you hear friends or family discussing something your child is doing and they say, "He is just looking for some attention" is their next sentence, your perfect response is: "He is?! Oh my gosh, I did not realize that. Thank you for the heads up; I'll get right on it!! Thank God you guys noticed that! Gotta go: Got some major huggin' to do!!" And then go have some fun at the park!

Imagine if you were to shower your child with praise for their greatness, affection, and quality time together, how little they are going to need to do bad or off-putting things in order to get the attention they need–because they will already be getting it! It only takes a moment to acknowledge your child at the dinner table for something they did, some contribution to family life they have made. That small acknowledgment will move mountains for your child, and those mountains will stay there for a lifetime. You have no idea how deeply you touch your child with your kind words, your words or praise, and your acknowledgment of their greatness.

CHAPTER 14

··

NO FAVORITES ALLOWED

It is easy, and oftentimes unconscious, not on purpose, involuntary, for a parent to have a favorite child. If you notice yourself having a favorite child, find yourself wanting to tell one of your children that they are your favorite and being extra happy to see that particular child over the others, that is something that needs to be examined, in depth, and healed.

either an aversion or an attachment

Having a favorite child is caused by either an aversion or an attachment: An 'aversion' being something that we just feel not good about, and don't necessarily know why we feel that way; an 'attachment' being something we really, really like and want and maybe even desperately need. I just made those definitions up on the spur of the moment – pretty clever, eh? Anyway, Oftentimes, we will have a knee jerk reaction to something or someone, and more times than not, at the root of it is something from our past – something that happened to us in our childhood, feelings that infiltrated our fetus in the womb, something that happened in a past life – who knows? Something happened to us that caused us to have either an attachment or an aversion.

For example, let's say you're in school and there's a redheaded kid who really likes you, is paying you extra attention, gives you compliments, and wants to be your friend. Something like that might give you an 'attachment' to redheads. So then if you meet a person who has red hair, you will get extra excited to be their friend, because it conjures up memories of the schoolmate from when you were in the second grade who thought you were the whole world. You know, you were his whole world; he just lived and died by you. He thought you were the cat's pajamas. He loved being around you, really had fun with you, wanted to hang out with you and go to the park with you, and do all kinds of stuff together. This redheaded boy just made you feel really good about yourself. When you were around him, you felt loved, you felt wanted, you felt approved of. And maybe that was something you never got from your parents or perhaps didn't get enough of or wished you could have more of. So if that was your experience of having a redheaded friend, if you now have a redheaded child of your own, it's a strong possibility you could have an attachment to that redheaded child as being your favorite.

Or take the antithesis of that: Let's say you're in the first grade, and there is a brown haired girl who is very mean to you. She calls you names, tears you down – about anything and everything. She just manufactures non-issues to tear you down about in front of the other kids and recruits other kids to gang up on you. You will never know why but this girl simply cannot stand the sight of you, and every time you come near her, she makes fun of your name, calls you "Ugly" and tells you, "You are so stupid". She's maybe a "popular" girl, and she persuades the other kids not to hang out with you and to make fun of you as well, tells them you're a geek or you're stupid or you're a social reject. She leads a posse to call you names and put you down until all the time you feel unwanted, unloved, rejected, ostracized, stupid, and like a total social reject. So now, if you have a brown haired child of your own, you might not like him. Because he reminds you of that awful brown haired girl in the first grade and takes you back to those awful feelings of being bullied. Those are the unconscious reasons why you can't shake this attachment or aversion – you most likely will not readily understand why it is happening to you. You won't know why you prefer one child over the others; the feeling will just be there, and you won't be able to get it out of your mind; you won't be able to get it out of your body.

In order to let this favorite or least favorite ranking of your children go, you have to realize that it is all about something in your past that either hurt you or made you feel extra special. And what you need to do for optimal parenting is to get to the bottom of it. You must say to yourself, "Oh my goodness, I'm having a favorite child" or "Oh wow, I'm having a least favorite child, and that is not healthy. That's not a good attitude to have when parenting my children. I need to look and see what it is from my past that is causing me to do this." And then you get out your journal, and you write on the first line: "My redheaded child. Hmmm. When do I remember a redheaded child that made me feel extra special?" Or "When do I remember a brown haired child who made me feel about an inch tall?"

look for triggers

I know I have singled out redheaded and brown haired children, but a favorite or an involuntary dislike of a child can come in any form. So if you find this happening to you, look for the characteristic that seems to trigger these feelings, whether it's the redheadedness or something else. The first step is to look for the triggers. It could be a child who has a face full of freckles. It could be left-handedness. It could also be that one of your children reminds you of yourself when you were that age. Do you have any judgments of yourself from when you were 7? Was there something you did not like about yourself or something you did or mistakes you made at that age? These are the questions you need to ask yourself when you make your journal entries.

It is quite possible that one of your children reminds you of you at the age you are now. Is there something or some things you dislike about yourself now? Are there some habits you wish you could let go of? Perhaps you see those same habits that you don't like in yourself in your third child. Let's say he's a procrastinator and he won't do his homework until the very last second. And then he rushes through it and then doesn't get a good grade on it. And he won't study for the history test until the night before at 10 p.m. when he starts cramming, but then he ends up failing it.

Maybe one of your children is a 'free spirit'. And you loved that about your 7-year-old, but you weren't allowed to express it because you were judged for your free spirit, put down for it, criticized for it. Let's say you were a free spirit and didn't want to wear shoes when you played in the backyard; you wanted to feel the soft, cool grass underneath your feet. You felt a sense of freedom walking barefoot. But when you did, your mom said to you, "Don't walk around barefoot; go put on some shoes!" Maybe you were a free spirit in some other way: Maybe you saw people for who they were and didn't judge them for anything. You saw the beautiful spirit inside them, and you didn't hate anybody, you didn't find fault with anyone. But your parents thought you should judge people, that you should only hang out with the popular kids or the 'beautiful' people, the 'rich' people. Free spiritism can exhibit itself in a number of ways.

we all long to be free to
love those we wish to love

Let's say your child wants to be friends with the 'geek', the 'social reject', the child that everybody puts down and nobody wants to hang out with. (I'm allowed to say that because I was that child. But, of course, that child is nothing but precious and adorable; he or she just hasn't yet realized it.) And when you were a child, you wanted to be friends with the 'social reject', the one that nobody liked and nobody wanted to hang out with. And your parents said to you, "You can't be friends with him: He's 'unpopular'! You should only make friends with the popular students. It could be that the other kids in the class put you down for being friends with that 'social reject', that underdog, the one nobody liked or wanted. The kids in school said, "Oh, you want to be friends with him? Well you're a geek too then. You're a loser too then." And you were browbeaten into ostracizing yourself from the child that you wanted to be friends with.

Fast forward 25 years, and now you see your child wanting to be friends with that unpopular kid, and you think to yourself, "It's not fair! I wasn't allowed to be friends with the 'unpopular' kid, so my child doesn't get to either!" How do I know this? No, I was not kept from being friends with the geek. I *was* the geek. At least that is what the kids at school pounded into me every minute of every day until I couldn't take it any more and joined them in believing it. They convinced me I was a burden on society for being a social reject and had no right to be happy. And I know if I were to have children, I would have some major charges around my child being both 'popular' or/and 'unpopular', because they could be one or the other at different times of their life. I guarantee either experience on the part of my child would come into play for me so as to fill me with a major charge on what their experiences were in a social context at school. And I would have to be verrrry conscious of my attitude towards that child in that respect.

what to do if you find yourself having a favorite

Get out your journal and write the question: "What are the characteristics of this child that I don't like as much as the others? Or if it's the other way around: What are the characteristics of this child that I am favoring over my other children? And then you write down the characteristics. Then you sit for a few minutes looking at your list, and then write down this question: Who does this remind me of in my past? Me, another kid, a parent, an uncle, somebody I loved, somebody I didn't like, somebody who was mean to me? What does this remind me of? Who does this remind me of? And you just sit and think about it. Get quiet, close your eyes. And then you can just write about it and just say, "Let me see." And then try to figure out who it was in your past that was mean to you or extra nice to you or yourself, what you didn't like about yourself. What is it about this child that makes you like them extra or like them less? And then tap on it. Refer to the Tapping for Parents chapter.

samples for tapping

"Even though I have an aversion to Jimmy because he has brown hair, just like Johnny did in the second grade, I deeply and completely love, accept, and forgive myself." Whatever it is that you feel is causing you to have an aversion or an attachment to one of your children, tap on it. Tap on everything and anything about it. And be conscious of it. Be very, watch yourself. Watch your mind. Be very conscious of it. And then give that child extra attention. Or give the other children extra attention. So that even though you see yourself doing it, you can get a head start on yourself and compensate for it so you make sure every child feels loved equally, because there is enough love to go around. There is abundant infinite love from a parent for their children, and it is not appropriate or healthy to have one be the favorite. A parent's love is equal for all the children.

my own personal experience with having a favorite

I noticed myself having a favorite. One of my kittens has a freckle next to her nose. And I find myself not liking her as much as the others. And I say to myself, "Janet, that's crazy. Because of a freckle?" And it keeps coming up for me. And I'm thinking, "What the hell? This kitten is precious and beautiful. What the hell?" And so that's what I have to do for myself. I have to compensate and tell that kitten, "I love you so much!" and know that it's something in myself that's not healthy, and I don't know where it's coming from, but it's about me and not about Simba. It's not about Simba's freckle. It's something about me. And I still have to figure out what it is. But I do compensate for it and make sure she gets equal love. Because I know it's something deep inside myself.

What it all really boils down to is parenting from as conscious a place as you possibly can. If you see yourself having attitudes your gut tells you are not healthy for you or your child, do your introspection, write down everything about it that you can think of in your journal, and, if it so warrants, do the Tapping for Parents explained in Chapter 4 of this book. If you do that and you still have unwanted attitudes towards one, or all, of your children, seek out a qualified therapist with whom you feel comfortable and who you believe can help you get to the bottom of things, and do the work. You will be amazed at how much staying conscious, introspective, and corrective will heighten your parenting experience and you will be thrilled with what a fantastic parent you will continue to be!

CHAPTER 15

HELPING YOUR CHILD THROUGH THE DEATH OF A LOVED ONE

The best time to introduce the concept of death to your child is when death happens. Or when they ask you. Children don't need to know about death until they're ready to know about death. It's not something you need to volunteer: "By the way, there's death." If you introduce it too early, your child won't understand or won't be ready to hear something so dark, and they could become traumatized, like I did when my parents took me to see *Bambi*. I didn't need to see *Bambi* at 3. It upset me so badly that I felt sad for a year. It was too traumatizing, too shocking to my heart, and too dark for a 3 year old. Knowing me, I probably would have been traumatized and sad for a year after seeing *Bambi* at any age. So maybe don't show your kids *Bambi* at all. Just sayin'.

the dogs went to the kennel

I have a sad story about my dad as a child. He used to tell me stories about how my grandfather drove an ice truck for a living. He would drive from one house to the next delivering blocks of ice for people's ice boxes. That is why they called it an "ice box" rather than a refrigerator. My dad and his younger brother would ride on the back of the ice truck as my grandfather delivered the ice. Those were the happy times he remembered. He also told me that the only time he ever remembered his father talking to him was when my father had Meningitis, and his father sat down next to him as he laid in bed and told my father was going to die of Meningitis soon. Well, my dad didn't die of Meningitis. But my grandfather died shortly thereafter of a heart attack. My father was 11.

My grandmother decided it was not appropriate for my 11 year old father or his two younger brothers to attend the funeral, and she had the boys stay with a babysitter for the duration of the funeral. My father was devastated for the rest of his life that all the strangers got to go and say good-bye to his father, grieve the loss of his father, and commiserate together over the loss of his father, but he was not allowed to go. My dad lived to 92, and he never got over it. Every time we'd talk about his dad and his dad dying, he'd say, "They sent the dogs to the kennel. All the strangers got to go to my father's funeral, but not us; they put the dogs in the kennel." He said, "I don't even know for sure that he's dead." My father never got over that. He saw a therapist for 40 years, and he talked about it frequently in his therapy sessions, but he never got over it. He cried every single time the subject came up.

What happened to my father taught me that if somebody dies, especially a parent, God forbid, but also a grandparent or other close family member, it is important that the child be allowed to go to the funeral to say good-bye. If there is a viewing, they need to be escorted up to view the body so they can process the fact that the loved one is truly gone, with a family member there to walk them through it and be there with them. When a child is introduced to the concept of death as it comes up naturally, they will be able to understand it and see that death is simply a part of life, and they will not be devastated by it. I mean, let's face it: death happens.

When there's a death in the family, sit your child down and say, "I need to tell you that your grandma died." "What does that mean?" Depending upon who old they are, if they know about death, you just tell them, "We lost Grandma. Grandma died." But if they're very young, and they don't know about death, then you have to explain the concept of death to them, in a matter-of-fact, gentle way. Without a heavy emotional charge, and with the attitude that death is a part of life, and it happens to everyone at some point, and it is nothing to become distraught over, you can simply feel the sadness and accept that part of the program over which we have no control.

You might just say, "Your grandma passed away. Grandma went to Heaven." You can explain it in whatever way represents your truth about death. "Grandma finished her life here on earth and went to be with Jesus," "Grandpa's body was old and stopped working for him, and he left his body. But you will see him again one day in Heaven." There are no wrong answers, as long as the explanation is delivered with tenderness, patience, and love. You explain to them what death is: "We all have a body and a spirit. Our spirit keeps our body alive – it is the energy source that runs our bodies. Like if you have a car, you can't run that car without gasoline. Well, you can't run a body without a spirit. Sometimes young, but usually old, a body stops working: Too many parts are broken or worn out, and it isn't able to continue keeping the spirit on the earth any longer. If a person's body gets old or really sick and stops working, the spirit leaves the body and goes to Heaven. It's not a bad thing; it's just how nature works. It happens with our pets – pets don't live nearly as long as we humans. But we can focus mostly on how wonderful it was that Grandpa could be with us for so many years and that you had the opportunity to get to know him and love him. We of course feel sad when we lose someone we love, but we try to look at the positive aspects of their life. Most times, when a person dies, their family and friends will organize a gathering to honor that person's life. Sometimes it's called a funeral, sometimes it's called a memorial, sometimes it's called a 'celebration of life ceremony'. With these gatherings, people get together and talk about all the wonderful ways their loved one touched their life – all the fun times, the funny times, the emotional times, the highlights of their life. In that way, family and friends are able to have closure and support each other in saying good-bye for the last time to their loved one. They have a chance to say good-bye, a chance to commiserate, a chance to hug each other and cry together. They get a chance to acknowledge how happy they were to know that person and bring to light all the contributions that person made to their lives. The close relatives are going to need comfort. And casseroles. Lots of casseroles. Cookies are good. Especially the moon shaped ones with the sugar glaze. Well, to be honest, I find the chocolate cake with the chocolate frosting to be the best for comfort.

"Death is simply a part of life. It is healthy to feel sad when we lose someone we love, and then eventually we realize that their death is a happening along the spiritual timeline, it was going to happen sometime, and our loved one would not want us to feel sad for too long; they'd want us to go on and live our life and be happy. They would want us to be happy that we knew them and happy that they were a part of our life. Grandma's funeral is on Sunday, and we'll all be going. I'll hold your hand so that you can see her body. Some people are going to be wearing black, some people aren't. Some people are going to go up and look at the body; some aren't. But the body in the coffin is just the shell that housed Grandma's spirit. And though she is no longer in her body, Grandma's spirit is here right with us."

Your child will have questions, and you'll answer the questions effortlessly as you speak from your heart, as you learned about death yourself or at least wished you could have learned about it when a loved one passed away. It will be a big help to your child to give them the emotional support and the physical closeness they need as you walk them through the process, holding their hand, giving them hugs, having your arm around them in the painful or scary times. In that way, your child can be introduced to death with an "it's just a part of life" philosophy from you, with love, comfort, and support. When they see you taking it in stride and walking through the feelings with courage and confidence, they will in turn learn to handle death in the calm and accepting way in which you have modeled it for them. You never want to make a child feel alone or scared during the death of a loved one. It's the same with a pet they have grown up with.

the perfect situation to teach about death will present itself naturally

If a pet dies before a family member, that will be the perfect time to explain to your child about death. And then it's not just an explanation – it's not just cold, hard facts: It's a life experience during which they are learning from you how to deal with death and other painful life experiences – without allowing the grief to bowl you over. Your child will learn that there is no need to become depressed or devastated. Teach your child that it is okay to feel sad: It is appropriate; it is healthy. "Here, let me give you a hug. We all feel sad sometimes. But we don't have to feel sad forever. We feel the sadness, we get a hug, and we give each other comfort. And then we can move on from sadness to remembering the joyful times."

It is vital that you never let your child experience death alone or from a place of discomfort. It is imperative that you be there to support them every step of the way – answering any questions they might have and explaining things from a calm and philosophical perspective. Death can be scary for a child – traumatizing, in fact; but when children see their parents taking it in stride – feeling sad but not depressed – that is the perfect lesson for them and the perfect way to support them to make it through unscathed. You can even explain the difference between sadness and depression: Sadness has a certain uplifted quality to it; it's one of the feelings we have the honor of feeling on account of being alive – for now, and we will get over them and then we will feel better, laugh even.

Depression destroys you. Depression keeps you from enjoying life and walking effortlessly through painful feelings to the other side with your healthy coping tools. Sadness is just another emotion on the feelings spectrum. Depression is heavy and not healthy. It's harder to pull yourself or another person out of a depression. Depression can be considered a mental illness: It's called "clinical depression". Therefore, you want to make sure your child understands that they don't have to feel depressed out of obligation or be devastated over the death of a loved one. It is important that they understand that death is a part of life – that it is the natural progression for a life here on earth.

Children need to be shown in no uncertain terms that they are not alone and do not have to go through the painful times alone; that they can ask for hugs, have you hold their hand, talk to you about their feelings and what's going on. I can't emphasize enough how important it is that you let them know you'll be right there holding their hand. Always.

so grateful to my parents for their love
and support through family deaths

My parents were there for me every step of the way when their parents passed on. I loved my grandparents like crazy from the time I was born, and they were crazy about me as well. When my grandparents died, my parents were right there with me, holding my hand as we viewed the body, interested in my feelings and thoughts and answering questions all throughout the ceremonies. And believe me, I held on tight. But I never felt alone or scared. I felt sad, but not alone, and not devastated. After I recovered from the *Bambi* debacle, I grew up with a healthy attitude towards death; I learned that it's just a part of life and you simply have to experience it – go to the funeral, feel sad, seek comfort from other loved ones and give comfort to the others – but you don't have to let it destroy you.

a good story to tell

Stories are a wonderful vehicle to help children understand life and death. Every year when I went to summer camp, from 7 years old to 26 years old, at some point during campfire, a counselor or director would tell the story of The Sparrow Wanting to Meet God. I cried then and I cry now when I hear it. Feel free to steal it for a precious moment of comfort with your child.

> There was once a sparrow, and this little sparrow in the worst way wanted to meet God. He wanted to meet God. He wanted to ask God questions about life and give him a hug. The sparrow was determined, and one time he said, "I'm going to meet God." He took off and flew as high and as far as he could. Well, he got tired, and had to come back to earth. But he tried again. This time he went a little further, but again he got tired and it was too much to get all the way to Heaven, so he came back to earth. Again he tried. The sparrow never gave up; he kept trying -- each time traveling further and

getting closer to God. Alas, he was too small to get all the way there, but he refused to give up: This last time, he pushed harder than he had ever pushed before. This last time was too much for him: The sparrow returned to earth and he died. And now every time you see a star in the sky, every little light up there is one of the times the little sparrow tried to reach God.

you can't spare your child
pain by leaving them out

Death may be hard for your child to accept, but you can't spare your child pain by leaving them out of the loop when there's a death in the family. You have to invite them into the loop. They will understand death; they will understand losing someone they love. You are not going to spare them their pain by, as my father put it, "taking the dogs to the kennel." You must bite the bullet, set them down, explain to them about death, and know that with your comforting support they will make it through and be better equipped to handle it the next time it comes up, and then every time they encounter a painful loss.

When someone I care about passes on, I have a healthy response to it and get over it in a reasonable amount of time, because my parents included me in all the family rituals and held my hand during the frightening parts, like going up to view the body, and sitting through the funeral. When someone I love dies, I feel sad, but I do not feel "depressed" or "devastated". I instinctively know that death is a part of life, we are all going to die someday, and it is not something to be devastated over. I know that taking it in stride and feeling all the feelings along the way is the more constructive path. Even when both of my parents died, yes, I was sad, but I was able to carry on with my life and wind up their affairs. I was able to talk about it and laugh at the funny things I remembered from my time with them and recall the good times. I attribute that to the fact that my parents included me in every single family event related to a death and supported me in each moment through talking to me about my feelings, and making sure I felt comfortable crying about it if I felt like crying. Yes, I miss my loved ones, but I know they are in a better place and that they are at peace. I know that one day, I will see them again. It's not good-bye; it's good-bye for now.

CHAPTER 16

THE GIFT OF PETS

In addition to needing to be loved, children need to be able to give love, and lots of it – unconditional, unadulterated love with all their heart, no holds barred. What better being for a child to have alongside them growing up than a pet? Pets add a different type of love than having parents to love or siblings to love. There are dynamics that go on between parents and a child and siblings and a child that can be oppressive to an open channel of love, but pets and a child will share unadulterated, unconditional, unbridled, expansive love. Because animals vibrate at such a high level, and, I believe, are more enlightened than humans – straight from Heaven, growing up with pets will enable a child to feel consistent, ongoing, never-ending love that will last a lifetime. They will learn what deep love feels like, and they can then transfer that love to their relationships with humans as they grow.

Think about when you have had a pet – a cat, let's say. When you were holding that cat, there was nothing but unconditional love pouring from human to cat and cat to human. The same with a dog. All pets, rats included. I mean, stuff can always happen, and you can get angry with a pet. But didn't you always realize after a time that the pet meant no harm, and that they were just being them: a happy go-lucky, playful, at times protective and possessive, animal, and find it hard to stay mad at them? So when a child becomes angry with a pet, the lesson of forgiveness will be an easy one to teach, and your child will come to understand that people do what they do because that's their nature, just like when the dog chews up only one shoe from their favorite pair of shoes.

co-ownership only

It is never a good idea to have your child "own" a pet such as a puppy or a kitten. You don't ever want to say, "Oh, this is my two year old child Jane's Beagle". The time for a child to own an animal is when that child is an adult, with the maturity and where-with-all to make their pet a number one priority. Children are not grounded enough or wise enough to understand and make the commitment to being 100% responsible for the life of a living . But your child can be a co-owner of a pet. Of course, you parents will be responsible for making sure all the needs of the pet are taken care of: that the pet is fed, is kept warm and clean, gets the necessary exercise, stays healthy, and receives lots of attention and affection!

There's nothing wrong with the pet being a family pet that the child can pour their unbridled love out to, without the, unsustainable for the child, responsibility for the life of that pet. That love and affection between child and pet keeps both parties vibrating at a very high level, feeling good about life and happy to be alive. It accustoms the child to opening their heart and loving others. It introduces the child to the concept of having an open channel of love between them and another creature.

the beginning of social responsibility

Being a co-owner of a pet is the beginning of social responsibility for a child. It helps them develop a social conscience and begin to understand the concept that it is a good thing to help those who need assistance. Your child will begin to feel good about themselves when they donate time to a charity or help the less fortunate. Having a pet to love, nurture, and help take care of will teach your child to enjoy caring for another. Their mindset will broaden from thinking only about themselves to wanting to give love, affection, caregiving, and attention to the feelings and needs of another. They will have a live being besides their parents and siblings to love when times get hard and can focus all their love and attention on this other being, saving them from falling into the pit of self-pity and depression. Long story short, taking care of and having a pet to love teaches a child to get out of themselves and their own needs and ego and focus on engaging with another being.

The hope is that when we grow up and have a spouse or an aging parent or friend that needs our help, we can feel comfortable and, in fact, quite enjoy giving of our time and energy to care for them. Having a pet around also prepares a child to give to the world in whatever way they feel strongly about – to help make the world a better place.

When it feels natural for us to give to another, and we give to another, it gives us a sense of accomplishment and fulfillment that we have helped another being survive and live happily. When you give your child the opportunity to love, cuddle, and receive love and affection from a pet as the beginning of their sense of social responsibility, that child's world modulates from centering around themselves to looking outward to how they can help the other living creatures on the earth to feel happy, safe, loved, and well taken care of – and enjoy it! There is no end to the tremendous rewards your child will reap when he or she is given the gift of growing up with a pet, or pets (I have always had several – I live for my pets!). Having a pet or two to love will enable your child to associate giving with enjoyment and love and affection.

Holding an animal that is loving being held releases an inordinate amount of endorphins into your brain. It triples the level of your vibration and makes you feel happy, joyful, loved, centered, appreciated, calm, and at peace. Sharing love and affection with a pet has unfathomable rewards, for both children and adults.

Rocky, Porfirio, Bucky Pepito, Mo, and Beggys I-III

Throughout my childhood, I had dogs, cats, and hamsters, all of whom brought me abundant joy and happiness. My father wrote a column for The Monterey Progress Newspaper. One Saturday when my father went to the Progress headquarters to turn in his column, there was a tiny puppy wandering around, lost and all alone, on the sidewalk in front of the building. My father brought him home and he became our family dog. My parents named him Rocky. Rocky had distemper – my parents guessed he had been roaming the streets for quite some time in the cold. My parents took him to the vet, but the vet didn't have anything to cure him. Well, my mother gave Rocky lots and lots of love and affection. They really let him know that he was wanted and how much they wanted him to get well and live to be their dog. She hand-fed Rocky little pieces of hamburger rolled up into a ball. My parents literally gave that puppy all the love a puppy could ever want. Sure enough, Rocky recovered. The next time my parents took Rocky to the vet, the vet said to them, "I wasn't expecting Rocky to live. I am so happy that Rocky lived that I'm not going to charge you for this visit."

Rocky was a medium size German Shepherd Heinz-57 mix, and when I was born he was already part of the family. There are all kinds of pictures of me holding Rocky's mouth open as a baby and me lying next to him on the living room floor, both of us on our backs, so cute! I remember Rocky. I loved Rocky so much.

We also had a cat named Porfirio, and we have all kinds of family stories about Porfirio. One time my parents put a can of sardines out for Porfirio and left to go to a movie. When they returned home, Porfirio had taken a newspaper and made little tiny strips out of it and covered the sardine can with the strips in a criss-cross pattern. I guess Porfirio didn't like sardines. There are pictures of me with Porfirio when I was a newborn: We were both lying on our backs right next to each other, and he was bigger than me! (I was 5 lbs. 6-1/2 oz. when I was born – my mom never omitted to include the 1/2 oz.!)

When Porfirio died, my parents got another cat: Porfirio's son. A neighbor came over to our house and told my parents, "This kitten is the spitting image of Porfirio, so you're taking him." I guess that was proof Porfirio was the dad, and the least we could do was take the kitten. My mother let me name him. My favorite cartoon at the time was the one in which a fellow smells a hamburger cooking and it smells so good that he raises up and floats through the air. It was part of the "Bucky and Pepito" cartoon series. I was 3. My mother asked me in front of the whole family – grandparents, aunts, uncles, cousins, "Janet, you get to name the kitten. What name would you like to give him?" Without hesitation, I announced loudly to the crowd, "Bucky Pepito". My mother laughed and said, "Okay then, Bucky Pepito it is." I don't know why she laughed; I think that is a great name for a cat!

Brother Matthew with Bucky Pepito

All the members of my family showed overflowing love for animals. My parents adored animals and treated every one of our pets like a member of the family. I remember one time my dad took my brother and me to Taco Bell for dinner. We tied Rocky to the fence next to where we were eating at one of the outdoor tables. When we finished eating, we got in the car and drove home. When we got home, my dad said, "Where's Rocky?" Well, Rocky was still back at Taco Bell tied to the fence by the table where we had just eaten. We rushed back to the Taco Bell, and he was still there. He sure was happy to see us!

One Sunday my father took my brother and me hiking in the Angeles National Forest. My brother and I were sliding down a huge rock in a stream, and Rocky lost his footing and went sliding down out of control. Luckily, I was at the bottom of the slide. I waited for him to reach me at the bottom of the slide and scooped him up and saved his life! It was like butta'. I still remember that God-sent rescue clear to this day as if it were yesterday. Like Got placed me there at that moment to save Rocky's life. I felt like *such* a hero!

My mom got my brother and me a pet hamster. I named him Beggy because he was beige. What a perfect name for a beige hamster if I do say so myself! Everyone in our family took turns holding Beggy – petting Beggy, letting him crawl across our shoulders, all through our hair, under our shirts. He was so soft and sweet. Everyone was in love with Beggy. Well, Beggy had a problem with the lower half of his little body, and he probably was not going to live much longer because of it. My brother and I were devastated – both of us crying a river. My mother called the vet, and the vet told her to bring Beggy in and he would operate on him and hopefully be able to cure him. My mother drove my brother and Beggy to the vet, where the vet performed surgery on him. You should have seen Beggy with that little plastic collar around his neck afterwards so he wouldn't rip out the stitches.

Beggy lived a little while longer, but the problem recurred and he died. All three of us were beside ourselves. So my mother bought us another hamster. Another beige baby hamster. Guess what we named him? You guessed it! Beggy. Beggy II, actually, because he, too, was beige. We felt again that Beggy was the perfect name for a hamster who was beige. To this day we remember with great fondness Beggy I, Beggy II, and Beggy III.

Mo

When I was a junior in high school, my friends and I went to the pound and adopted a darling Border Collie puppy for our math teacher, Mr. Morehead, who had just lost his dog. We named the puppy "Mo", as that was Mr. Koiles, the other math teacher's, nickname for Mr. Morehead. My poor mother – she had to live with all the crazy names I gave our pets. I named one of our dogs Madison Avenue, 'Maddie' for short. Anyway, Mr. Morehead didn't want the puppy, so we offered it to Mr. Koiles. No go: He lived in an apartment. So I brought Mo home. I walked in the door and greeted my mom with, "Hi Mom, we have a new puppy!" At first my mom was a little miffed that I had brought home a puppy without her permission, but by the next day my mom had fallen madly in love with Mo, and Mo was our new family dog. Mo was the *best* dog – *so* well behaved and loving. We still had Rocky – he was a senior dog by then. Mo used to terrorize Rocky, trying to get him to play with her all the time. We loved them and Bucky to the moon and back. Matt and I would put the leashes on Rocky and Mo and they would pull us around the block – like the Iditarod. They really loved it, and so did my brother and me! I remember that like it was yesterday as well.

Janet, Matt & Mom with Mo

Our pets added so much love, so much fun, so much adventure, and so much character to our lives. I will never stop appreciating having animals growing up.

Parrie

When I was an adult, I had a cat named Paraskeva. I named her after my Bulgarian grandmother on my mother's side, Paraskeva Karastoyanov. I called Paraskeva "Parrie". Parrie was a gorgeous little tabby who used to sleep on my chest as I cuddled her while we napped, and when we slept at night. I think Parrie was an angel in a cat's body.

pets rock!

Yes, I love my job teaching dance aerobics to the seniors at the gym. Yes, I love writing my books. Yes, I LOVE dancing and singing and performing stand-up comedy. But my animals are my life. They bring me en-ending joy, affection, and love. They are the loves of my life. They make me laugh. They go everywhere with me. I am madly in love with all of them. They are all my heart. My pets provide the love – unconditional love and affection – that I crave, 24/7. They give it to me and I give it to them. They are happy creatures, and I am thrilled to be able to take care of my animals and hang out with them. We go on a walk every day. We throw the ball. We cuddle together. My little Wiener-Beagle Bengie sleeps under the covers at night and cuddles with me. I took Burt, my big Bernese Mountain Dog Rottweiler mix, to Hollywood Paws to learn tricks because he was so cute, so much fun, and *so* smart and had *so* much personality: Burt is now a trained actor – he knows all the production tricks and has made two t.v. shows. Every now and then, I get a phone call from a friend who says, "I'm watching you and Burt on *The Animal Planet*."

I am so busy teaching my Silver Sneakers class, walking my dogs – with Mrs. Bojangles the cat ("Bo" or "Mrs. B" or "Kiki") on my shoulders. Mrs. B just LOVES being out in nature with us watching the world from the perspective of my shoulders. I love writing my books. I don't really spend much time with other humans. I have friends and acquaintances, but I don't get together with them very often. It's mostly me and the dogs and the kitty: They're my family. I don't have children, but my animals provide me with all the love I need – all the love and affection and play and humor – Mrs. B is SO funny: She does that thing where if she gets close to Bengie, she arches her back and jumps sideways all the way across the room. She tries to tackle Bengie when we play fetch. And when she can't tackle him, she bats him in the face with her paws and bites his legs. And then Bengie looks at me and mutters, "Maaaawmie! Kitty huuwt me!" She really didn't hurt him, Bengie's just a big baby and loves hugs and kisses from Mommie.

living in an animal-loving
family is SUCH a blessing

My parents adored animals, and by bringing pets into the home, they enriched my life to the Nth Degree! Pets are a super-charged asset for a child. Growing up is hard, but with a pet as a constant companion to love and cuddle, life gets a whole lot easier. Pets are a tremendous gift to a child. They are an added benefit to the family and to the quality of life for a child. They bring abundant love, affection, fun, and laughter to family life. No family's going to be perfect: Every family has challenging dynamics and issues. But when there are pets along for the ride, there's always somebody that's there for you to give you unconditional love and acceptance.

animals raise the vibration of the family, and the planet.

Animals raise the vibration of the whole family, because pets are so close to God; they are beautiful, Heavenly beings. When a child is sad – let's say they're not getting along with their parents. But the dog and the cat: They're there for them. Unconditionally. Pets will give your child comfort and affection, something children need desperately when they're down. And when they're up, a pet will instill that love in their heart that every child longs for every minute of every day, everywhere they go.

having pets teaches children compassion

Being raised with pets in the home teaches a child to have compassion for animals, not just in the home, but all over the planet. It gives them a one-on-one close relationship with an animal, complete with touching and a heart connection. It teaches a child that animals all over the planet – both wild and domesticated – are living, sentient beings.

Pets give a child the gift of vast amounts of love they get to feel when they are around them, petting them, cuddling them, talking to them, watching them play, feeding them, and having them always there by their side. Pets show a child the vast amount of love they are capable of feeling and giving to others for the rest of their life.

our pets helped me through
a very painful time

When I was eleven, my parents split up. It was a nightmare for me. I would not wish that on anyone. I watched my family life crumble before my very eyes into two miserable, lost souls for parents, with us kids left to do our best to try and survive the fallout. But through thick and thin, I was blessed with Rocky and Porfirio and Bucky and Mo and Beggys I-III, whose love, affection, and fun were a constant in my life. Those guys helped me stay afloat during my hard times. Not every family experiences divorce, thank God, but I think every family experiences challenging times; every family member experiences emotional difficulties. You can hugely bolster your child's morale – throughout the good and times and the bad – with the gift of a family pet. Or pets! The more the merrier! Bring on the goats, the pot bellied pigs, the rabbits, and the hamsters. And don't forget the hamster wheel! All night, every night. But don't worry: After a while, you get used to it, and it becomes a rhythmic, lulling sound that helps you fall asleep. Pets respond to your love and affection and nurturing in like kind. Even with those trying pet days, the benefits of having a family pet (or pets!) will last a lifetime for the entire family.

Long live the Beggys and the Rockys and the Mos and the Porfirios and the Bucky Pepitos of the world. LONG LIVE FURRY LOVE!

CHAPTER 17

....

MAKE 'EM LAUGH

seeing the humor in situations

What happens when the stock you decided not to buy shoots up from $30 a share to $1 million a share in one year? Do you get pretty mad at yourself when you think of how different your life would have been if only you had known...or do you laugh at your total ineptness to get your life path to go in the direction of large quantities of money? Well, I start out with the one – Bitcoin – and then I go to the other – an if-I-don't-laugh-I'll-cry kind of thing. We can choose to react to challenges, mistakes, and losses by getting angry with ourselves, criticizing ourselves for making the "wrong" decision, putting ourselves down, and judging our actions as wrong or stupid. Or we can find the funny, find the humor, in every situation – excluding, of course, grave situations like the death of a loved one or a pet, or cruelty. There's nothing funny about those things. But for the most part, a parent can find humor in every mishap, misstep, and mistake. You can laugh at yourself – make fun of yourself for making such a silly mistake. I have learned to approach each and every mortifying situation from the viewpoint of a stand-up comedian.

my funny life

I have learned that it is much easier to cope with life and things go much more smoothly – especially on the inside – when you can laugh rather than cry about stupid things that happen. We all have foibles. We all have idiosyncrasies. It's not embarrassing to have faults or idiosyncrasies or weaknesses. I believe that God gave us humor to help us cope with life, to make life fun, to give us a means to keep our vibration high, and to help us stay healthy and happy through thick and thin.

my hilarious family

My Uncle Dick, on my father's side, always came to our family holiday celebrations with a joke ready to tell us. Like this one:

One day in church, the priest arranged for Little Joey to be part of the service. When the choir sang, "And the angels lit the candles," Joey was to sneak over and light the candles. When it came time in the service, the choir sang, "And the angels lit the candles." Nothing. No Joey. The choir director raised his arms again, and the choir tried it again, "And the angels lit the candles." Again, no Joey, no candles being lit. The choir director tried a third and final time before giving up, directing the choir to sing loudly: "And the angels lit the candles!" All of a sudden, Joey's voice rang out: "And the cat peed on the matches!"

We used to laugh a lot in my family growing up. When I was seventeen, my mother was appointed to the municipal court bench. In addition to being a Judge, my mother was a stand-up comedian. She used to have entire courtrooms in stitches.   When my mom was appointed to the bench, she'd have the

When my mom was appointed to the bench, she took her stand-up routines with her to the courtroom. She'd have the jury laughing, she'd have the audience laughing, she'd have even the defendant laughing. One criminal case my mother heard ended up having a lot of humorous things happen during trial. At one point, when my mother was *voir diring* the jury, she asked the jury, "Have any of you ever been the victim of a crime?" One juror raised her hand. My mother asked, "What crime were you the victim of?" The juror replied, "Evangelism." "Evangelism?" queried my mother. "Yes," replied the juror, "My car was evangelized." My mother asked, "What kind of car was it?" The juror replied, "Yellow." My mother asked, "What color was it?" Juror: "Chevrolet."

One of the days during that trial, the air conditioning went out during lunchtime. When the jury came back from lunch, my mother said, "I have a very important request to make of all of you. It seems our air conditioning has gone out, so NOBODY EXUDE ANY BODY HEAT." Well she had the jury laughing, and then they expected her comedy, and looked forward to it. At the end of the trial, they all said they had a great time sitting on the jury. The defendant told my mother, "Thank you, your honor, I had a great time. I would have had an even better time if I hadn't been the defendant."

My mother was just finishing her coffee in the break room before court one morning, and two male lawyers came in and said, "Can ya get us a cup of coffee, Dear?" My mother, deadpan, replied, "Well, what you do is you get your own coffee and you put a quarter in this coffee can right here. And then when you're finished, you wash your coffee cup and put it in this rack." The lawyers insisted, "Aw, c'mon, Hun, can't you just get it for us?" My mother said, "No, I can't: I'll be late for work." And with that, she left the break room, went to her chambers, put on her robe, and went out and took her seat on the bench. And court went into session. A few minutes later, who waltzes into the courtroom? You got it. The two lawyers. My mother said that when the two lawyers saw my mother sitting on the bench about to hear the case they had come to argue, they just turned white. My mother smiled, and in her kind and concerned tone, asked, "Did you find your coffee all right, counsel?" "Oh, yes, we did. Thank you, your honor, thank you." When my mom got home that night, she told us that story, and we laughed and laughed. That story stood my family in good stead for 30 years. We never ran out of ways to make people laugh at any and every gathering we ever attended. We never got tired of telling that story, and no one in the family ever got tired of hearing it.

My mother told a defendant, "You need to either pay the fine by June 6th or else return to court on June 7th. The defendant whispered something in her lawyer's ear, after which the lawyer said, "You Honor, my client doesn't understand what she's supposed to do." My mother said, "Okay. So, if your client wakes up on the morning of June 7th and finds that she has not paid the fine, she needs to come to court."

Another time, my mother asked a defendant if he wanted her to appoint an attorney to represent him, and he said, "I don't know, do you think I need one?" My mom responded, "Well, let's see," as she opened up his file and plopped it down on the bench, "You have two drunk driving charges, a marijuana charge, and a failure to appear. I'd say you need an attorney." The defendant said, "Okay." I remember going to watch her that day, and she was just on a roll, having the time of her life. I had to stick a Kleenex in my mouth to keep from laughing out loud. The people sitting next to me were laughing, and I said, "That's my mom." They said, "She's funny." I said, "I know."

There was a doctor on the witness stand testifying. When it came time to break for lunch, my mother announced, "All right, we will take a recess until 2:00, at which time we will resume the examination of the witness." The doctor protested, "Can't we finish up now? I can't come back after lunch: I have patients." "No. I am hereby ordering you to come back this afternoon to finish up your testimony." The doctor insisted, "Well, I'm not coming back." My mother took a breath and then recited the poem she had just made up: "Doctor, ours is not to question why; ours is but to testify." And then she turned to the audience, held up her right index finger and said, "Hmmm. Not bad." The doctor still objected, "Your honor, I have patients, I can't come back." My mother said, "You see that door over there? The one you entered the courtroom from this morning?" "Yes." "Well, if you don't come back this afternoon, you will be entering the courtroom from that door over there – the one the defendants enter from when they come in from the lock-up." She always just made stuff up on the spur of the moment.

My mother found the humor in every situation. She would use humor to diffuse what was looking to be a potentially grave and tense situation. She had everyone laughing, just when they were expecting to be stressed out and afraid of her. Many of the lawyers who worked in my mom's court – both the prosecutors and the defense attorneys – told my mom, "This is the most fun I've ever had in my whole career, and I look forward to coming to work every morning.

the Glendale Bowl

My first time performing my stand-up routine was at The Glendale Bowl – in the bar of the bowling alley. It took me six months of stand-up comedy workshops before I felt ready to get up. I was *really* nervous, but once I got on stage, I had the time of my life. One at a time, both of my parents decided that they, too, wanted to get up. So, one after the other, they both went to the same Greg Dean comedy workshops that I had taken before my first time going up – at the Bowl. Both my parents were really funny. You should have seen it: An entire bowling alley nightclub full of lawyers and judges there to see their fellow judge perform stand-up.

My dad was very funny, too, when he did his showcase. He had this routine in which he said, "I'm a lawyer. My clients are so upset by the invention of the cell phone – they complain to me that every time they go to rob a bank, before the money's in the bag, every customer in the bank has called 911 and the police are at the door to greet them. Now they have to file for unemployment. They ask me, 'What should I say I do for a living?' It's a real problem."

My brother was funny, too. Especially when I was sitting on his lap with my hands behind his back while he did the arms as I told the story of Horace. He always tried to put his finger in my nose. I had to move my head all around to stop him. The whole camp was in hysterics.

The family that laughs together...keeps talking to each other.

learning to find the humor in all situations

Growing up, I learned to find the humor in every situation, and it got even more ingrained in me when I started performing both improvisational comedy and stand-up comedy. I spent 26 years in comedy improv and stand-up workshops. I became a stand-up comedian and an improvisational comedy artist, and I learned to laugh at all my foibles. When I laugh at my own foibles, others can laugh with me because they've got foibles too. It takes away the tension. So whenever there is a time when I can laugh at myself or what is happening to me or the stupid thing I did, I do, and it makes life a whole lot easier and a whole bunch more fun. If you like, you can catch the culmination of my 25 years of stand-up comedy workshops, going to open mics, and waiting hours to get up to do 10 minutes, and finally producing my own comedy show in Hollywood. You can watch it on YouTube: It's called "Janet Stegman Starring in HBO Here I Come!". It's kid-friendly – I made sure it was, because there were children in the audience that night.

Humor and laughter can change the tambour of a situation from tense to fun in an instant. It just takes letting go of any hope that anyone will ever think you are perfect and also of the need for anyone to ever think you are perfect. Once you've made it clear to yourself and those around you that, well, you are okay even when you do stupid things, make mistakes, are not perfect, you can run with that. And I'll tell you what: When you do that, the folks around you are relieved that they can be themselves as well – their imperfect selves – right along with you. You can all laugh together at your foibles, at the stuff life throws at you and the lack of any idea whatsoever of what to do with that stuff, and at your complete and utter deer-in-the-headlights manner of dealing with life and its obstacles.

It is important never to laugh at a child – for anything, whether they fall down, accidentally run into a closed door, or forget their homework. Whatever they do, always remember that no one is perfect. We all make mistakes; we all have weaknesses. It is imperative to never ever laugh at your child or make fun or point and laugh or find fault and then laugh. That will pound their self-esteem into the ground so far that you will not be able to recognize them. But if you can laugh at yourself, if you can laugh at situations, if you can find humor in things that happen in public or things that happen at home – without making the child the butt of the joke, your childrearing will go a whole lot easier.

Frequent laughter in the home will teach your child to find the humor in life's challenges. And then they will find the humor in their life challenges for their whole life. Once you introduce your child to the worlds of humor, laughter, and funny, you will have given them the gift of being able to go through life mostly laughing.

what parents can do to bring
humor into their child's life

Start off by buying a joke book. Kids *love* to hear jokes – even if they're corny or not funny. If you laugh, they'll laugh. Children *love* it when you laugh. Memorize one of the jokes from your joke book, and then when you're driving in the car, say, "Why did the elephant paint his toenails different colors?" "I don't know, why?" "No." "So he could hide in the gumball machine. Have you ever seen an elephant in a gumball machine?" "No." "See? It works!"

"Knock, knock." "Who's there?" "Banana." "Banana who?" "Banana banana." "Knock, knock." "Who's there?" "Banana." "Banana who?" "Banana banana banana." "Knock, knock." "Who's there?" "Banana" "Banana who?" "Banana banana banana banana." "Knock, knock." "Who's there?" "Orange." "Orange who?" "Orange you glad I didn't say banana?"

You can all watch some good stand-up comedy together as a family. You can take your family to an improvisational comedy show, or watch comedy movies together. Some funny things to watch together:

On YouTube – on The Carol Burnett Show:

- "The Dentist from The Carol Burnett Show (full sketch)" with Harvey Korman and Tim Conway or any other sketch with Harvey Korman and Tim Conway. Harvey Korman can never keep from laughing when Tim Conway is making stuff up as he goes.

- "The Oldest Man: Clock Repair from The Carol Burnett Show"

- "The Carol Burnett Show - Mama's Family Taking Care of Mama"

- "The Family: Sorry! From The Carol Burnett Show (full sketch)"

- "LUCY AND ETHEL CHOCOLATE" from "I Love Lucy"

- "Abbott & Costello - Who's on First?"

- "Hello Muddah, Hello Fadduh (Camp Granada Song) with Lyrics Sing-Along, Allan Sherman, 1963, updated"

- Movie: *It's a Mad Mad Mad Mad World.* My family watched this movie a hundred times together, and loved it every time.

tag freeze

You can do improvisational comedy together in your living room. Tag freeze is an easy one. You get two people up in front of the group, and they ask for an activity and a location. The audience members yell out activities, and then when one of the two has accepted the activity, they say, "Now I need a location," and the audience members yell out locations: "A volcano in Hawaii," "The bottom of a well," "The zoo." And one of the two says, "Okay, we're at the zoo." And then the two do a funny scene, making it up as they go along. At an appropriate time, maybe two minutes later, someone from the audience yells, "Freeze!" and the two actors freeze in their positions wherever they are. Then the person who yelled "Freeze" goes and taps one of the actors on the shoulder, that actor leaves the stage, and the new actor takes their place. The new actor then begins a completely different scene with a completely different location and activity, which the new actor must reveal with their first line. The second actor must then pick up exactly as though they had been in the new situation the whole time. The exercise can be over when everyone has gotten up at least one time. You can play Tag Freeze as long as you want – as long as everyone's laughing and having a good time!

Tag Freeze is a wonderful exercise to help children come out of their shell and be able to act without fear in any new situation. They will have their "Tag Freeze" skills and will be able to "just go with it" – make life up as they go along. Isn't that just what life is anyway, making stuff up as you go along and having fun with it? And feeling part of a family? When you play Tag Freeze, you parents can play funny characters and do comedic voices, and your kids will follow suit. It's just all around good, clean fun and will provide you with an evening of laughter and quality time together.

'Poets'

'Poets' is a wonderful exercise as well. Kids *love* 'Poets' because everyone gets to make up a silly poem right there on the spot. One person gets up in front of the group and asks for a first line for their poem. One at a time, everyone yells out a first line of a poem. The performer then chooses the first line they like the best and begins. The first line is also the title of the poem. So it goes like this: "Leaves are Pretty in Autumn, by Janet Stegman. Leaves are pretty in Autumn. It makes me want to sit down on my bottom. And watch the leaves turn from green to red and purple. Leaves are pretty in Autumn. I hope my parents like it too and get me a turtle. Leaves are Pretty in Autumn by Janet Stegman." And the crowd goes wild. There are no wrong poems: each is brilliant and fun and gets thunderous applause. Like you're at a real poetry reading and everyone is oohing and ahhing at every poem and every poet. 'Poets' is really fun, and it teaches children that they can be creative in the moment and not care if their poem is silly or doesn't rhyme. Because no matter what they create: It's perfect! Everyone must get up and recite their spur-of-the-moment poem. Some of my best comedy moments have been spontaneous, spur of the moment genius. You can serve popcorn and fruit juice and spend the whole evening laughing and playing together.

aren't we a silly family?

When something happens and people in the family are somber, and they're criticizing and judging the situation saying, "Oh, if I had only done this," or "How could I have been so stupid?" take a breath, step back, and say, "Aren't we a silly family?" or something to open the door to finding the humor in the moment.

"Right?"

"Right?" is my favorite response when someone points out the stupid thing I just did. "Why did you spend all that money joining the gym and then never go?" "Right?"

"Right?" stops everyone in their tracks. You know why? Because you have just admitted that you did a silly thing, a nonsensical, illogical thing, and you are not defending yourself, you are laughing at yourself. Who can argue with you when you agree with them and laugh? "Dad, why did you wash the car when you knew it was going to rain tonight?" "Right? Well, I said to myself, 'Self? What's the biggest waste of time you can think of to do today? I know! I'll wash the car, right before a rainstorm." You're done. Everyone laughs, and then asks, "When's dinner going to be ready?" Like I said, humor can diffuse the most embarrassing of moments. And when humor is a constant in a family, children learn that they don't have to feel embarrassed when they do something embarrassing: They can simply laugh at themselves and admit louder than anyone that they are human and did a silly thing.

the more you laugh the lighter you feel

The more you laugh with your child, the lighter your child will feel – even in the hard times. Laughter and humor raise a child's vibration, raise the vibration of the family, add lightheartedness to growing up, and help a child cope with hard times and difficult situations. They teach a child never to judge or criticize themselves, but rather to find the humor in what they have just done or what has happened to them. A child will then learn to laugh at themselves, without the fear of another laughing at them.

my mission statement

Being a stand-up comedian has made me an exceedingly happy person. Everywhere I go, I make it my mission is to make people laugh. When I go to the market, when I go to the shoe store – wherever I go, I try to find something funny to say or do to make people laugh. When they end up smiling or laughing, I know I have made their day. Mission accomplished!

make yourself laugh

When you find yourself feeling angry with someone at the grocery store for butting in front of you or grabbing the last roll of toilet paper off the shelf, turn around and say, in your best Gilda Radner voice, *"Never mind."* Or "Missed it by *that* much." or "Thank God I still have yesterday's newspaper at home!" You'll be so glad you didn't spend your afternoon mad at someone who doesn't even know you're mad at them! Instead, you're chuckling all the way home at how clever and comedic you were!

People of all ages, not just children, can benefit from applying the principles of humor and funny to situations and turn what could be a heavy and painful encounter into one of lightness and laughter, not just in the home or with the family, but everywhere they go. Wherever you go, there you are! When you can't find a Tupperware top to fit the bottom half in your hand, make up a poem about your Tupperware lids.

"Tupperware Lids"
by Janet Stegman

My Tupperware lids are nowhere to be found
Like socks in the dryer, they're nowhere around
Darn it, I can't find a lid to fit
Oh how I wish I had a pillow to hit
"Tupperware Lids" by Janet Stegman

people mimic what they grow up with

We all mimic what we grow up with. If we grow up with anger, we mimic anger when we're adults. If we grow up with criticism, we mimic criticism. If we grow up with humor, we laugh and laugh every chance we get, forever. Laughter is contagious.

Go and find the funny, share the funny, be the funny. It will help your child appreciate humor and give them a lighter outlook on life. You too. It will set the stage for a happy and lighthearted child rearing experience for both you and your child, and for the whole family as well. Forever.

CHAPTER 18

∙∙

KEEP YOUR MOUTH SHUT

need-to-know basis

When it comes to your personal life, your child should be on a need-to-know basis. You don't want to force them to grow up too fast. If you share adult content or adult problems with your child before they are old enough to be able to deal with those types of things – before they have formed solid coping skills – it can give them deep emotional scars. When a parent complains to their 8 year old about their relationship or shares their money worries with them, it is not only not helpful, it can severely damage their tender and vulnerable undeveloped psyche. A child will naturally gravitate towards wanting to solve their parents' problems for them and will feel responsible for making them all better. They will feel it is their job to save you from whatever mess you've gotten yourself into because, well . . . HAPPY PARENT, HAPPY CHILD. Children long for their parents to be happy. Think about it: When you are pleasant to be around, you give off a joyful, positive vibe – a nurturing presence. If you feel uplifted, your child knows they are safe and that there is no chance you will be venting your anger or taking your frustrations out on them.

A child's core emotional strength is not sufficiently developed for them to be able to hear about bad things – painful things – and not be devastated. I literally, *literally*, went into a deep depression after I saw *Bambi*. I was 3, and it upset me horribly. I did not need to see *Bambi*. Really ever. I mean, the mom was killed right in the beginning just bam, here, tiny ones, watch this baby's mother be tragically murdered in front of her baby – feel her baby's heart be crushed. I thought about it for years, and every time I would think about it, I would feel sad and cry. So, no, I did not need to see *Bambi*. *Bambi* is an adult-themed animated film. My 3-year-old heart did not need to see a mom being killed leaving her baby all alone and traumatized.

if you would share it with a therapist, leave it out with your child

As I said, my parents got divorced when I was 11, and shortly thereafter, my mom began using me as her therapist. I guess I saved her a lot of money on psychiatric fees. I imagine she liked the idea of not having to admit to another adult that she had allowed herself to be a victim – to be shamed and controlled – for 18 years and that she was miserable. My mother would sit me down on our carpeted spiral staircase and make it seem as though she was spending quality time with me talking just the two of us – gifting me with what the Oxford Dictionary defines quality time as: "Time spent in giving another person one's undivided attention in order to strengthen a relationship, especially with reference to working parents and their child or children". Like I said, a nurturing mother-daughter bonding experience. I thought she was sitting me down with the intention of showing me the love and attention I was so desperately craving. But what she was really doing was using me for a therapist – telling me in great detail all the mean things my father had ever said and done to her during their marriage. I could recite in living color every single solitary mean word and thoughtless deed my mother ever saw my father say or do. To this day, I can tell you line and verse all the reasons my mother stopped loving my father and decided to divorce him; she left nothing out.

give them their time to sleep – uninterrupted

So here I am, 11 years old, inconsolable and crying myself to sleep every night, my father having just moved out – I missed him so badly. And as if that wasn't painful enough, often times at night, my mother would come to my doorway as I was lying in bed trying to sleep, and, after reciting to me a whole litany of things I had done wrong that day, complain to me, "I'm so worried about money. I don't know how I am going to pay the bills. Your father hasn't paid me any child support." For gosh sakes, she was a lawyer with a well-paying full time position in the city prosecutor's office. Well, I ended up taking on all her money worries, because I loved her so much and couldn't bear seeing her in such distress. I couldn't go out and get a full-time job to make enough money so she could feel not-worried. I felt powerless and impotent to help.

I needed to know about, you know, Math

I really didn't need to hear about all my mother's problems. I needed to know about, you know, Math. How to get along with the kids at school. How to be happy. My mother's focus needed to be on me and my well-being. She needed to be asking me questions about how I was doing in school – did I have friends, did I need to talk about the bullying I was experiencing, was I having trouble concentrating on my homework with all the hideous bullying I was having to endure at school? Did I need help being good at making friends, did I know the difference between a flat and a sharp on the violin (No, no I didn't. Oh my poor orchestra teacher.)? She needed to be concerned about *my* welfare, not constantly complaining to me about *her* life, *her* problems, or *her* pain.

Mom's marriage misery sessions
made me grow up too fast

My mother's marriage misery sessions made me grow up too fast; they took away my childhood. Because now I was her therapist. Now I was a venting board for my mother's problems. My childhood was no longer light and happy and full of kid stuff.

So you see, terrible things can happen from stealing a person's childhood – from telling children things before they are ready to hear them. It is detrimental to the well-being of a child to not be burdened with adult subject matter before they are mature enough to handle it. They'll have plenty of time to be an adult when they're an adult. Let them be a child while they're a child.

My father shared things with me no daughter wants or needs to know about her father. I did not need to know the intimate details of his relationships with women. I did not need to know everything a man would share with a buddy or a best friend about his life. TMI, really, TMI.

okay to answer questions

If your child has questions about you, by all means, answer them – providing they legitimately want to know something about you. You can always couch your answers in generalities so as not to burden them with your troubles. If they ask, "What's wrong, Mama?" Tell them, "Oh, Mama just feels a little sad. I'll feel better in a little while. It's not your fault, don't worry." Something like that, where you assure them that you don't need them to fix you, that it's not their responsibility, that it's not their problem. "Please don't feel bad for me: I'll figure it out. I just want you to be a kid and be happy." Parents need to have the attitude that their child's feelings are 150% important to them – that they care 150% about their child's feelings. It is advantageous to a parent to think about how what they are saying to their child is affecting them before they start talking. Ask yourself, "Is what I am about to say to my child something they can't do anything about and don't need to know?" If the answer is yes, pick a new topic for discussion. Remember: A child is naïve and impressionable and not a licensed therapist. Children have not yet learned not to take things personally. They will believe their parents' pain is their fault and then feel like a failure when they can't take their pain away.

what to focus on for a parent

The best thing you can do for your child is focus on their activities, their life, what they are learning, and the things they are doing. Your child needs to be thinking about and focused on kid things. They are not at the stage where, "Oh, you tell me your problems and I'll tell you mine, and we'll commiserate." They're not at that stage. It's not that they don't care: It's that they need to not know about adult subject matter: They're not equipped to handle that. Children don't know how to filter adult subject matter and steer it towards a positive outcome. It's like shrapnel hitting them. They have not developed the defense mechanisms to keep out the sadness, the powerlessness, and feeling they are to blame for it all. A child cannot stop their parents' adult problems from overwhelming them.

it is possible and even appropriate to handle and let go of depression without the help of your child

You might say, "But if a person is depressed, it's not their fault. They complain to their children because they need to vent and don't know who else to turn to." The belief that people who suffer from depression can't help it and therefore can't be held responsible is a common one. However, I am living proof that depression is curable. I spent many years working with therapists and practitioners and am here to tell you that you can be healed of depression, and you don't need to seek comfort for it from your child; there are healthy alternatives to seeking comfort from your child.

healthy alternatives to seeking comfort from your child

While you are in a good place emotionally and have a few spare minutes, jot down a list of friends and siblings who would enjoy commiserating with you about each other's challenges, missteps, and bumps in the road. Perhaps there is someone you know who wouldn't mind exchanging understanding and supportive listening ears, so that you can both vent your frustrations to a mature adult capable of handling your frustrations and fears without becoming adversely affected. You can always ask them in the beginning, "Please, I don't want you to worry about me or get upset about what I am about to tell you: These are my problems, and I will handle them. The last thing I want is for you to think I want you to feel bad for me or solve my problems for me. I mean, I welcome any suggestions you might have that you think would help me, but mainly, I just need a listening ear right now so that I don't go crazy and take it out on my kids." "Okay, sure." "Perfect, thanks! Well, here goes..."

just hire a damn therapist

How many times have I wished my mother had hired a bona fide therapist to vent her problems on instead of me. I'm pretty sure what she did to me was what her mother did to her and that she didn't know any different. But now that we know all this, I am asking you to think outside the box and imagine other scenarios besides the ones you were raised with, because those weren't necessarily the best parenting methods. Approach all your parenting decisions and communications with your child with conscious caution and thoughtfulness, so as to avoid slipping into auto pilot because "that was the way you were raised." I'm not implying in any way, shape, or form that your parents raised you wrong: I am simply saying that the best parenting comes from thoughtful reflection and putting yourself in the position of your child and imagining how it would make you feel if someone treated you the way you are about to treat your child. Right now, in present time: How would it make you feel? Would it make you feel hurt, flawed, and defective? Or would it make you feel expanded, joyful, and brimming with self-esteem – like you can do anything you put your mind to because you're brilliant and fantastic!! You can learn *so much* by putting yourself in your child's shoes in each moment, or at the very least, when you sense your child is feeling not good about the way you are dealing with them.

a guide for sharing with your child

1. Keep the conversation and focus of your relationship to their needs, their feelings, their activities, and their accomplishments. Keep the sharing of your own pain, problems, and worries on a

need-to-know basis. Ask questions in relation to what's going on in their life. Have them tell you about their challenges. Ask them if they want your help.

2. Do everything in your power to care more about your child's feelings and well-being than your own – force yourself if you have to.

3. If you are in a position in which you are completely incapable of giving your child a modicum of activity, conversation, love, and affection, get on the horn and ask a family member or close friend to come over and spend some time with them. Ask them to shed some light to your child on your situation in a gentle, kind, and compassionate way so that your child can understand in general and simple terms what you are going through.

4. Worst case scenario, if all else fails, be honest and apologize to your child and help them find an activity they can do by themselves, like an art project, and tell them to come and show you the finished product at the end. A kind word and some accolades for an art project will go a long way in building your child's self-esteem and belief in your love for them. Practice taking a moment in each situation to look at yourself and your actions from the point of view of someone else watching you from outside your window. Leave your ego and fears at the door for a moment, and decide what parenting actions will serve your child the most. See in your mind's eye your own actions that you feel would be the best ones to take in order to teach your child the lesson you want them to learn. Be the best role model you can be; be the role model you wish you had been blessed with when you were growing up, or perhaps did in fact have. Show them how much you care about their feelings and their well-being by the decisions you make for them.

5. If you feel you have made a mistake in your parenting, don't worry, you can *always* have a do-over. You can say sorry, ask

your child how you can make it up to them, let them tell you how they felt when you made your "mistake". Children are very forgiving of a parent who makes the effort to right their wrongs, learns from their mistakes, and makes up for the hurt they caused by giving their child their heart's desire.

6. If you find yourself wanting to vent your problems on your child, stop yourself on a dime before it happens, or if it's too late, mid–sentence and say, "I'm so sorry; I was being self-obsessed. Note to self: 'Don't do that'." And then laugh at your faux pas. Continue with, "Please, tell me something about your day. Anything – let's get off of me and onto you. Did I tell you lately how much I love you?" "No." "Well, I do. SO MUCH!! Okay, fill me in, I'm listening."

resources for healing damage
caused by parents' inappropriate behavior

If you would like additional insights and guidance on this subject, I highly recommend *The Emotional Incest Syndrome: What to do When a Parent's Love Rules Your Life* by Dr. Patricia Love and Jo Robinson and *Silently Seduced: When Parents Make Their Children Partners* by Kenneth M. Adams PhD. Those two books have been instrumental in helping me heal from the damage caused by my parents' inappropriate behavior with me.

not your friend

In addition to refraining from using your child as a therapist, it is also a good idea to refrain from making them your "best friend". When something is bothering you, call your real best friend to vent your frustrations and get understanding and comfort. But your child is not your friend: They are your child. They're not an adult: They're a child. They are not ready to know about adult things. You can answer their questions if they have questions, but it is better not to burden them with adult-type problems. Their lives will not be hampered if they don't know everything about your life or about you. They will not be harmed in any way if you seek outside help to deal with your frustrations. It's okay to only share your inner–most thoughts and feelings with a mature grown-up. A child needs you to help them grow into a healthy, happy adult; they don't need to know everything about you in order for that to happen.

Parents, do your best to help your child keep their innocence intact for as long as possible. I had no ability to stave off the sadness, powerlessness, fear, and anger my parents shared with me about themselves. I had no filter to keep myself from taking on my parents' grief, so I just absorbed it into my little psyche, where it stayed, until years later, when I was able to clear it. I had no ability to compartmentalize: Those are her problems; I don't have to think about that. I just took them on. Children are little sponges. I absorbed my parents' problems, and they became a part of me. If you go through a hard time, make sure you are clear with your child that IT'S NOT THEIR FAULT AND THAT YOU WANT THEM TO BE HAPPY AND NOT FEEL IT'S UP TO THEM TO FIX YOU. Pay more attention to your child being happy than to your own feelings, because children don't have the ability to realize it's not personal and to always see it that way. A child is not a therapist; they should not have to deal with therapist types of issues. It will not detract from your child's life if they do not know what kind of worries you are experiencing or pain you are in, or what your problems of the day are. It will be most helpful to your child if you are concerned with protecting them and making sure they aren't burdened by your problems.

go and live with them in the
snow globe on the mantel

See that snow globe over there on the mantel? See your child inside that snow globe with all the majestic mountains, towering trees, shimmering streams, and fluorescent flowers. Go live in that world with them and let them see only the beauty in life – for as long as you can. They will learn for themselves how to navigate through the trials and travails of an adult life – when they are ready. But their innocence and childhood will have been kept intact by their wise and discerning parents. It will be satisfaction enough knowing you have been a wonderful parent and given your child every chance to grow up unfettered, well balanced, conscious, and free.

well gosh darn it, when is it okay for me to share my life with my child?

You may ask, "How old does my child have to be before I can make them my best friend?" "When is it okay for me to lean on my child for help with my problems and share the details of my personal life with them?" And the answer is...drum roll please...Never. There is never a time for that; there is no age at which it is appropriate for your child to be your friend. Your child is not your friend, they are your child, and you are their parent. They will always be your child and you will always be their parent. It is never appropriate or healthy to put your child in the position of acting as your counselor or confidant. You can tell your child "need-to–know" facts about yourself, like if you're going into the hospital for surgery, or if you're making spaghetti for dinner – subjects that do not put your son or daughter in the position of being your best friend, your therapist, or your confidante.

You know that "my daughter my friend" thing?" Forget it; it's a myth. It's a mistake. Do light, fun, what movie do you want to see, where shall we go for dinner, here's a funny thing that happened to me today types of things with them. Never begin a sentence with, "I'm so depressed..." Go see your therapist, call a friend, or write about it in your journal until your fingers ache. Keep your conversations with your child light, fun, and on a need-to-know basis. Always. I promise, once you are introduced to and contemplate this concept, you will agree that this is the healthy and loving way. It is the appropriate way to always treat your child. I guarantee that one day you will thank me for my impassioned insistence. Think funny stories, questions about their day, long hugs full of *all* the love, and reading the *best* books together!

CHAPTER 19

DEALING WITH DEPRESSION

a parent's depression can adversely affect a child

We all get depressed from time to time. I can't think of anyone who can say they have never been depressed. Life can be difficult. Feelings get hurt. Sad things happen. Life can be one big roller coaster of happy, sad, depressed, and challenging. I would never want to criticize someone or make them wrong for feeling depressed. It is a natural part of life – part of being human. However, when there are children involved, and the children have to watch Mama go through her days depressed, it can have an adverse effect on their little psyches.

A child will sometimes feel responsible for their parent's depression. They will want to bring them out of it; they will want to spend all their time cheering up a parent and making them happy. Let's face it: It's more fun to be around someone who's upbeat, cheerful and excited to be alive – someone who is enjoying the adventures life has to offer - than it is to be around someone who's depressed and wallowing in self-pity.

In order to protect your child from the possibility of a life of fear and guilt, it is important for you as a parent to handle your depression, if you do encounter it, outside the presence of and without the help of your child.

my experience with a depressed parent

My mother suffered horribly from depression. I remember her being depressed much of the time. My mother told me of the time the family went to Disneyland and she wore sunglasses the whole time because she didn't want people to see her crying over how mean my father was to her. I wanted to say, "So why didn't you just leave him? You weren't dependent on him: You were a lawyer and could support yourself no problem!" I never understood why my mother stayed for so long in such a miserable marriage. She stayed married to my father for eighteen years before finally divorcing him. My mother told me that the day my father moved out was the day her headaches went away.

a box of Snoopy stationery

I remember one time, shortly after my dad moved out, it was a Saturday, my dad's day to pick my brother and me up to go and spend the weekend with him. It was also my mother's birthday. I was so traumatized from the bullying at school and then my parents splitting up and both of them being heartbroken and despondent that I didn't have the where-with-all to plan a birthday party for my mom or buy her a present. Long story short, I hadn't done or planned anything to celebrate her birthday when my dad came to pick us up. I got in the car with my dad and brother, but as we drove off, I realized how bad my mom must have been feeling, because I knew how bad I would have felt if my family had forgotten or, worse, ignored my birthday. I turned to my dad and said, "Today is Mommy's birthday." He said, "Yeah, I know." I said, "Well, I don't want her to have to spend her birthday alone. Can you please take me back so I can spend the weekend with her?" Which he did.

When I got home, I rode my bike to the neighborhood pharmacy and bought my mother a darling little box of Snoopy stationery. I came home, wrapped it, and took it up to where she was in her bedroom. I said, "Happy Birthday, Mommy!" and gave her her present. She opened it, said "Thanks," and laid back down in the bed. I said, "I came back to be with you on your birthday." She said, "Oh." We didn't do anything that weekend. She stayed in bed all weekend. I always believed it was my fault that she was depressed, because I hadn't thought to stay home with her in the first place. I hadn't said, "I'm not going to go to Dad's this weekend because it's your birthday; let's go celebrate!" I didn't have a birthday present for her or a card.

Looking back, I think the air in the Stegman house was so laden with grief and hostility that I could barely take a breath, much less behave like a mature eleven year old and have a birthday party all planned out for her and presents. Instead, I got in the car to go with my dad and then felt sad for my mother, made my dad turn the car around, and came back to spend the weekend with her. But that wasn't enough. It didn't do anything for her. She never got out of bed the whole weekend, and we didn't do anything together either day. All my mom did the entire weekend was be depressed. She didn't seem to appreciate at all what I had done to show her how much I loved and cared about her.

What my mother didn't do was say, "Ohhh. Ohhh. You came home to celebrate my birthday with me!? That's *so sweet*!! I have the *best* daughter!! C'mon, let's go out to lunch. And then we'll go out to dinner later. We'll see a movie." Nope, she didn't do that. She just stayed in bed the whole entire weekend. I always believed it was my fault that she was depressed, because I didn't have the consideration to stay home in the first place and have a present already wrapped and ready to give her. I always blamed myself for not having that consideration and have never forgiven myself for it. Maybe it's time to forgive myself. I was eleven. I made a mistake. Divorce is hard – on everyone. Depression is not caused by your eleven-year-old doing something insensitive. It is caused by years of emotional neglect and hurt feelings – probably during childhood.

you can be healed of depression

You might think, "Well she couldn't help it. Depression is a mental illness and cannot be cured." Yes, that is a very common belief in this country. But here's the deal: I healed myself of depression. And addiction. And so can you. So can anyone else you might know that suffers from depression.

my magic formula for healing depression

When I was in the throes of addiction and depression, I was introduced to three types of energy healing work: the journaling, the tapping, and the inner child work. I would work with one therapist, and just when I would start to feel like I had gone as far as I could with them, all of a sudden, there was another healer presenting himself or herself in my life, and I would go with them. I continued going to see whatever healers came onto my path – listening to them and following their suggestions. And then what do you know? Lo and behold: No more addiction and no more depression. So you can't tell me it's impossible to heal from depression. Even a little crack in the illness after some healing work will improve a person's outlook on life to where they can see they have made progress and that there is hope that they are doing all the right things.

I spent many years in the presence of EFT practitioners and inner child workers helping me release the pent-up emotions that were causing my depression. I feel very strongly that parents have a spiritual fiduciary duty to their children to do everything in their power to handle their own personal depression so that it does not spill over into their childrearing and adversely affect their children. If you suffer from depression, it is imperative that you make every effort to reach out for help to heal it. Find a local EFT practitioner. Have sessions by phone if you can't find one locally.

Could my mother have done something about her depression? Certainly. She could have found a bona fide therapist to bare her soul to and handle her depression between the two of them. But she didn't do that. Instead, she burdened me with it. That is not a good way to parent. It hurts the child when a parent doesn't handle their depression outside of their parent/child relationship. When I look back, I can't help but wonder why, if she knew she was morbidly depressed and was going to stay in bed her whole birthday weekend, she didn't take one minute to think about my feelings and say to me, "Listen, I'm really depressed, and I'm probably going to stay in bed all weekend. I know you gave up your weekend with your dad to be with me because it's my birthday, but why don't I drive you back to your dad's so you can have a fun weekend with your dad and brother rather than stay here with me and do nothing?" It would have taken an hour and a half of her bed time to drive me to my dad's apartment.

Look, I know people get depressed. I know depression can overtake a person's life and render them immobile and dysfunctional until hopefully it passes or until they have to get up and go to work on Monday.

you are dealing with tiny lives
with feelings and impressionable psyches

But please people, *PLEASE* take into consideration that there are tiny lives with feelings and impressionable SO IMPRESSIONABLE psyches that one weekend in bed from depression with no attention or love or appreciation forthcoming can cause a child to believe for a lifetime that their feelings don't matter, that their parent's depression is their fault, that they are bad for it, that no one will ever care about their feelings or well being, and that there are only depressed people out there to form relationships with – happy people don't exist so why bother holding looking for one. With the utmost understanding and compassion, I beseech you: If you are depressed or addicted or having feelings of wanting to abandon your child and get away forever, please reach out for help. It doesn't matter what kind of help you reach out for – a simple reach will lead you to the exact right modality for your healing. John Bradshaw once said, "To bring forth your dreams, simply do what you *think* you need to do, and they will come."

I promise that once you take a step towards healing your heart, your higher self will lead you to the exact right people and/or programs and/or workshops that will restore you to optimum mental health and happiness. By doing so, you will become a super-parent. Not only because you will be parenting from a place of excellent mental health and happiness, but also because you will have pulled yourself through a difficult time and will now be able to help your child get through their difficult times. Also, in addition, your child won't have to reinvent the wheel: They will watch you being unashamed to reach out for help and doing whatever is necessary to get yourself through the difficult times, and living the transformation that reaching out for healing brings. There are a myriad of valuable lessons for your child as you give yourself the gift of a life that is "happy, joyous, and free," as they say in the 12-Step programs.

be willing to reach out for help
– without ceasing

My saving grace was that I was willing to keep on reaching out for help – to a therapist, a 12-Step Program, any workshop that hinted at recovery – until I got better. I said yes to whatever rescue vehicle came my way. I continued reaching out: to a therapist, a 12-Step Program, any workshop that smelled like it could help me. I found a therapist who gave me writing assignments and then had me read what I had written to him. He taught me how to turn my depression and self-judgment into "lessons" for myself. "Hear what your inner-self is trying to tell you so that you can take better care of yourself the next time." He introduced me to Siddha Yoga, the spiritual practice that taught me to let go of judgment and fear and moved me INSANELY QUICKLY along in my recovery. In our sessions, my therapist would have me close my eyes and see Little Janet and then have nurturing conversations with her and hold her. Then I found another therapist who did The Tapping with me and taught me that skill so that I could continue clearing grief and terror and any other painful feelings that were contributing to my depression, as they came up.

By reaching out for help and saying yes to any reasonable modality of healing that flew into my life, I was successful in lifting myself out of my depression. Don't get me wrong: Life can still be *very* difficult at times. I *still* have two energy healing sessions per week! And thank God I read the book *Sandcastles: Tools for Letting Go of Addiction and the Pain of the Past,* because now I have tools to pull myself out of difficult and/or painful situations. It may take me a while to become willing to reach into my magic bag of tools and ease my angst, but I definitely know they're there, and I only have to sit in fear or depression until I become willing to write them down and tap on them. Sometimes, if I don't have time for the whole enchilada, I just tap real quick, and it is hugely calming whenever I do.

do not be ashamed or embarrassed
to reach out for help

For the sake of, at the very least, your child's mental health and happiness, do not be embarrassed or ashamed to reach out for help. *Never* stop reaching out for help. Never give up. There is help out there, and all you have to do is reach out for it and take it. Find an EFT Practitioner and be honest about your true innermost feelings. Painful feelings are *never* something to be ashamed of. We all have them, I PROMISE. It is more noble to share your honest deepest darkest secrets with a therapist and heal them than it is to appear "fine" to the world. If you do what is necessary to expose your feelings to the light of day by sharing them with a professional, you will be less likely to express them in an unconscious, inappropriate, and hurtful way to your child. I assure you: YOU ARE NOT ALONE IN HAVING PAINFUL FEELINGS, MEMORIES OF THINGS YOU ARE ASHAMED OF, THINGS YOU HAVE DONE THAT YOU FEEL EMBARRASSED ABOUT. It comes with being alive. You can't escape it: It's the human condition.

If I can only remember the name of that author who wrote *Sandcastles* . . . who was it? Let me see . . . Oh yes – it was me! Not because I want to sell more books (although that would be so bad – let's be honest), but because I truly believe that following the methods, suggestions, and tools it has to offer is the quickest and most effective way to deal with depression. So that your child doesn't have to. Let your child be a child. Take responsibility for your emotions and be a cheerful, loving, and attentive parent. When you've got it, you can give it.

CHAPTER 20

A NEW BABY

A new baby is on the way – how exciting!! Soon you'll have a brand new baby in your arms, ready to raise: to be cuddled, fed, changed, sung to, read to, made to laugh. Ready to make you laugh and fall madly in love with you. It is *so* exciting to be bringing home this tiny new addition. Let's face it: Babies are just little pieces of Heaven – to hold while they sleep, make silly noises at, and make them laugh. They're adorable and cute and fun and funny: everything good. Except to the child who's been your one and only for the past two or three years. To them, not so much. After all, they have been the center of your world their entire life. That's the only life they've ever known. Enter new baby, and all of a sudden, poof! It's over. Mom and Dad bring home this rolled up blanket, and everything's changed. There is an inexplicable and abrupt shift in the amount of attention and focus they are getting. It's the largest shift they've ever experienced. One minute they're the center of your world; the next minute they're demoted to second string, playing second fiddle to this foreign little creature. At least that's what it feels like to them.

It is easy for parents to get caught up in the excitement of having a new baby. But all the two year old feels is, "Hey! What happened to all my love and attention? Instant jealousy, grief, confusion, and sadness, and now the two year old is constantly hitting the baby and getting in trouble for it. Not a pretty sight.

But wait! Do not be discouraged! There are steps you can take to facilitate a smooth transition – one in which your child will feel excited and enthusiastically included in the upbringing of your new baby. Pay close attention to these steps, because if you are not vigilant and mindful of your older child's feelings and do not heed these warnings, you may find your older child traumatized, ill-prepared for only half, or, Heaven forbid none, of the attention, affection, and love they've been used to getting, and in great emotional distress. Suffering in quiet desperation, they will not know what to make of this sudden shift in their place in the family and will feel they have done something to make you pull away or turn against them. They will feel at a loss for what they have done to deserve this punishment. It will be extremely disarming to them; they will feel lost and severely and irreparably traumatized. If you aren't painstaking in compensating for the shift in your focus and attention, it will hurt like Hell for your older child. Think back on the times you got rejected by a boyfriend or a girlfriend or God forbid a husband or a wife – or perhaps a parent. It hurts like Hell, right? At any age. But the rub for a child is that they don't have the necessary tools to handle the magnitude of confusion and the baffling and painful feelings they find themselves experiencing. A child does not have the experience or understanding to put the puzzle together and see logically what is going on: that it's not that there is less love for them, it's that the novelty of a new baby is taking the portion of their parents' attention that used to be all for them.

If you don't make every effort to ensure your child is showered with effulgent love, attention, and affection, there is a possibility your child will go their entire life having debilitating jealousy as their baseline emotion. Like they will be forever bubbling underneath with jealousy. And loss. And lack. And rejection. They will lead from those emotions in everything they do for their whole life. Parents don't realize how hurtful and what a shock it is to a child to have such a sudden change in the amount of love and attention they receive from their parents, even though it is unintentional on the parents' part.

Because a child is young and impressionable, they don't have the inner strength or wisdom to handle a stranger usurping their place in life, and they end up feeling insanely jealous, deeply hurt, and woefully rejected, and they don't know why. They are frustrated because they have no idea what they did to cause their parents to pull away, and they become angry with themselves for whatever they did to cause it, even though they don't know what it was. They are baffled over the reason for the sudden abandonment, and will carry this abandonment and guilt around for the rest of their life. This is the time your child is forming the underpinnings for the emotional state from which they will lead in all their future endeavors. This is unconscious, unless and until they seek recovery, at which time they will hopefully have an opportunity to see it and heal it.

and now for the good news!

The good is that there are simple steps you can take to circumvent the painful reaction your child might have to the little bundle of joy that has just graced your doorstep. These simple but important preparations and actions will establish the groundwork for your child's loving relationship with each of their siblings for the rest of everyone's life. As soon as you become aware that your new addition is not affecting your child or children in the same way as it is affecting you, you can adjust and accommodate accordingly and give your older child or children what they need to feel equally loved, wanted, and cherished. You will be doing your child a huge favor by taking conscious care with this aspect of your parenting, because if you prepare your child properly for the arrival of the new baby and continuously show them equal, if not more, time and attention, you can subvert any chance of them being saddled with a lifetime full of prodigious and insidious jealousy.

FIRST, It is imperative that you be mindful of this information – hold the awareness of these practices in your heart and mind at all times.

SECOND, as you hold this awareness in your heart and mind at all times, actively counteract any potential unequal portions of love dispersed to your children, younger and older. Remain vigilant of your children's feelings and go out of your way to pay extra attention to the older child, giving them gifts from the baby and gifts from you. Explain to your child that you don't love them any less just because there's a new kid in town: You love them INCREDIBLY SO MUCH – the same amount as you always did – the same amount as you love the baby. Tell them the new baby will require constant supervision and will be a novelty to friends and family, but they will not be losing one iota of your love or attention. In your talks after the baby arrives, reassure them that if they feel confused or usurped, it does not in any way mean that they have done anything wrong. Remind them that you love them to the moon and back, and "C'mon! Let's play a game!" Immediately remedy the situation with extra "I love you"'s and games.

THIRD, spend *extra* quality one-on-one time with your older child: Go out of your way to shower them with love, affection, attention, laughter, stories, and reading good books to each other.

"What color should we paint the nursery?"

Before the baby comes, involve your child in the preparations for the new baby. Bring the child into the nursery and ask them what color you should paint it. Decide together, so that even if you don't take their suggestion, they will feel included in the decision-making. Excitedly invite them to go with you on outings to the toy store to buy them a present and also to buy the new baby a present – that they get to pick out. At night before you tuck your child into bed, read them a story and say, "Let's read this together now, and then when the baby comes, you can read it to him." If your child is old enough, you can read books with them about pregnancy and getting ready for a new baby.

one very important role!

You want to make sure your child understands how important their role as the older sister or brother is. Let them know what a huge impact they will have on the baby, both when it's a newborn and when it's all grown up, because they are going to be the older brother or sister. In some instances, an older sibling can have more of an impact on a baby than the parents. Babies LOVE to be adored by their older siblings. It adds such love and fun to their childhood, which they will remember and carry with them forever. Conversely, the opposite can be devastating. I had a client whose older sister was abusive – verbally, emotionally, spiritually, and physically, and that affected her deeply – as though her parents had beaten and criticized *her.* The scars from the abuse my client endured at the hands of her older sister stayed with her for years, and she had terrible abuse issues. So an older sibling hitting their younger sister or brother or calling them names or tearing them down will leave scars that last a lifetime. To nip this in the bud, you must, in addition to teaching your older children how important their role is in the upbringing of their younger sibling, do everything in your power to protect your older child from feeling jealousy over the younger additions. Shower your older children with attention, affection, love, compliments, and quality time with you without the baby. In doing this, the older children will not resent the younger child and will naturally form a loving relationship with them.

Janet with baby brother, Matt

"I'm here for you"

It is important to impart on your child that if they have a problem with their young siblings, they need to come to you rather than take matters into their own hands. They need to know how important it is never to criticize, bully, or belittle any of their siblings. In order to facilitate loving relationships between siblings, parents must be conscientious in going above and beyond the call of duty to monitor each of their children's feelings and be cognizant of any signs of jealousy or feeling they are being left out or slighted – in ANY way. If you do, swoop Little Jimmy off his feet, put him on your shoulders, and announce to him – if at all practicable – where you and he are going together – just the two of you, right now and what present you will be buying him – or if he will be picking out his own present, and what fun improv game you will be playing together once you're on your way to the toy store.

'I Spy'

"I Spy" is a fun game and safe to play while you are driving somewhere. The driver picks an object and announces to the passengers, "I spy with my little eye something beginning with a 'C'." The passengers then try to guess what the driver is referring to. "I spy a Corvette!!" "Yup! You got it!!" "I spy with my little eye something beginning with an 'F'." "That Ford!" "Nope; guess again." "The Fountain!" "Nope; guess again." "Those Flowers over there!" "Very good!"

**they need to know they can relax
cuz you got this**

Let your child know that whatever problem they are having with the baby, you will handle it and that they will not be left in the dark trying to fend for themselves with their younger sister or brother. Tell them that no matter what, you will advocate for them and make sure they are satisfied with the outcome. Assure your child you will make it your priority that they feel heard, their feelings will always be cherished, and they will always be cared about and taken care of.

lessons on being a good human being

As you give your child all these reassurances, you will not only be facilitating a healthy relationship between them and the new baby; you will be teaching them how to be a good human being and establishing quality values in them. You will not only be preparing your child to welcome the new baby into the family; you will be giving them the most valuable of skill sets for dealing with people. It will make it easy for your child to trust those who earn their trust, believe that it is safe to open their hearts to love, and circumvent any potential fears and anxiety. You will be setting a foundation for their relationship with their siblings that will go on forever, and will also be teaching your child how to deal with hard-to-handle emotions.

Remember that you are not simply trying to appease your child: This is an opportunity to teach them invaluable life lessons. You will be relieved when you see your child calmly and happily watching as the new baby receives special love and attention, because they know there will be plenty o' love and attention coming to them as well.

"I'm happy for you! Really I am!"

When you give a child the love, attention, and affection they need when the new baby comes, you are ushering in a healthy and uplifting attitude towards all of their future relationships, because they will now be able to feel emotions other than jealousy. They will now feel expanded love and sincere happiness for the successes of others. They will organically be glad for a friend or relative when good fortune graces the friend or relative's doorstep. It's SO GREAT never to feel jealous of a friend or family member, but rather only empathetic glee!

my brother my joy

I remember driving home from the hospital with my parents, holding my brand new baby brother on my lap. It felt wonderful!! And then when we got home, there was a present waiting for me from the baby. I was 3 years old when my brother was born, and I immediately fell madly in love with him. I taught him how to walk, how to talk, even how to do a cartwheel. I was thoroughly involved in his upbringing; I was like a third parent. I don't remember ever feeling jealous of him. Except for one time with my grandmother; apparently, she didn't get the memo. My grandmother was babysitting my brother and me while my parents were out on a social event, and when my parents got home, I climbed into my brother's crib and pulled the covers up over my head. When my mother asked me what I was doing in the crib with the covers up over my head, I said, "I'm a baby. Grandma likes babies better than little girls!"

I mean, sure, I've felt my share of jealousy; it's hard not to. But I can spot it a mile away when I do, and I call myself on it, because it doesn't run unconsciously deep. Why? Because my parents made a monumentally conscious effort to make sure I didn't feel usurped with my brother added to the family. I really appreciate that. And I had a BLAST raising my baby brother! We have home movies back from 1961 that are just hilarious. My dad ran the movie camera while I was teaching my brother to walk, and every time my brother would fall down, my dad would pause the camera. So it looks like a Keystone Cops routine with one fall after another, no breaks.

My parents would ask me every night to show them what word I had taught my brother that day. I would turn to my brother and say, "Say TAPE RECORDER", and with this adorable little one year old voice, he would recite the word I had spent the entire day teaching him: "TAPE-WE-COE-DOE" – even though he had no idea what it meant. All four of us would just bust up laughing – including my brother!

three earth-shattering, change-the-world things parents can do

1. Get your child involved in the preparations before the baby arrives and include them in all the festivities for the new baby.

2. Have talks with your child to prepare him or her for the new addition who is going to need just as much love, attention, and affection as the older one. Explain to them that you don't want them to feel slighted when you show the new baby love,

because . . ."There's enough love to go around! We have an infinite amount of love for both you *and* the baby. Please don't ever think we love the baby more than we love you; we love you both equally! SOOOO MUCH!!"

3. In the presence of the baby, shower your older child with attention and affection.

some extra one-on-one time

Remember, your child is an individual: He is not merely Janie's older brother. He will need some of his own time with you. In addition to needing to be included in the preparations and festivities for the baby, he will need individualized time with you. Do your best to shower him with one-on-one attention – just your older child and you.

Those are some cracker actions to take to insure a healthy, happy child in the process of having their life turned topsy-turvy by an invasion of a pesky younger sibling.

Remember:

1. The baby gives Junior a present when he first meets Junior;

2. Junior is praised incessantly for his kind, gentle, and loving treatment of the new baby;

3. Junior sits on Mom or Dad's lap when the baby is playing by himself or in the high chair eating;

4. "I love you's ring through the air!;

5. Playing games and singing with the older child while baby naps.

Kids don't come with a manual, and parents don't always have the exact right instructions for every situation. Your job as a parent is to be observant and thoughtful of your child's feelings, to be an empath for your child, to always be putting yourself in the shoes of your child, and to anticipate and then cushion how upcoming life events will affect them. And to be conscious and caring of how your child is feeling in each and every moment. Be patient with your child: They are work-in-progress and want only to please you and to make you proud.

Kumbaya, my Lord, Kumbaya

CHAPTER 21

DANCE TO THE MUSIC

Three things saved my life growing up: humor, music, and dancing. Whatever else was going on in my family growing up, we always had music, we always had humor, and we always had dancing. For those three reasons, once I was able to heal my addictions and let go of the pain of the past, after my pets of course, every aspect of my life is infused with some form of music, dancing, and laughter. The other day, someone asked me, "If you could do *anything* you wanted to do in your life, what would it be?" and I said, "Singing, dancing, acting, stand-up comedy, and musical theatre. All day every day." These are the things that take me to my highest bliss, and I now know that as a beautiful child of God, I am entitled to live at my highest bliss. The reason I can grasp this concept is because, growing up, my parents sang with me, gave me dancing lessons, danced with me, and shared their senses of humor with me. By infusing my childhood with music, dancing, and humor, my parents set the stage for me vibrating at my highest bliss in my adulthood. Music, dancing, and humor are what carried me through the dark times. They gave me hope and the knowledge of how happy I was capable of feeling.

The vibrations of music, dancing, and humor are SO high that whenever you are feeling down or discouraged, if you start singing or dancing, or playing the saxophone, or finding the humor in your problems *du jour* and telling your friends, or (my favorite) seeing the humor in your painful situation and spontaneously adding it to your stand-up comedy routine, you will feel instant relief. Your psyche will rise to the vibrational levels of whatever creative activity you are doing, whether it be making music, singing harmonies, dancing to inspirational, spirited music like Swing, Country, and Rock 'n' Roll, or making *mia culpa* comedy routines out of your problems *du jour* – which are HIGH HIGH HIGH!

Robert Myers, PhD, in his article, "Music is an Important Ingredient for Child Development and Parent-Child Relationships" in the February 26, 2019 issue of the Child Development Institute web page, *https://childdevelopmentinfo.com*:

> Several recent articles in scientific journals point to the wide range of significant effects that learning and listening to music has on the brain development of children and adolescents. Other studies reveal that when parents share musical experiences with children and teens, including listening and/or dancing to music, as well as singing songs together, it has a positive effect on parent-child relationships. Music's Effects on Brain Development Based on the use of various neuroimaging techniques, research shows how early music training (before the age of seven) produces actual physical changes in brain structure and function. One study found an increase in the white matter in the corpus callosum (the switchboard in the center of the brain) which results in increased brain connectivity. Einstein learned to play the violin as a young child, and a study of his brain showed unusually strong connections. Another recent study determined that early musical training increased the gray matter in the cerebral cortex, particularly in the sensory-motor area of the brain. The improved coordination this produces was also found to improve emotional regulation and the ability to inhibit responses to events. This, of course, enhances a child's ability to handle frustration and avoid over-reacting to difficult situations. Yet another finding from neuroimaging was that even brief musical training results in an increase in

blood flow in the left side of the brain. This is thought to result in improved language processing ability. In March 2018 at the National Institutes of Health Kennedy Center Workshop on Music and the Brain, a panel of scientists highlighted research findings showing that from infancy, children are responsive to listening to music, and the experience significantly contributes to language development. The group also noted that in addition to promoting language development, music has a positive effect on the development of other cognitive functions including attention, visual-spatial perception, and executive function.

no bad apples in that bunch

Have you ever watched The Osmonds perform? GUESS WHAT?! THEY GOT THE MEMO!! In every one of their concerts, they get up on the stage and deliver the magical combination of singing, dancing, humor, and joy to BAM! whip their audience into a tornado of ecstasy – in a matter of minutes. These folks are not just dancing, they're dancing *together.* They're not just singing, they're *singing harmonies together.* They exchange playful banter between numbers, and they smile! It is obvious they are having the time of their lives, and that their vibrations are contagiously HIGH HIGH HIGH. Whenever I am feeling down or discouraged, I put on an old Osmond Family Christmas Special – in the middle of July, who cares? Or an Osmond Brothers concert. After I do that, I feel all my tension and worries subside. I mean, I know their religion promotes clean, healthy living, so you know that, rather than putting their energy into mind altering substances and unhealthy habits, they have devoted their time to mastering the performing arts. As a result, they vibrate in music, delicious harmonies, dancing, and fun, and in turn, they create loving, happy relationships – even Marie: Once her first husband healed his addiction, she married him all over again! From watching their children perform with them, it is clear they as well have come out creative and accomplished. It appears that every member of the Osmond Family is in love with every other member.

You don't see any of the Osmonds on Larry King criticizing another Osmond or revealing some "feud" they're having. You don't see them appearing on Jerry Springer screaming at and hitting each other with a stuffed fabric baseball bat! There is no way The Osmond Family could consistently transmit that kind of effulgent joy for 40 years if their lives were immersed in animosity and dysfunction. But what *are* their lives full of? Hard, hard work to keep their finely tuned, masterfully trained singing voices, harmonies, and dancing skills in tip top shape, love of family, laughter, fun, and an appreciation for the gift of life. Even when there was dissonance in the family, they came together and worked it out. Their parents made sure they were constantly exposed to complex harmonies, adorable dance routines, joyous humor, and contagious laughter. Take a lesson! A music lesson that is!!

it is never too early to introduce
your child to music and dancing

If you begin singing and dancing with a child by 6 years old, they will be ear trained their whole life, meaning that they will be able to hear a pitch and then sing that same pitch. They will be able to know whether they are on pitch or flat or sharp. In all my years of teaching singing, I have only fired one student, and it was an adult. He did not sing a single note on pitch, and it was him or me. I chose me. It was apparent his parents had not exposed him to singing as a child. I can't ever remember teaching a child to sing and having trouble getting them to sing on pitch.

I had a boyfriend named Michael, whose parents piped classical music – Bach, Beethoven, Chopin – into his nursery when he was a baby – in the afternoon while he was napping and at night as he was falling asleep. At 5 years old, he demanded his parents buy him an organ, so they bought him a miniature organ. At 10, he was ready for a full size organ, which they got him, and requested organ lessons, which they gave him. His legs couldn't reach the foot pedals, so his parents attached some type of contraption to them so he could use them. Michael grew up to be a world class organist and piano player. He could play by ear: I would play him a recording of a song, and he would turn to the piano and play the song perfectly. And he had perfect pitch when he sang. He played for my *Pirates of Penzance* that I directed (see "The Pirates of Penzance directed by Janet Stegman" on YouTube). The songs were not in an appropriate key for a child, so he transposed every single song in the show into the exact right key for each child. By ear. This is what piping classical music into a child's nursery when they are an infant can do. Michael's parents gave him the gift of an innate ability to play music by hearing it, sing on pitch, feel the beat, and have an appreciation for beautiful music. In a genius kind of way.

It's never too early to introduce music into your child's life. Nothing jarring to the spirit like rap music or hip hop or acid rock; no Stravinsky: Listening to music that is jarring to the spirit or promotes hatred will upset a child's young psyche.

My parents loved music; it was a staple in our home. My father had a Lincoln Continental with an 8-track tape player and all the classic American musicals on 8-track tape: *Carousel, The Sound of Music, South Pacific, Peter Pan*. He had a Herb Alpert tape too. I fell in love with those musicals and Herb Alpert's music. My dad always played some type of uplifting music whenever we drove in the car. My mother played music on the radio every morning while she was getting ready for work. She sang with my brother and me in the car every time we went somewhere. She taught us to sing harmonies to "Michael Row Your Boat Ashore" and "Take Me Out to the Ball Game". She taught us to sing rounds like "Row, Row, Row Your Boat" and "White Coral Bells". We'd drive to shopping, lessons, and dinners out singing rounds and harmonies.

two songs to be sung in rounds

"Row, Row, Row Your Boat"

Row, row, row your boat
Gently down the stream
Merrily, merrily, merrily, merrily
Life is but a dream

"White Coral Bells"

White coral bells upon a slender stalk
Lilies of the valley make my garden walk
Oh don't you wish that you could hear them ring
That would happen only when the fairies sing

**dance lessons at 5 gave
me poise and coordination,
and swing & ballroom dancing
came easily to me as an adult**

My parents gave me dance lessons starting at 5 years old – ballet, tap, and acrobatics, which have stood me in good stead my whole life. I feel confident and coordinated when I move, and I constantly get compliments on my Swing, Ballroom, and Country dancing, into which I incorporate *all* of my classical training. I can quickly and easily learn a new dance routine; I can dance to whatever music is playing – with panache! My parents taught me the Jitterbug at 7, and my dad would do all the aerials with me whenever we went somewhere where they had Swing music.

Singing and dancing brought great love and fun to our family and compensated for the feelings of sadness and low self-esteem I went through. Music and dancing helped to soothe whatever my parents were going through in their marriage, and individually from their own wounds. Song and dance uplifted our spirits and raised our vibrations.

When I was in the fourth grade, the school sent out a notice that we could sign for ... a violin class". "Okay!" I was a "yes" kid. My mom got me a 3/4 size violin. In the fifth grade, I played in the elementary school orchestra (the ultimate contradiction in terms). I was so bad. SO bad. I feel sorry for the music teacher because I didn't know what a flat or a sharp was. I can just imagine him sitting up there on that stool waving his little baton as I played every other note off pitch and the rest of them probably the wrong note. I don't remember ever practicing – not one time – I didn't understand the concept. And then in the sixth grade, the school announced they were canceling orchestra and only teaching band, and I needed to learn a band instrument if I wanted to continue playing an instrument in a musical class. I think they did that to get out of having to listen to me play every note out of tune on the violin every day. I then set aside my violin (thank God) and learned the clarinet. I finally learned the difference between a flat, a sharp, and a natural. I marched in the junior high school marching band, and then in the high school marching band – SO MUCH FUN!! In high school I also played in the pit orchestra for *Bye Bye Birdie* and *West Side Story* and learned musical theatre watching and playing for all the rehearsals and performances. I had a blast in band and pit orchestra, and my ear became superbly pitch-trained, and to this day, my body is a metronome. When I dance and when I sing, I am ALWAYS on beat. ALWAYS. It's not up for discussion.

I only applied to one college: UCLA. With my 3.8 GPA and high SAT scores, they took me in a heartbeat. After I received my acceptance letter, I called the band office and said, "I want to be in your marching band." They said, "What instrument do you play?" I said, "Clarinet." They said, "Learn the sax." I said, "Okay." I spent the summer taking alto saxophone lessons and practicing (yes, *I* was practicing!). I practiced every day!! At the end of the summer, I went to the UCLA campus and auditioned for the Marching Band. GUESS WHAT!? I GOT IN!! I GOT IN!! That was the second happiest day of my life. I had SO MUCH FUN in the UCLA Marching Band, and my body became an even better tuned metronome!

Dancing touched my life as well!! I told you about the second happiest day of my life. Well, the happiest day was ... So, I studied the Lindy Hop with the Pasadena Ballroom Dance Association after watching people Lindy Hopping at Swing Camp Catalina that Michael had taken me to our first summer together. I thought, oh, I could never learn that: It's too complicated! But I decided to give it a shot. First we took the beginning class, and then we took the beginning and intermediate classes one right after the other. At the end of the intermediate class, the teachers would give us the lecture that we could take the advanced class, but we had to take the intermediate class for at *least* six months first, usually a year and a half. Some people even took three years to be ready for the advanced class.

Every Saturday morning, I took the beginning and intermediate Lindy Hop, and then I would stay and watch the advanced class. Sometime in here, Michael and I realized we weren't right for each other, but I KEPT STUDYING AND DANCING THE LINDY HOP!! SO FUN! After five weeks, I COULDN'T STAND IT ANY MORE, and I snuck into the advanced class. At the beginning of every advanced class, the teachers would say, "Okay, everybody dance," and they would watch us dance. They would yell, "Change partners!" They were making sure everybody there was ready for the advanced class. The Lindy Hop was MY HEART – MY BLISS! I was ECSTATIC dancing the Lindy Hop. So the day I snuck into the advanced class after only *five weeks*, I danced with the different partners as the teachers watched, nervous yet ecstatic that I was there. Well, GUESS WHAT?! They didn't say a word!! I stayed and took the advanced class!! I left there higher than a kite. That was the best day of my life. I continued taking the intermediate and advanced Lindy Hop class for six years and went to their dances every Saturday night. I also went dancing two to three times per week and practiced and loved it. To this day, when I dance The Lindy Hop, it brings me unbridled joy. So that's the day I found my bliss – dancing The Lindy Hop in the advanced class at PBDA and not being kicked out!

There's always going to be some challenges in a family raising kids. You can't escape some difficulties and hurt feelings. But I'll tell you: Through all the dark days, through all my parents' problems, and through all my family's problems, I had band, I had my dancing lessons, and I had my dance performances: ballet, tap, acrobatics, folk, and gymnastics. My whole family – parents, brother, aunts, uncles, grandparents – came to my dance recitals. My parents and brother came to all my band performances. Everything I was ever in, my parents and brother were in the audience cheering me on. Those were some special times.

Besides the fact that music and dancing raise your vibration and bring you joy, they bring a family together in love and fun.

When I went to college, I studied voice and joined Opera a La Carte, a traveling Gilbert and Sullivan opera company. I got my first lead role in *Godspell* at a community theater. After college, I went on to star in all kinds of musicals, including playing Peter Pan in *Peter Pan*, Molly Morgan in *Girl Crazy*, Meg in *Brigadoon*, and Cousin Hebe in *H.M.S. Pinafore*. I had so much fun doing musical theatre and singing. Don't just take my word for it, watch me fly *Peter Pan* at "Janet Stegman Starring as Peter Pan" on YouTube. I didn't even have to act: I am Peter Pan! And then I was a voice teacher. I taught kids musical theatre and directed them in musical productions.

Janet starring in *Peter Pan*

Janet performing at the Los Angeles County Fair

harmonizing with my mom

Some of the best times I remember were harmonizing with my mom – Christmas carols, "Michael Row Your Boat Ashore". And singing rounds with my brother and my mom – "Row, Row, Row Your Boat" and "White Coral Bells". I loved listening to the American musical classics and Herb Alpert with my dad.

playing the guitar and singing at campfire

My singing added to the wonderfulness of our campfires at summer camp. When dusk turned to dark, we would light the campfire. At that point, I would take out my guitar and play the few camp songs I knew, and the whole camp would sing with me. My camp friends still talk about that to this day – 40 years later – me playing my guitar and singing "Leaving on a Jet Plane", "Today", and "Where Have All the Flowers Gone" for the camp at night with us all singing together around the campfire, looking up at the stars. Music enhances a person's life and forever touches the lives of those around you. Music is just a naturally uplifting phenomenon.

advice for parents

Play music early and often in your family. Play music while you are preparing dinner, whenever you are hanging out as a family, and when you are driving in the car on your way somewhere. Sing together when your child is very young, and sing together often. Play a variety of music: Broadway, pop, classical. Gilbert and Sullivan is wonderful! And some jazz. Share it with your child when you're snuggling, when they're sitting on your lap. That way your child will associate music with love and affection. It will raise their vibration and help their brain develop, in a very calming way.

Take your child to the music store and let them pick out music for everyone to listen to. Or for them to listen to in their room. Listen to a variety of music on the internet before you go, and let them decide what they would like to come home with.

Take your child to live theatre. There's nothing like sitting next to your child watching his aunt fly out over the audience singing her heart out. There's nothing like sitting next to your child while they are enchanted watching beautiful singing, dancing, and acting, all the while teaching them a moral and a story. Sharing live theatre is magical. My parents took me to *Peter Pan* and *The Sound of Music* and other musicals starting at three years old, and I still remember the thrill of watching live theatre.

Take your child to a musical, and after the show, play the CD on the way home and sing the songs from the show that you just watched.

Learn songs with harmonies – simple songs – and teach your children the harmonies. Remember: When you sing with your child when they are young, when you play music for them early on, they will become ear trained and thus have perfect relative pitch, and that will make it easy for them to become proficient at singing in musicals and musical groups and solo performances when they are older. It's good to ear-train them before the age of 6: That will stand them in good stead for the rest of their life. Singing harmonies together will bring joy to everyone in the family.

Every holiday season, it will be fun to come together as a family and sing Christmas carols together and other holiday favorites. You can get a four-part harmony book of carols or songs, teach everybody their part on the piano – everybody learns a part, then you can sing Christmas carols or any holiday music in four-part harmony – every year – so joyful, so uplifting. Harmonizing together will bring a family together in love and fun no matter what is going on in the family. It will uplift everybody.

Music, dancing, and humor are what saved my life. I am a wonderfully happy person today, and when I sing and dance, even happier. I mean, people tell me, "We love coming to your class because the energy in the room is so fantastic, from *your* joy – from your singing and dancing." Once the mp3 player went down, and I just started singing from Queen, and they were laughing because I was singing to them while the music was on the fritz, yet we could keep on dancing.

so much fun singing together as a family

I produced and directed *The Pirates of Penzance* with the Santa Cruz Junior Theatre. I had 6 to 10 year olds singing opera. I had toured with the show in Opera A La Carte, so I knew the show like the back of my hand. The Santa Cruz Junior Theatre was doing this opera – little tiny kids putting on an opera.

I handed every cast member a tape – that was back in the days of the cassette tape – of *The Pirates of Penzance* performed by the D'oyly Carte Opera Company. I told them, "Take this home, listen to it incessantly, and learn the music." Two weeks later, one of the mothers came up to me at one of the rehearsals – there were two parents and two girls in the family – and told me, "I have to tell you, we have been driving around singing to the tape everywhere we go – and we've never had so much fun and felt so happy together!"

Music, Dancing, and Humor
Learn It – Know It – Live It!

CHAPTER 22

....

A HEALTHY BODY

happy child, happy body
– keep up the positives

Happy child, happy body. Think of your child's health as a puzzle, with the pieces all fitting together perfectly to make a beautiful picture of a healthy, perfectly functioning child. First and foremost, you must keep up the positives: love, affection, compassion, comfort, compliments, and praise, to insure your child has the self-esteem necessary to believe they deserve to be healthy and *naturally want* to search out viable preventives to fend off any possible health problems, and also any cures if ever any illnesses arise. The answer will always be there for your child if they know where to look and believe they deserve vibrant health. Also, when you keep up the positives, your child's heart will be happy and that HAPPY HEART will help keep their immune system strong.

We already know that constant sadness, anger, and low self-esteem wear away at our immune system. So first and foremost, you will want to do everything I've suggested in the way of love and support to keep your child's spirits up. A child who is happy will for their whole life seek effective ways to keep their body healthy, because they will love themselves so much. When you love yourself, you naturally want to stay healthy, so that you can feel good all through your life adventures. In addition, when a child feels good about themselves, they don't want to punish themselves with sickness.

I have met people who are sad and depressed and feel bad about themselves. Those are the ones who feel like they deserve to be punished and so don't take good care of their health. They may have destructive vices that they can't seem to let go of. They won't take supplements or go to a naturopath or a chiropractor, because they believe they deserve to be ill and not feel good. They are comfortable being ill and not feeling good – it's comfortable for them. When you raise a child to feel good about themselves, you're setting them on a track of staying healthy and feeling good their whole life.

Children have a mental, a physical, and a spiritual aspect to their being. First, there is the physical. We have gone over how to ensure your child has good mental health. Your child's physical health must also be a priority, because if they don't feel well, they won't be happy. When a child is in pain, they can't feel happy because they're only feeling the pain. For the physical aspect of your child's health, I recommend finding a skilled naturopath or/and chiropractor who is trained in nutritional supplements and familiar with how the energy channels of the body work so they can keep your child's organs healthy and the energy channels flowing freely by either being licensed in or else referring you out to practitioners who are licensed in the natural types of health care, including naturopathic medicine, chiropractic – which will keep the fluids flowing freely throughout your child's joints and nervous system, acupuncture, and nutritional supplements. Organic Superfoods, a green powder made from organic, vine-ripened, picked-right-when-they're ripe fruits and vegetables, contain phytochemicals which will help keep allergies and illness away. If you give your child half a scoop to one scoop, depending on their size, of Organic Superfoods every day in a glass of juice diluted with water, it will help keep their immune and defense systems strong, and there will be less chance of them getting sick.

There are two other nutritional supplements that are wonderful for children and they are called Alovéa HOPE Pops, all-natural, sugar-free, immune-building cherry lollipops that contain 50 mg. of "acemannan", the molecule in the aloe vera plant that keeps your immune system well regulated and working properly. You can purchase these supplements from my Alovéa website at *janetmariestegman.myalovea.com*. The aloe vera plant has been found to be the most healing plant known to mankind. The acemannan molecule is as close to the molecular make-up of mother's milk as any substance can get. It has the same saccharides – the necessary sugars for cell-to-cell communication – that mother's milk has to keep your cells communicating with each other. So the lollipops, and most of the other Alovéa products, are *really* good for children, and they are all good for adults. They have protein bars – mmmm yummy – I eat two of them every day. I give the lollipops to my friends and my friends' kids!

a problem with the mind will create sickness in the body

As I have stated, my mother suffered from clinical depression. She was criticized frequently by her mother as a child, and then by her husband as an adult. She was on antidepressants for the last half of her life. I watched my mother have every *single* procedure that every medical doctor she ever saw suggested she have and take every drug any doctor ever prescribed. When a doctor told her she had cancer of the thyroid and needed to have it taken out, I tried to persuade her to try natural remedies that I had seen work for other people to support their body in healing itself of cancer. By this point, I had been researching the subject for many years. I suggested she try a more natural approach before letting them take out her thyroid. Well, she screamed at me, "You can't heal cancer! I have to have this done!" She had the surgery, and it was the kiss of death. It was the beginning of the end. It did not go well, to put it lightly. She lost the ability to speak, and she never was able to breathe well after that, because the surgeon nicked her vocal cord during the surgery, and the doctor who inserted the trach, after ten days of her being barely able to breathe and having to be intubated with oxygen, crushed her windpipe during the tracheostomy. And then for the rest of her life, until the day she died, she couldn't talk, could barely breathe. She was never the same after that. I think it's best to, if at all possible, avoid a medical procedure if you can heal yourself naturally.

I figured out that traditional, allopathic medicine was like a religion to my mother. I think that medical doctors represented loving parents to her – nurturing parents that, I believe, she always longed for. The doctors touched her with the stethoscope, they asked her how she was feeling, they would praise her when she followed their instructions well. You see, her mother was not affectionate and was often critical. My grandmother didn't believe in praising a child. Her father was kind of quiet, and not demonstrative with affection or compliments.

When my mother had a doctor's appointment, she would get very excited. They meant the world to her. It was like a trip to Disneyland. I would drive her to her appointments, and they were the highlight of her day. She *loved* going to her doctor's appointments. Whatever drugs the doctors prescribed, she would take. I think she wanted validation for being a good patient. The doctor would say, "Did you take your medicine?" "Oh, yes I did." "Oh, good girl!" But the thing is, she ended up on so many antidepressants and anti-anxiety drugs it became a nightmare. The doctors handed out the opioids like candy, and I think she got addicted. It was a nightmare – for me, anyway. And then the cancer, and then the surgeries, and then she ended up severely handicapped and miserable for the last eight years of her life.

My mother had no interest in learning about natural medicine or how it had helped me and others I knew. She had no desire to know about true healing on a systemic level, even though I was brimming with information and solid research on it. I think it was because my mother believed she deserved to be sick, and also because she got so much attention from her doctors when she was sick: She felt nurtured by her doctors, and me, when she was sick. That is a story of how somebody who has clinical depression and has been criticized does not have an interest in being healthy, because, well, there's not much attention from doctors for being outdoors playing sports and *not* going to doctors. She turned to the doctors because for her, they were the caring people in her life. She did whatever her doctors told her to do and rejected any natural paths to healing. You couldn't even speak to her about natural medicine. Except that towards the end, when she kept falling, she did take the supplements I gave her, and then she didn't fall anymore. She also let me take her to the chiropractor, which she absolutely loved. Through it all, I loved my mother to the moon and back, and I accepted the way she was – since I couldn't change her or get her to see things from my perspective – and I am forever grateful to have had that time taking care of her before she left this earth to go share a green beer with

Jesus: My mom died on St. Patrick's Day 2017. People do what they do, and when you can't change them, you just love them.

let the sunshine in

We all need some sunshine every day. You can put a hat on your child if you're worried about exposure to the sun. I wear an all natural, chemical-free sunblock so I don't expose my skin to harmful chemicals contained in the conventional sunblocks. If it's super hot, I stay in the shade. Plus, I take nutritional supplements that allow my body to fight off any damage too much sunlight might cause.

steer clear of the legal meth

I counseled a man who has struggled with addiction his whole life. His name is Chris. He is a beautiful, intelligent, loving man who lives in the park in a tent. He has struggled with excessive drinking, marijuana use, and chain smoking since high school. I interviewed Chris regarding what he feels led to his life of drug addiction, alcoholism, chain smoking, and debilitating depression. Here is his story:

Chris' grandmother put him on Adderall and Ritalin at the age of four because he "had too much energy" and had trouble sitting quietly in his classroom in kindergarten. He strongly suggests parents not put their kids on drugs for having "too much energy". He believes the drugs he was forced to take as a young child caused him to become a depressed chain-smoking drug addict alcoholic living in a tent in the park. He feels that because the doctors and his grandmother put him on heavy duty drugs at four years old, when his brain was still developing, it negatively affected his brain. He says that being on the drugs at such a young age got him used to being in an altered state and being dependent upon the chemicals in the drugs, and his brain became accustomed to functioning with mind-altering drugs.

Chris stresses that if your child has "too much energy", enroll them in several different sports so they can kick the ball hard down the soccer field and get out all their energy, run around the playing field and get out all their aggressions, and wear themselves tired. When Chris got to junior high school, he stopped taking the drugs and insisted on playing soccer, volleyball, and football. He noticed how playing those sports helped him express his high energy. Chris was never able to sit quietly in school. Not everyone has the mental make-up to sit quietly at a desk eight hours a day listening to a teacher talk and raising their hand. Drugs are not the solution. Sports, love, patience, and togetherness: Your child will make it fine to adulthood with those.

Chris has a lot of anger left over from being forced to take what he believes to be legal meth at four years old. He advises parents to only put their child on medication if they have a life-threatening illness. Chris wishes his grandmother had put him in soccer and other outdoor athletic activities instead of forcing him to take heavy duty medication.

Remember that kids need sunshine. And a TON of exercise. So get them outside running around engaging in fun physical activities. That will be good for your child.

spiritual health

We have touched on the naturopath and the chiropractor and nutritional supplements for your child's physical health, and compliments and positives for their mental health. Now let's address your child's spiritual health. I don't have an opinion as to religion. What I believe is important is that you discuss matters spiritual with your child and let them talk about their thoughts and feelings on the subject. As they are allowed to play and make a garden, create art, dance, sing, and love a pet, their spirit will be just fine. As long as they are smiling and laughing and loving, their spirit will shine bright always. You should not worry about anything other than making sure their heart is happy.

nutritional supplement favorites
for parents and children

I believe in doing everything I can to keep my immune system humming and happy so I don't have to drop everything and go to the doctor every time I have a sniffle. What I do, for myself, is make sure my supplement pantry is well stocked with my "must-haves" – the nutritional supplements I can't live without, which support my (1) Immune System that helps me heal of . . . well . . . everything, (2) Defense System to help me fight off any illness, and (3) Endocrine System / Hormones that keep me looking and feeling young and vibrant. Those are the legs of the triangle of glowing health.

My favorite "must-haves" are: "Immun" by Alovéa for my immune system, "Orgain Organic Superfoods" for my defense system, "Balance" by Alovéa for hormonal support, and "Limitless" by Alovéa for inflammation. These are made from food and the aloe vera plant and keep your immune, defense, and endocrine systems running smoothly. I take "GenF20Plus" by Leading Edge to keep my human growth hormone replenished and "OPC3" by Isotonix for my joints and other health benefits, and "Pure Collagen" also by Isotnoix to keep everything supple. I take others as well, but those are the ones I can't be without.

the secret to anti-aging and happy hormones

When I was taking care of my severely handicapped 80 year old mother, I was so stressed that I had little to no energy and started feeling depressed and looking really old. I wasn't my old bouncy self. Just then I happened upon an article in a health magazine entitled, "Aging is a Treatable Disease", by Harolyn Gilles, M.D., a bioidentical hormone doctor. As you can guess, I was all over that. Before I had finished reading the article, I was calling Dr. Gilles to schedule an appointment! I drove six hours to Scottsdale, Arizona to see her. I would have driven across the galaxy to have my vitality and youthful bounce back. Dr. Gilles had me take a blood test before my appointment and have the results sent to her, which I did. I made the six hour trek to Scottsdale, and that turned out to be one of the best trips I ever made. At my appointment, Dr. Gilles said, "I can't even see your hormone levels in the test results, they are so depleted. No wonder you have no energy and feel depressed and old!" She told me that any time you have stress in your life or go through an illness, your hormones get depleted. But you can't take chemical hormones, because they will wreak havoc on your health. She prescribed compound pharmaceuticals made from soy and yam because they mimic your own hormones and your body believes they are your own naturally-produced hormones. She said that most women don't know this, but testosterone is the most important hormone for a woman and had me take a testosterone supplement and more of my GenF20Plus. Well, I took everything she prescribed and suggested, along with my aloe vera products, which she gave the thumbs up to, and voilà! I was back, baby!! Youthful, energetic, athletic, and happy. I tell you these things, because they have made *such* a difference in my life: When you feel good physically, you naturally feel better mentally and emotionally as well.

The other reason I feel it is important for parents to know about the supplements and bio-identical hormone treatments is because parenting can be *very* stressful, and your hormone levels and immune and defense systems can become weakened as a result. Parents do their best parenting when they feel good and are full of energy and vitality.

For children, taking the Immun or eating the HOPE Pops, both with the Acemannan, will keep their immune system well regulated, and the Organic Superfoods will keep their defense system strong to help fight off viruses and colds. From what I have seen, I believe those two supplements are the best baseline nutritional supplements to give children in addition to feeding them a nutritious diet. I mean, kids are never going to have a perfect diet. Just like I love my pie, they love their birthday cake and ice cream and whatever other treats that are fun for them. When the majority of their meals are nutritious, and you are perhaps giving them the Alovéa products, you can relax and not have to worry that they are not eating a perfect diet. *IT'S OKAY TO LET THEM HAVE TREATS!*

Because our food and water and air are of a little lesser quality than they were when we were cave people, it is important to fortify our diet with nutritional supplements. I cannot tell you how many people tell me how young I look, that they can't believe I'm 63, that they can't believe how athletic and youthful I am. Yup. Immune boosters, superfoods, and hormone support, baby, my life-savers! You can buy the Alovéa and Isotonix products on my company websites, *janetmariestegman. myalovea.com* and *isotonix.com/janethealsyou* websites. I am a distributor for both companies, because I love their products!

to vaccinate or not to vaccinate
– that is the question

I cannot tell you whether to vaccinate or not to vaccinate. There are arguments on both sides, and that is a decision you will have to make for yourselves. What I will do is give you some sources that I have found to be informative and credible on the subject. I will also give you some suggestions on how to help your child either heal from or have the best chance of never having an adverse reaction to a vaccine, if you decide to vaccinate. I've already talked about the organic superfood powder in a glass of diluted juice. I can't say enough about the Immun with the Acemannan for this as well. In addition, the OPC3 by Isotonix will detox toxic metals. Standard Process has a powder called "SP Detox Balance" and you would put that in a smoothie. For purposes of researching the subject of vaccines, so that you can make a fully informed decision, I recommend going to the AMA website and reading the articles they have posted on vaccines, and to the NVIC and ICAN websites and reading their studies as well. There are also some very good books on the subject by authors like Dr. Vernon Coleman and Tony Lyons. There are also two interesting documentaries: *Vaxxed* and *Vaxxed II,* both of which offer valuable information.

All I am saying is be cautious. Do your research; do your due diligence. Look at both sides of the equation and decide what is right for you. Make your decisions based on what you feel is right. See a naturopathic doctor and give your child the recommended supplements so that they can have a better chance of staying healthy and, if you do decide to vaccinate, avoiding any adverse reactions or injuries from them. What I am saying is don't follow either side blindly. Do the research, make your educated decision, and do what you feel is best for your family.

If you decide not to vaccinate, the nutritional supplements I am recommending will help your child stay healthy and most easily be able to fend off colds and flus. I consider them an alternative to vaccination. Also, a toxic metal cleanse would be excellent for your child's health no matter what you decide, because there are toxic metals in most medications, in the air, and who knows what else. Toxic metals can cause all kinds of interruptions in your child's health, so make sure you give them the detox supplements to counteract any poisons they might have ingested.

If you do choose not to vaccinate, there are effective ways to keep your child from getting a cold or a virus, and those are by building their immune system and their defense system and keeping their hormones replenished. All of the supplements I have been suggesting are effective for that. Bone broth is excellent for replenishing hormones, and strengthening the immune system, and avoiding cavities.

help with keeping away cavities

Bone broth is also known to help stave off tooth decay. If your child has an issue with cavities, I refer you to the book, *Cure Tooth Decay: Heal and Prevent Cavities with Nutrition*, by Ramiel Nagel. It talks a lot about drinking bone broth (I take enough bone broth pills to choke a horse) and taking a fish oil called "Green Pasture Blue Ice Royal Butter Oil/Fermented Cod Liver Oil Blend capsules". Symplex F by Standard Process is a good one for that as well. I also take wheelbarrows full of plant calcium, the most assimilable calcium.

Between your love, affection and kind words and some good nutritional supplements, your child's immune system will be through the roof healthy, and your loved one will have a much better chance of fighting off a cold or flu; They will be able to either stave off or fight off any virus or disease that comes along.

how to insure your child will not want to experiment with drugs

I would like to quell your fears of your child ever wanting to experiment with drugs, drinking, or smoking. If you follow the practices suggested in this book, your child will learn to express their feelings in a healthy manner and feel good. They won't feel the need to reach out for drugs or other mind or emotion altering substances. They won't feel the need to rebel to the point where they destroy their mind and body. Mind-altering drugs are mostly an escape. If you're teaching your child that their feelings are important and that you care about them, and they get to you about their feelings and are able to express them in a healthy way, they're not going to *need* to escape. Because they're just happy. Nobody feels the need to escape when they're happy. You just want to feel happy and live your life!

I promise that if you practice the principles in this book, it will seriously, *seriously* decrease the chance of your child ever wanting to experiment with drugs or other destructive behavior. If you put all of these things in place, your child will have the skills to talk to you about their problems and their feelings. If you make the home environment one in which they can talk to you about whatever is going on with them, you will drastically decrease the chance of them ever wanting to take self-destructive, dangerous substances or do dangerous, destructive activities.

a hug a day keeps the doctor away

Keep the doctor away: Shower your child with love, kindness, compassion, understanding, validation, compliments, humor, singing, dancing, comfort, hugs, praise, praise in front of company, and stories. And save some for yourselves as well. You deserve it!!

CHAPTER 23

CHEAPER THAN BAIL

outdoor activities

There is value in outdoor activities. You might be surprised to find out how expensive kids' sports are. But come to find out: They're cheaper than bail! If you involve your child in activities that keep them active, exercising, interested, taking on a challenge, working towards finishing a project, and growing their own food, they will stay interested in those activities as an adult. They will keep them occupied and . . . well . . . out of jail. I kid, but it's true what it says in the Bible that "Idle hands are the devil's workshop . . ." If a person is engrossed in a wholesome activity, obtaining a goal, fulfilling a purpose, and a fun time, well, let's just say: "NO BAIL FOR YOU!"

Organized sports are not the only outdoor activity your child can participate in. There are a myriad of other outdoor activities your child can choose from. They might love a sport that isn't necessarily at the "highest" level. There are sports kids can play together in the park, like tossing around a football or a softball or a frisbee. There are the jungle gym and the swings. How much fun did we have as children playing in the playground at the park?

Let's face it: We all need Vitamin D. We all need sunshine. We need fresh air and sunshine for our mental health. Think about people in Portland or Seattle where it's cloudy and rainy all the time. They have to sit in front of a light machine to keep from getting depressed. For our mental and emotional health, we need to get outdoors every day for a good amount of time. In addition, we need exercise. Aside from being necessary for our physical health, exercise is important for our mental health. Physical activity helps to bump up the production of endorphins, our brain's feel-good neurotransmitters. And the releasing of those endorphins lifts our spirits. Our physical well being and feeling good in our body is as important as eating good food and taking good nutritional supplements, and, of course, hearing good compliments.

exercise is one leg of the triangle
of your child's health

Exercise in any form is one leg of the triangle of your child's health. Whether it be walking with you through the neighborhood, riding a bike with their brother, sister or friend, playing a sport at school or flag football in the park with the neighborhood kids, it will suffice for the exercise vital to their mental and physical well-being. If your child is outdoors breathing fresh air and moving their body, they are getting the necessary exercise and enjoying the sunshine.

the martial arts are an excellent physical activity

Even though the martial arts are not considered "outdoor sports", they're still very good for a child because they help a child feel comfortable in their body, move with agility, and learn how to control their body in a positive way. A martial arts skill will help them to move gracefully through their daily lives and exude confidence. They will feel safe in their person, as they will know that, if a situation were ever to arise in which they would need to defend themselves, they could instinctively do so. They will lead from a position of strength and confidence in the knowledge they are safe in their person and can easily protect themselves and their loved ones if needed at any given moment. Most likely, nobody would ever dare challenge your child, as they would be giving off an air of, "Don't you even *think* about it!"

Martial arts are good all the way around. Taking martial arts classes and practicing outside of class will help your child keep their body in tip-top shape. They are good for exercising and strengthening their muscles and keeping their heart and lungs healthy.

don't forget about gardening!

And then there's gardening! When you're gardening, you're outside, you've got your hands in the dirt, you're communing with nature. Your child might not have the mental make-up or the physical ability to compete in sports; no worries, there are other outdoor activities like gardening that can be just as valuable. Gardening brings all the benefits of an outdoor activity, *and* it produces something *very* valuable: DINNER!! Gardening will give your child the satisfaction of growing their own vegetables and picking their own raspberries. There's nothing more delicious than a piece of fresh fruit picked ripe off the tree in your front yard! Growing our own food takes us back to our roots – to our natural human need to pick fruit off the trees and dig up roots from the ground to nourish our bodies. That is what our ancestors did. They didn't drive to the grocery store to buy food; when they were hungry, they went and picked an apple or dug up a carrot. Growing our own fruit and vegetables draws us into the cycle of nature in which we eat wholesome food right where it grew and understand that we are part of that cycle.

When you're planting a garden, you're communing with nature; you're touching nature; you're smelling nature. Your energy is mixing with the creator's energy in creating nature. You merge with nature. It's healthy to eat food you grew and picked; all five senses are aware of it. You can see it, you can touch it, you can smell it, you can taste it, and you can feel it. Eating organic food right out of the ground or off a branch of a tree is the healthiest way for your child to nourish their body.

but I don't know anything about gardening – yikes!!

It's okay if you don't know anything about gardening. Go with your child to the bookstore or the library and get a book on permaculture or how to plant a vegetable garden. Make it a family outing and go out for organic salads afterwards. Celebrate that you as a family are going to learn how to plant a garden and grow your own food together. You will be learning what kind of soil to use, where to get the seeds, what time of year to plant what, how to water your plants, how far apart to plant the seeds. You parents are going to learn how to make and maintain a garden, which is a necessary survival skill to have. Plant your garden in the backyard, if you have one – or the front yard – or the side yard. If you don't have a yard, perhaps you can get a community garden plot near where you live. Many neighborhoods have a community plot for families who want to grow their own garden. You can even get planters at your local hardware store or nursery, and dirt, and plant your garden out on your porch or deck.

Read your gardening book with your child. When you have finished the book, schedule a time for the whole family – whoever can make it – to go outside and plant your garden. Go on, get your hands in the dirt. Lie down on the ground and feel Mother Earth supporting you! Take a nap in the sunshine and then plant your garden. Have a ball creating your garden together as a family. Planting a garden with your child, or maybe even the whole family, will be the perfect bonding experience for all of you. As an extra added bonus, it will teach your child survival skills, and those skills will stand them in good stead for the rest of their life. Having a garden that you planted together will take you all back to your roots and give you something to talk about forever; it will give you a shared interest – a fun and nurturing activity to do together. It's the perfect project to share with your child. The idea of having a book about gardening and learning to grow your family's own fruit and vegetables includes your child reading to you from the book, which will be good for practicing their reading skills.

from the ground up

So you learn the whole process of making food together – from the ground up. When you and your child take part in growing the food and preparing your meals together, you are learning the entire process of feeding yourselves, from the ground up, and that's fun and exciting! There's nothing as exciting as having a salad made from lettuce that you grew yourselves. You don't have to have an acre of garden: you can do that with one small pot.

my own childhood garden with
my dad was a cherished experience

When I was a little girl, my dad made a little spot in the backyard for us to grow a garden. We planted corn, potatoes, and carrots. We planted them together. The corn grew probably 10 feet high. There's pictures of me as a little girl in my little red dress and little pointy black patent leather boots (it was 1966 – what can I say?) standing next to the stalk of corn, and the stalk is towering over me – three times as high as I was. When it came time, we dug up the potatoes and the carrots and picked the corn, and then my mom cooked them all, and we ate them at dinner. It was such a fun thing to share. And you can do that with salads, with lettuce or herbs or anything – anything you want to plant.

go on a picnic at the park with your
homegrown vegetables and fruit

It's the little things, you know, that kids remember and appreciate: the little ways that you go out of your way to make an occasion special. One idea that would bring jubilant joy to your child would be to take them to the park for lunch. Eat outside, in the sunshine, with family and friends. I guarantee your child will think it's the greatest thing ever – going to the park on a picnic with Grandma or Grandpa or Mom or Dad or all four! They will love it! Bring a special surprise: a homemade cake for dessert, a canned juice drink, to go with your home grown lunch. That would feel very special. It would make a memory your child will never forget. Especially since they helped grow the food!

a fun time at the park with dad

A few years after we planted our garden and ate the delicious corn and potatoes, my father started taking my brother and me to the park to throw the football. When I was eleven and my brother was eight, he taught us how to throw a football and how to catch a football. He'd say, "Think of the football as a baby. I'm going to throw it to you, and then you open your arms and pull it to you and cuddle it like you would a baby." We would play catch together at the park. That was incredibly fun and bonding. I remember that to this day, like it was yesterday. Believe it or not, when I played football on the UCLA Marching Band intramural football team – flag football – I was our star receiver! I would make all the touchdowns! All because my dad taught me how to catch a football when I was eleven. It was a skill that has stayed with me my entire life. It was a life skill. To this day, I hear from my band friends, "You were our star receiver! You did great!"

more fun outdoor activities

My father took my brother and me to Yosemite. We hiked all the way to the top of Half Dome and El Capitan. We had a great time going on those hikes and seeing all the sights. Those were some really good times with my dad. He took us go-karting, swimming, boating, and on many other wonderful adventures. He even set us on his lap, one at a time, of course, and let us drive his Lincoln Continental in the huge race track parking lot with no other cars around. I'll never forget that, either!

You can do the same with your child – spending time with them outdoors doing different things, trying all kinds of different activities. You can make wonderful life-long memories with your child on all your outdoor adventures and capers!

if they want to participate in
school sports, have at it

Aside from the slight expense of school sports, there's absolutely nothing wrong with enrolling your child in them: soccer or baseball or basketball, wrestling or swimming. Any one of those would be good. Football if they promise to always, *always* wear a helmet on their head and a pad over *every single* part of their body! Let them try whatever sports they express a desire to play. You don't ever want them to get injured, so you will want to spend time learning about and stressing to them the importance of taking every safety measure and learning how to play safely. You might even let them try a little bit of everything when they're little. If they decide they want to enter competitive sports, if they say to you, "I really want to do it; I think I would love it!" support them – pay the millions of dollars for their uniform and entry fees. But seriously, any wholesome sports will be good for your child. And cheaper than bail!!

encourage and praise your child for playing, not for winning

Encourage and praise your child for playing and trying their best, but steer clear of making winning the most important thing. Make sure you don't take the attitude or even hint that the only way for them to succeed is by winning. Does it really matter who wins? The point is that they participated; they had a good time; they did their best. Those are the things that matter, and those are the things I encourage you to praise and encourage them for. I mean, if they won the game, yay! Great job! High five! But if they didn't win, ask them:

"Did you have a good time?"
"Yes."
"Yay! Great job! High five!"
"Did you do your best?"
"Yup!"
"Yay! Great job! High five!"

It's all good! As long as they have fun, get some exercise, spend time outdoors, and have social interactions with other players, you have done your job. Yay! Great job! High five!

a family of rabbits

I know a mom who was elated to be planting a garden for the first time with her four year old son. She bought raised beds for the backyard. She went with her little boy and bought carrot plants and pea plants. They spent the next Sunday afternoon transferring the plants into the ground. Well, by the next day, a rabbit had moved in. And then, of course, the rabbit had little ones. Well, you can't throw a rabbit out of her home – everyone knows that – especially not if she has babies! So there it was. So much for the carrots and peas. But they did enjoy the learning experience of having a family of rabbits living in their garden. And the little boy loved getting to watch the baby bunnies grow up. And eat all the vegetables they had planted. That's *almost* as good as growing a garden, or maybe even better. You never know what cherished memories will come from a backyard caper with your child that includes bunnies.

something for everyone

The thing to remember is that there is something for everyone. If your child is competitive and loves playing competitive sports, let them play competitive sports. But competitive sports are not for everyone; there are other activities they can participate in, like throwing a frisbee around the park, or freeze tag, or Pickle, or swinging on the swings and playing on the slide. Any outdoor fun will be wonderful and beneficial for your child. Throwing a softball or a football, kicking around the Hacky Sack: It's about being outside and breathing fresh air and soaking up some Vitamin D. It's about running around, playing and laughing and having fun with friends and loved ones.

Thank God for children – they help us get back to our carefree childhood roots and play outside, not a care in the world, just everyone out having a blast together!

CHAPTER 24

WHAT TO DO IF YOUR CHILD IS BEING BULLIED

this is my chapter

I write this chapter with the wisdom of an adult who, from the fifth grade through my junior year in high school, was bullied – horribly, horribly bullied – every minute of every day at school. After one week at my new elementary school, every ounce of my body took on the belief that I was a loser, a social reject, and undeserving of friends, success, or happiness. I did not feel that way about myself when I was little. It wasn't until I was ten and my family moved to San Marino, an extraordinarily affluent community, and I entered the fifth grade at the elementary school there. That was when it was pounded into me that I was the most socially inept loser that ever lived.

After spending a lifetime wondering what it was that made me different and why did the kids choose me to zero in on and make the designated victim, I have come to believe it was because I was a sensitive little girl, heart open, full of love, feeling my feelings, 'quiet', and therefore vulnerable. I was not familiar with the concept of being verbally abused every minute of every day. I was *'quiet'* because my father told me to be 'quiet'. The night before the first day of school, he told me, "Don't go shooting your mouth off. Be quiet. Hang back until you get the lay of the land". Really? How is a 10-year-old supposed to know what 'be quiet until you get the lay of the land' means? I have no idea what my father was thinking. He wasn't; that was the problem.

He didn't say, "Janet, you are a beautiful little girl with an adorable personality, so loving, so fun, such a precious, free spirit. Just go and be yourself, your happy, fun, smart self, and you will have no trouble making friends." That would have been good advice.

So the other students took my 'hanging back until I got the lay of the land' as me being insecure, shy, and lacking self-esteem; when in fact, it was quite the opposite. I was a happy child with tremendous self-esteem, *very much* a free spirit. I remember riding my bike to school that first day. I had on this darling little brown *faux* leather jumper with a little white ruffly blouse and a little *faux* leather British cap that matched my jumper. I felt like a million bucks, like I was the cutest little thing that ever lived. I was riding my pink Stingray with a banana seat and a big basket in the front. I could ride all the way to school with no hands, which I usually did.

the unwelcome dragon lady

When I got to school, the teacher, Miss Stuart, assigned a Welcome Wagon Lady to me, a classmate named Marion, who was tasked with acquainting me with the other students and seeing to it that I felt 'welcome'. I was *so* excited to be starting a new adventure at my new school! Little did I know, Marion had other plans for me. Instead of welcoming me, she told the other kids to put me down and make fun of me every chance they got, which they did, and which pleased her very much. Marion turned out to be the *Un*welcome Dragon Lady. In one year, I went from feeling like the world was my oyster to believing I was a worthless social reject.

One day, Nadine, one of the students Marion recruited into her band of bullies stood, up in front of the class to give a report on the 'Missing Link'. At the end of her report, she unveiled the poster size drawing sitting on the easel and said, "This is a drawing of what scientists believe the Missing Link looked like. And, no offense, but I think it looks like Stegman." (The kids never called me Janet. When speaking or referring to me, they always called me 'Stegman' or 'Steggie' or 'Stegbutt' or 'Steggiebutt' or 'Stegosaurus', or some other very original, creative derivative of my last name. I don't think anyone even knew what my first name was.) The teacher, in an attempt to deflect the baseless insult, announced to the class, "Janet's such a good sport." And that was that. That was all the support I got – from the teacher or anybody else. "Janet's such a good sport." I died a thousand deaths sitting there at my little student desk there in the back of the room. I felt so humiliated. It was excruciating. But I was quiet, like my dad said. I sat there, crushed, humiliated, embarrassed, not saying a word – I didn't know I could. It was not in my box of tools. I had never been taught how to stand up for myself or that I could walk out of an abusive situation and say, "Thanks but no thanks." There I sat in my own private hell, drowning in a pool of anguish, not moving a muscle, not knowing what to do other than sit there and pretend I was alive. I have often wondered how much less scarred I would have been had the teacher turned to Nadine and, loudly and for all to hear, said, "Nadine, that was a very cruel and hurtful thing you just said to Janet. I'm sure it hurt her feelings; it would have hurt mine. I think you owe her an apology." And then she could have waited for Nadine to say she was sorry and assure it was not true.

dreams do come true

The Missing Link disaster was never spoken of again. Until my 20th reunion. Twenty-eight years later, at my 20th high school reunion, I joined a group of about six classmates standing around talking about how some kids were mean when we were in school. I don't remember exactly what was said, but I remember it paralleled exactly what happened to me in the fifth grade. I turned to Nadine and said, "Yes, as a matter of fact, Nadine . . ." She looked at me, full of emotion, and said, "Oh, Janet, I am *so* sorry. Marion put me up to it. I remember I said it, and then she started laughing, and nobody else was laughing, and I felt terrible. I have never forgiven myself for that." After carrying that pain around for 28 years, Nadine's words were music to my ears. I immediately replied, "I forgive you, Nadine." And I did. After all those years, it turned out she didn't really think I looked like the Missing Link. Good to know.

I'm thinking it might have saved me a lifetime of self-consciousness and hurt if the teacher had announced to the class: "Janet, you don't look like an ape. You are a very pretty little girl. Please don't listen to what Nadine said or take that personally: It was just a mean thing for her to say, and it's not true. Here's a piece of chocolate for your troubles." That would have done wonders for my self-esteem if she had done that. Especially the chocolate part.

Interestingly enough, after feeling such intense hatred for Marion for causing me so much pain and turning me into the 'unpopular one', as well as feeling endless envy for how 'popular' she was, I found out that the entire time she was torturing me, she was being physically abused by her father at home. And then I understood. Unbeknownst to anyone at school, Marion was living her own life of quiet desperation, doing her best to navigate herself through this living Hell, angry and powerless to stop her father from abusing her. And she took all of that out on me. Because I was a vulnerable, sweet, unsuspecting 10-year-old with no idea how to advocate for myself, or enlist an adult to do so, or even that it was an option. She did it because she could, because she needed a whipping board for her anger, and I was someone upon whom she could vent her frustration with no risk of further abuse.

The next year, Marion transferred to a private school and I never heard from her again. But the damage had been done. I was one of the three whipping boards for our class – one of the *'unpopular ones'*. And when word got out, it was just a mean ol' free-for-all, until my last day in that city. The dye was cast, and my caste followed me around all the way through my junior year in high school. (My senior year, I had had it and went to live with my father in Santa Monica, where I started afresh and thoroughly enjoyed myself.)

Looking back, I have come to realize that back then, teachers were not trained in how to deal with bullying in the classroom. I don't think they were aware how sensitive children are and how bullying leaves lifelong scars on them. So all the teacher could think of to say was, "Janet's such a good sport." Back in the 60s, people were just not aware of how damaging being bullied is. It was common practice. Bullying was just accepted as a part of going to school. Unless it was extreme physical bullying, it didn't count for bullying. It was simply called name-calling. You were 'teased.' People said, "A little teasing never hurt anyone," and "Sticks and stones will break my bones, but words will never hurt me." Parents would say, "Kids can be mean," "Well, that's what kids do," "Those rotten kids." It was just accepted and never questioned.

out of adversity springs wisdom

So as you can see, I had a very difficult time as a little girl with being bullied. Truthfully, in retrospect, I see that it taught me compassion and understanding for anyone being bullied – adult, child, animal, spider – and that it is appropriate to stick up for those who are being abused. It is the loving thing to do. Experiencing such intense emotional pain and quiet desperation from the fifth grade until the end of my junior year showed me how important it is to treat others with love, understanding, compassion, and respect.

Now you understand why this chapter is such an important one to be included in this book. I don't ever want another child to have to endure the kind of cruelty I did through for most of my childhood. Did I say, "Thank God for summer camp?!" Literally, summer camp, my yearly one-to-two-week haven where I was treated with the utmost love and respect, saved my hide. I truly believe I am the person I am today because I was shown such unconditional love and acceptance every summer by everyone at YMCA Camp Ta Ta Pochon.

teachers need to nip bullying
in the bud – at every turn

My parents had no clue how to deal with my being bullied at school. Nobody even called it that. All my parents could think to say was, "Those rotten kids." My freshman year in high school, my mother went to talk to my speech teacher because I was being so badly bullied in speech class. SO bad. There were about eight boys who sat on the couches in the back of the room, and every time I turned around, they would say, "Turn around, ugly." "Shut up, stupid." And when I gave my big speech, those boys spent the rest of the year making fun of me for it. I gave a speech about women's rights. And the whole rest of the year, everywhere I went, the boys called me *"Mizzzz* Stegman (parodying the "Ms.") and "Miss Women's Lib". Still no one ever called me by my first name.

A short while later, I was asked to speak at a N.O.W. (National Organization for Women) meeting. My mother was a city prosecutor in Pasadena, and was a member of N.O.W. It was quite an honor to be invited to speak at a N.O.W. meeting at the young age of 14. I think Gloria Steinem was there; Gloria Allred too. I gave a wonderful speech about being an independent girl. I brought the house down, I made everybody laugh. I was really proud of myself. It was such a wonderful speech that I made it onto the radio the next morning.

That day at school, one of the kindest and sweetest girls in my class, Daralee Gowan, said to me, "I heard you on the radio this morning!" I replied, "That wasn't me." I never lied. I always told the truth. Except that morning, because I couldn't bear the thought of being made fun of *some more* for being for women's rights. Daralee said, "But Janet, it was your voice. They said your name." "Nope. Wasn't me." I mean, here, somebody was actually being nice to me, but I was still being ripped to shreds by those rotten kids, and I did not know how to handle it. Because of the bullying, I missed an opportunity to share an accolade with a friend, and perhaps continue the friendship. To this day, I thank Daralee for treating me with such love and kindness when we were growing up. But back then, I could not accept the accolade. I could not say to Daralee, "Yeah, that was me on the radio. Pretty neat, huh?" Because I was so sensitized to being made fun of for being . . . *whatever.*

My mom took time off of work to go and talk to the teacher, Mr. Austin, about how those boys on the couch were treating me. Because he was just letting them be so cruel to me. He never said a word to them; not one time did he ever advocate for me. Nothing. Nada. Crickets. He never said to them like, you know, "Knock that the heck off. The next one that says *anything* the least bit mean to Janet is out of the class, and you will get an F on your report card."

My mom always wanted me to be a debater like her and enter debate tournaments, but I had no interest. I participated in one debate in that stupid class, and because I had so little self-confidence and such low self-esteem, I couldn't forgive myself for not doing a very good job – right out of the gate like my parents. So I never entered any debate tournaments. Let's be honest, the first time you do something, you're not going to be good at it. But if you work at it, you can get good at it. But I didn't want to. I'm pretty sure I would have been an excellent debater – I'm really smart and well spoken. But because I was being bullied so badly, I couldn't take the chance of being made fun of – for anything more. I was sensitized to being embarrassed. Like right underneath the surface was, "I'm so embarrassed for who I am." Honestly, I can't even remember whether my mother's talk did any good. It was just one big disaster, that class.

My senior year, I had had it with those rotten kids in San Marino and went to live with my father in Santa Monica. I got a fresh start and had a really fun time there. No one 'knew' I was 'unpopular' (what a stupid word, 'unpopular' – it means nothing). All I can say is thank God for Santa Monica High School and thank God for Camp Ta Ta Pochon!

I tell you all of this, not because I am going to rename this book *Janet's Tales of Woe in Bullyland,* but rather because I want to impress upon you how incredibly serious it is when a child is being bullied. I want you to fully comprehend the magnitude of toll it takes on a child to, at such a young age and being so vulnerable and impressionable, be faced with such immeasurable and undeserved cruelty. Even high school kids can be hugely negatively affected by bullying – the damage to their tender psyches, as well, can be unfathomable. Children have no clue how to stand up for themselves, so you must do it for them. At all costs.

Now that you know how passionate I feel about no child being bullied – anywhere – ever, you're probably wondering, "Okay, so tell us, Janet, what should we do if our child is being bullied?" Well, I'm glad you asked. Because now I am now going to tell you how to deal with their child being bullied.

Here it is:

Don't let it happen. Whatever you have to do to stop it, do it. If talking to the teacher or the principal gets you nowhere, tell the teacher, "If you can't stop the kids from bullying my child, I am going to take my child out of this class, take my child out of this school, and sue you." Go to the principal and say, "If my child comes home one more time and says she's been bullied at school, I'm going to sue you. You, my child's teacher, the school board – for harassment, severe emotional distress, intentional infliction of emotional distress, and other torts. You need to handle this so more children aren't scarred for a lifetime." Use your best judgment, of course, but whatever it is, advocate for that child. To the death. Don't stop until your child is no longer being bullied. If you have to get a restraining order, get one. Go to the newspaper and tell the story of how your child's school is unable to control its students and the bullying at the school. Make shit up. Just do something. Have the intention of stopping your child from being bullied at all costs.

If you have to pull your child out of school and get them into homeschooling or a private school or a charter school or a Montessori School – a school where the children are loving and the teachers are kind and compassionate and advocate for all their students, do it.

It would be good to read "The Calf and the Giraffe Go on a Picnic" to your child. That's one of the stories from Chapter 25 of this book. It will help you impress upon your child never to take bullying personally. You want to tell your child, "Bullies are very miserable, sad people. Rather than hate them or fall victim to their abuse, pity them, feel sorry for them, pray for them. When one of those miserable, sad children begins to bully you, simply say to them: 'I'm so sorry you are so miserable. I hope you feel better soon. I'm praying for you.' Bullying has nothing to do with the one being bullied. Do not let it tear down your self-esteem. A person who is bullying you is telling you exactly who they are: a very angry and jealous person with a big hole in their gut. They want to push you down so that they can feel superior to you. But it's a fake superiority. It is the desperate grabbings of an extremely unhappy person in an attempt to find something to feel superior about, *albeit* false. Now that you understand why the bully is trying to hurt you, here is how you can deal with the situation: Simply say: 'You are not allowed to talk to me that way. I will not allow you to talk to me that way. You talk to me in a respectful manner, or I will be forced to take further action.'"

Impress upon your child: "Never take bullying personally: It has nothing to do with you and everything to do with the bully." If you instill that wisdom in your child, they will always lead from that place when they encounter a bully, if they ever do. That way, no matter where they are in their life, they will always know it is not about them. Arm your child with the knowledge that any time they are bullied, it has nothing to do with them and everything to do with the bully. *That* is a lesson we *all* can be reminded of, every minute of every day.

teach your child the type of communication
That allows them to retain their power

Teach your child how to communicate in a way that allows them to hold on to their power. Teach them to say, "You will not talk to me that way, ever. Or I will be forced to take action." And then they walk away. Just walk away. And then if they have to take further action, they can come to you and you can take action.

It is also important to teach your child that, although they may want to punch the bully for being cruel to them, violence is never the answer. Violence always comes back to you in a negative and regretful way. I guarantee that if you engage in violent behavior, *you* will be the one blamed, and *you* will be the one that gets in trouble, even though you were provoked. I have seen it a hundred times.

If your child tells you one time that they are being bullied, that they are being made fun of, that they are being called names, being put down, being torn down, teach them how to defend themselves with those non-violent, high road, assertive, leading-with-self-esteem methods. In fact, it would not at all be a bad idea to teach them those skills when there is no current bullying going on, preventively.

advocate for the child in *front* of the child

As sad as it seems, it is far too often the case that a child will be bullied by a parent. If this is the case, and the best you can do is try and convince the other parent to treat the child in a respectful and loving manner, do it in *front* of the child. Advocate for the child in front of the child. You might think that you don't want to 'undermine' the other parent's parenting, but in the case of abuse, whether it be raging at the child, berating the child, making fun of the child – anything that feels abusive, that makes you think, "This is just wrong," "This is hurting our child and could very well be scarring him for life," that is the time to do your best to advocate for the child and say to the other parent, "You're hurting Paul's feelings. He doesn't deserve to be talked to that way. Can you please be more respectful in the way you treat him?" Then, even if the abusive parent continues with the hurtful treatment of the child, at least your child will feel he is not alone and that someone is on his side and is sticking up for him: namely, you. That will go a long way towards helping your child make it through the painful and unkind treatment he is receiving from the other parent.

it matters

Following is a quote from Gabriel Russo, D.C./Energy Worker:

"When I was growing up, my father was very abusive to me. His anger towards his own life came out at me, and he would criticize me about anything. If I dropped a fork on the floor, he would ask, "What's wrong with you?!" As a youngster, this was very painful, because I didn't understand that it had nothing to do with me, and it left me feeling demeaned and with a low self-esteem. When I was young, I didn't realize there was anything wrong, but I now realize that my father's abuse affected my sense of self in a very destructive way. Forty years later, my mother told me that the only thing she and my father fought about was how he treated me so hurtfully. I asked her why she didn't tell him to stop in front of me. She said she didn't want to undermine my father. I believe that having an ally back then would have made a big difference in my life."

once more with feeling

Whether your child is being bullied at school or at home by another parent, it is important that you advocate for the child in front of the child. In that way, no matter the outcome of the situation, your child will feel you cared deeply about their feelings and their well-being, and they will feel supported and advocated for. Then, however the situation works out, your child will not have felt all alone and left to fend for themselves. Rather, they will know they were loved, cared about, and advocated for. Armed with that support and love, they will be able to get through anything, unscarred.

Even in the case of one spouse tearing down the child, it is more important that the child feel supported and advocated for and that they are not alone and have an ally in one parent than one parent not "undermining" the other. It is different from when one parent is instructing or telling the child they can't go over to Johnnie's tonight. That would be undermining. But standing up for your child while they are being verbally abused may seem to the other parent like you are 'undermining' them, but I assure you the 'undermining' you are doing to the abusive parent is *nothing* compared to the damage you will do to your child if you do not stand up for him or her and do your absolute best to stop the verbal abuse from happening. Even if you can't stop it, your child will know that you tried your best and will feel loved and supported – just because you stood up for him or her.

Being there for your child and showing them love and support, in front of the bully(ies), in all cases of adversity will work wonders for your child's happiness all through their life and infuse them with the feeling that they are never alone and can get through anything, no matter how hard.

CHAPTER 25

A COLLECTION OF STORIES

Children LOVE stories. Children get lost in a story. And while they are mesmerized by the story of the handsome prince and the smitten princess, they glean the lessons cleverly woven into the story, and those lessons become ingrained in their moral conscience forever. I remember sitting around the campfire at eight years old at summer camp, surrounded by majestic mountains, listening to the camp director masterfully tell stories. I especially remember, like it was yesterday, the story about the little sparrow flying as high as she could over and over again in an effort to talk to God. Now, every time I look up at the twinkling stars, I remember that each one of those lights was made by one of the sparrow's Heaven-bound attempts to meet with God, and I feel inspired to want to know God. And I am filled with the good feelings I had while I listened to the story and loving being a part of a camp family that sang with me, laughed with me, and accepted me for who I was. Warm feelings. Precious memories.

To make it easier for you parents to have a variety of stories readily available for bedtime, I am providing you with some wonderful stories full of helpful life lessons, which will stand your child in good stead for the rest of their life. Tell your child stories everywhere you go and often: while putting them to bed, driving in the car, preparing dinner – whenever your child begs you to tell them one of your enchanting stories.

My father tucked my brother and me into bed every night, and he always either sang us some songs or told us a story that he had made up just for us. My favorite story was "The Calf and the Giraffe Go on a Picnic". I have cherished my dad's stories about "The Calf and the Giraffe" my whole life, as not only was it created by my father just for my brother and me, but also because I loved it when his animal characters came to vibrant life to teach us valuable lessons about friendship and love.

You can make up your own stories for your child. You can even tailor them to your child's challenge du jour. It's not as daunting as you might think – all you have to do is sit down at your desk with a pen and 10-11 pieces of paper in front of you and sit quietly as you close your eyes and see what story pops into your head: Maybe it's a ladybug having a conversation with a beetle, and they are deciding whether to climb a tree or swing on a branch in the backyard. Maybe the Lady Bug wants to swing on the branch and the Beetle wants to climb the tree, and they have to come up with a compromise if they want to hang out together. I just this second thought of that story, because I was reminded of my Grandma Harriett telling us the story, "Lady Bug, Lady Bug, Fly Away Home":

Lady Bug, Lady Bug, fly away home;
Your house is on fire and your children are alone.

Cheery, I know, but at least she was holding our hands and engaging us in a story! In a poem no less! We loved it! So you maybe don't want to tell a story about a bug whose house is on fire and her children are alone. But you can easily come up with a story about a scene playing in your head, laughing all the while at the silliness of your story. Once you begin making up stories on the spur of the moment, it will become effortless for you to come up with a bedtime story to tell your child, if you simply let it flow, and have a valuable life lesson in mind! Your child will be thrilled hearing the story you've made up just for him, and the more stories you make up, the easier it will get!

I also understand how busy parents can get maintaining a home and raising children at the same time. Finding the time to write a story can be out of the question some days. So for those days, I am sharing with you, for your ready reference, a few stories I have up my sleeve. The first is entitled, "The Calf and the Giraffe Go on a Picnic", made up by my dad – I added the pre-story when I put it to paper 20 years later. After that is one I wrote after I grew up, using the same characters, as a present to my father.

THE CALF AND THE GIRAFFE GO ON A PICNIC
by Edwin Stegman, prologue by Janet Stegman

There once was a boy whose name was Jonathan. His full name was Jonathan Martin, but his mommy and daddy called him Jonnie for short. Except when his mom was mad at him, then she called him Jon Martin. He had a neighbor, Butch, who liked to call him J.M. Jonnie liked it when Butch called him J.M. – it made him feel grown up.

But mostly Jonnie liked being a kid and making sandcastles in the sandbox his parents built for him in the backyard. Jonnie didn't even mind going to bed at night, because every night when his mom tucked him in, she had a new story to tell him. Unless he felt sad or confused or angry or scared: Then she would just sit with him on his bed and talk to him – in a sweet kind of way – a way that always made him feel better.

This particular night, Jonnie was feeling frightened. "What's got you so frightened, precious Jonnie?" his mother asked. "When you turn out the lamp and leave after my story, I get scared because I'm all alone in here and it's dark."

"Oh," said his mom, thinking about that one. "But Jonnie," she said, "You're not completely without light. Because you're my shining star!" "I am?" Jonnie asked. "Yes, you are," his mom answered, gently kissing him on his forehead, "You see, Jonnie, inside of you shines a bright light filled with love."

"But how come the kids at school don't see that bright light of love inside of me the way you do?" Jonnie asked. "What do you mean?" his mother asked; she was puzzled as to why Jonnie would say such a thing. "Well, today at school, some of the kids were mean to me. They were calling me awful names, like 'stupid' and 'ugly', and it really hurt my feelings," explained Jonnie. "Don't they see the light of love inside me and know that they should be kind to me instead of mean?" Why do they say all those awful things?"

Jonnie's mother thought for a moment, and then she answered, "I don't know why those kids were being mean to you. Only they can answer that: Maybe their parents are mean to them and they were taking it out on you. Whatever the reason, the most important thing you need to remember is that if you believe in yourself, no one can tear down your self-confidence. You know what a beautiful person you are. People may say all kinds of things to you or about you, but if you believe in yourself and know, as I do, what a precious and handsome and brilliantly intelligent little boy you are, that's all that matters. People say or do mean things for all kinds of reasons, and all it means is that they aren't very happy with themselves. I'm not sure what the right way to handle that kind of situation is, but I think you can say something like, 'I'm sorry you are so miserable that you feel the need to be mean to me. I hope you feel better soon." The main thing is to always remember that you have a right to be treated with respect and kindness and to stand up for yourself. Do what feels right in the moment. You can't go wrong if you hold your head high, keep your dignity, and say your truth. You can always use quips and quibbles filled with truth bombs to deflect criticism and insults. And always remember to keep your sense of humor and have compassion for the less confident, the ones among us who are hurting."

"Oh, wow. I hadn't thought of it that way. I can do that. Thanks, Mom." Jonnie answered, amazed at how wise his mom was and how she always made him feel better with a little mommy wisdom. "And if you would like, I will go and talk to those kids' parents and the principal of the school to let them know they need to do whatever it takes to stop those kids from bullying you like that. You think about it and let me know what you would like me to do to make sure you feel protected and safe."

"Thanks, Mom. You always know how to make me feel better. Story please!" Jonnie demanded, knowing it would be the perfect ending to a beautiful day!

Jonnie's mom began telling her favorite story – the one about two dear friends, a calf and a giraffe:

One day, the calf and the giraffe set off for their weekly picnic in the park. Their moms had fixed them each a delicious lunch. The calf had a sprouts sandwich with pickles and Jello made from wheatgrass juice, and the giraffe had a leaf casserole that his mom had sprinkled with apricot twigs, just the way he liked it. Their dads had given them a quarter so they could buy an ice cream from the ice cream vendor.

> The calf and the giraffe walked a good three miles to the park, and by the time they got there, they were plenty hungry. They spread their blankets out under a big shady oak tree, as it was pretty warm that day, got themselves a cup of cold water from the rushing stream, and sat down for their special luncheon. "Mmmmm!" said the calif, "My mom is the *best* cook in the whole world!" "No way José," argued the giraffe, "My mom makes the most *delectable* leaf and twig casserole in the entire *universe*! Would you like a taste?" "Oh, definitely," said the calif, and he took a big bite. "Yum! Would you like to try my Jello?" "Certainly!" cried the giraffe. See, he had hoped the calf would offer him some of his yummie wheatgrass Jello. "Yummmie!" exclaimed the giraffe, "I guess both our moms are pretty darn good cooks!"

The two sat together on their blankets eating their lunch and watching the animals and human kids playing together. They played all sorts of games like frisbee and tag and freeze tag. Then the calf and the giraffe laid back and drifted off to sleep, feeling the warmth of the sun on their skin. "What a life," thought the calf as he drifted off to sleep. "This is a giraffe's paradise," thought the other.

After an hour or so, the calf and the giraffe woke up to the jingle of the ice cream cart passing through the park. "Ice cream!" yelled the calf; "Ice cream!" yelled the giraffe, as they ran to buy their favorite ice creams. A drumstick for the calf and a chocolate covered vanilla ice cream bar for the giraffe. Their mouths watered as they walked back to their blankets and took their first bites. All of a sudden, a bully jumped out from behind a bush and grabbed both of their ice creams. "Hey!"

239

yelled the calf. "Hey!" echoed the giraffe. "Those are ours! Our fathers gave us money to buy them! Give them back!"

But the bully only laughed and said, "They *were* yours, and now they're mine. Yum!" and he started eating their ice creams, a bite from one and then a bite from the other.

Just then, their old friend Mr. Pig ran over to where the three were standing. He himself had been picnicking under a shady cedar tree nearby. "You give my friends back their ice creams right now!" demanded Mr. Pig. But the bully refused, and in fact, laughed at Mr. Pig. The bully took one more bite of each ice cream and then turned to walk away so he could finish eating their ice creams without Mr. Pig haranguing him. As the bully was turning around, he tripped over a branch lying on the ground and fell down, ice cream flying everywhere. Embarrassed and nursing a scraped knee, the bully ran away. The calf and the giraffe started to cry. "That wasn't nice," protested the calf. "I was really looking forward to my ice cream," cried the giraffe. "I know," said Mr. Pig, in his understanding way. "It was very mean what that bully did to the two of you. Maybe I can help you feel a little better. The reason that boy was mean to you was because he feels sad inside. Any time a person is mean, it is because they don't like themselves and don't have it in them to be kind to others. They are mean to others in an attempt to make themselves feel superior, because inside they feel inferior. And they feel that since they feel sad inside, it's not fair that others don't, and that makes them feel jealous, so they try to bring them down so they don't have to feel jealous."

"Somehow that makes sense," said the calf, drying his eyes. "Yeah," agreed the giraffe, sniffling a little, "I understand. And ya know what? I feel kinda sorry for that bully and glad that I'm so happy inside and like being kind and generous with others. And ya know what else? I feel happy that I have a good friend like the calf who shares his wheatgrass Jello with me. And an understanding friend like you to stick up for us!" I bet that bully doesn't have any friends who share their yummie green wheatgrass Jello with him. Thanks, Mr. Pig."

"You're welcome. And secondly," added Mr. Pig, as he took two shiny new quarters out of his pocket, "I have been saving these for just the right time. This is the perfect opportunity to cheer some friends up, and I would like to buy you each other ice cream. And don't worry, I'll go with you and see to it that Mr. Bully stays away."

"Gee, thanks, Mr. Pig," exclaimed the calf, with a brightly beaming smile on his face. Mr. Pig escorted the two back to the ice cream cart, bought them their ice creams, and sat with them while they gobbled up their ice cream bars – with aplomb! When they had finished their ice creams, Mr. Pig bid farewell to the calf and the giraffe and headed for home. "What a story we have to tell our folks when we get home!" said the calf. "I'll say," agreed the giraffe. Then they gathered up their blankets and picnic baskets and headed for home as well.

As Jonnie's mother finished her story, she looked over at Jonnie, who had drifted off to sleep. "Good-night, my precious little boy," she whispered, as she planted another gentle kiss on his forehead, being careful not to wake him. "I love you." And with that, she tiptoed out of his room and closed the door, content in the knowledge that she could send him off into a peaceful and contented sleep. As Jonnie's mom left Jonnie's room, she turned off the light. She knew he would not be scared if he woke up, because Jonnie's heart shined bright and lit up the whole room!

THE CALF AND THE GIRAFFE AND THE POTATO ART
by Janet Stegman, idea by Edwin Stegman, her dad

Jonathan Martin Belmont was an adorable little boy who was a delight to have around. He had great fun playing with his friends, going places with his family, and learning at school. And sometimes Jonnie felt confused about things that happened to him. On this one particular evening, as his dad was tucking him in, Jonnie said, "Daddy, am I a handsome boy?"

Jonnie's father of course was surprised by his son's question, because he had always thought Jonnie was an extremely handsome boy, and he thought Jonnie knew how handsome he was. He answered his son with a very enthusiastic, "Absolutely! You are the most handsome little boy I know! And the smartest, kindest, and the most fun, too! Why would you ask such a question?"

"Because I'm the shortest boy in my class. Some of the kids call me 'shorty', and sometimes they call me 'ugly' too," Jonnie told his father. "It makes me feel sad, and I wish they wouldn't call me that."

"Jon," Jonnie's father said quite seriously, "You are an adorable child. Besides that, you have plenty of growing to do, and each child grows at their own pace. Your body's just taking its time so it can be sure it gets it right. About you thinking there's a chance those kids are right about you being 'ugly', well, there isn't. You are quite a beautiful little boy. Don't you believe a single word those bullies said. Remember the story your mother told you about the calf and the giraffe on their picnic? Remember what Mr. Pig said about why people say mean things? Because they're sad inside and are trying to make themselves feel superior? Even though being mean doesn't really make anyone feel any better.

"Well, I have another story for you that I think you'll really like."

"Oh, tell me the story, please!" Jonnie beseeched his father, "And I hope it's about the calf and the giraffe again! I like those two." Jonnie's father was glad his little boy loved his mom and dad's stories, because that was one of his favorite things about being a dad. Besides that, he had made all his stories up himself!

Jonnie's father, with great joy, told Jonnie another story about the calf and the giraffe, only this one started out with two dear friends at school. It went like this:

One day the calf and the giraffe were at school – they were glad to be in the same class that year, since they were, after all, best friends.

That morning, their teacher, Mrs. Stevens, stood in front of the class with a tray full of Idaho potatoes. Just ordinary potatoes. They were all different shapes – some were large, some were small, some were skinny, some fat, some had lumps and bumps.

What was their teacher doing with a tray of potatoes? Well, Mrs. Stevens got the class' attention and said, "Today we are going to decorate potatoes. If you will notice, we have a crafts table set up in front here, piled with all sorts of arts and crafts materials." She pointed to a long table with all kinds of decorations. "You can use as many of these as you wish. It's not a contest: Each person's potato will be as appreciated as the next. You have an hour. Oh, and you can help each other with ideas if you wish. Have fun!" And with that, Mrs. Stevens walked down the aisles and handed each student a potato.

The students were all very excited. There were so many fun crafts to choose from! As the hour went on, the students began cutting out felt shapes, gluing, painting – all the while talking and laughing, and admiring each other's work. The students were amazed at how talented and creative their classmates were. "What are you doing with your potato?" Billy asked Jane. "I'm making an elephant, see? I rolled the pieces of construction paper into a trunk and legs, and this little piece of felt will be its tail," answered Jane. "Oh," said Billy, "That's pretty neat. It makes me feel like I'm in a deep, dark jungle in Africa, with wild animals all around."

"What's your potato turning into?" the calf asked the giraffe. "It's a bush with flower blossoms all over it. I'm using these sequins to make it look like a plant," said the giraffe. "It makes me hungry for some of your mom's leaf and twig casserole!" joked the calf. "And the red, pink, and yellow tissue paper cut into tiny pieces and wadded up are going to be glued on for flower blossoms!" explained the giraffe, so proud of his exquisite potato art. "And you?" he asked the calf. "I'm designing a fancy, flowing gown for my potato. First, I'm making a pattern out of tissue paper just like my dad does when he makes scarves for my mom. Our long necks can get very cold sometimes, you know. Then I'll get some crepe paper and stitch the dress together and put eyes, a nose, hair, and a big smile on its face!" Said the calf as he busily cut out his crepe paper dress.

"Oohhhh, I can't wait to see it," exclaimed the giraffe, his voice fluttering with anticipation.

As the nightshade adornment hour drew to a close, the students put the final touches on their art work. "Is everyone about done?" asked Mrs. Stevens, tickled by the masterpieces she was seeing.

"Yes!" answered the class.

"All right then. Mr. Calf, Will you please come to the front of the class and show us your potato?"

The calf went to the front of the class and showed off his fancy potato. It was dressed in a flowing crepe gown and had a cheery smiling face. The calf explained that he used beads for the eyes, beige felt for the nose, brown yarn for the hair, some red wax for the lips, and had painted in the teeth with white paint. The class and Mrs. Stevens applauded.

After the calf sat down, Mrs. Stevens called on the giraffe, and he explained how he had created his colorful bush. Again, the audience applauded. Mrs. Stevens had each student come up and show off their potato. The class admired the way each potato was decorated and had a wonderful time seeing all the different versions. They felt like they had been to a potato art museum.

After that lovely show, Mrs. Sevens said to the class, "My, this was fun. We'll have to do it again soon. Next time we'll decorate . . . avocados! But I want you all to notice something. Did any of you think that one potato was more attractive than the others? More valuable than the rest?" Some students shook their heads; some answered, "No."

"You felt that each potato was beautiful and unique in its own way; that they were all very different, but each was lovely just the way it was, correct?"

"Right!" exclaimed the students.

"Did any of you dislike your potato, or think it was 'ugly'?"

"No!"

"The potatoes came in all different shapes: Some were large, some were small, some were skinny, some fat, some had lumps, and some had bumps. Did any of you feel your potato was unattractive or unworthy in any way because of its shape?"

"No way!" answered some. "Nope," said the rest.

"All were equally worthy and equally beautiful, right?"

"Right!" echoed the class. "Mrs. Stevens, what are you trying to teach us?" Billy asked.

"Well," Mrs. Stevens answered, with a twinkle in her eye, "People and animals are like potatoes. They come in all shapes and sizes. And all are deserving of beautiful decoration. Some people have an image in their mind of what a 'perfect" body looks like, but the thing is, there is no such thing as a 'perfect' body. Each one is attractive in its own way. Just like with the potatoes. Each one is different, and each is worthy. Each one can be dressed up and look stunning. Always remember that, no matter what you look like, no matter if you're tall, thin, short, fat, no matter the color of your hair, the color of your eyes, or the color of your skin, you are magnificent and deserving of love and respect."

Jonnie's father kissed his little boy on the forehead and said, "Good-night, handsome."

"Good night, Daddy . . . thank you," Jonnie said as he set his head on his pillow and closed his eyes, hoping his mom would make eggs and hash browns for breakfast in the morning. He felt like the most handsome and beautiful little boy in the whole world.

THE STAINED GLASS
Told at campfires at YMCA Camp Ta Ta Pochon and Memorialized by Rockin' Camp Director Kim Garber

A famous artist was busily decorating one of the most prominent cathedrals in France. He had boxes of strained glass of every color lying around for him to use to create his most magnificent piece of artwork - front and center of the church. It was huge and it took him months to construct. In one of the boxes of stained glass was this one small and insignificant piece of glass. Every time the artist rummaged through the box, the little piece of glass tried to "polish itself up and shine in a spectacular way" so that the artist would see it and use it in his holy work of art.

The months rolled by, and day after day, the little piece of stained glass was left in the box, feeling it had surely been forgotten. Instead of giving up, the little piece of glass decided to look for a ray of sunshine so that its beauty could be noticed by the artist. Still feeling ignored as the project was rolling to a close, the little piece of glass wanted to cry. After all, this beautiful mosaic would be there throughout time, and the little glass was sad thinking it would not be a part of something so special to honor God. Resolved that it would never be noticed, the little piece of glass started to cry. Just then, as the artist rummaged one last time through the box, he saw it and brought it to the top. It could see the sun! It wanted so badly to shine as brightly as the sun! Trying to emulate the sun, the little piece of glass threw its rays of light around the church, beaming with all its might. With one final burst, the little piece of glass beamed as hard as it could hoping against hope the artist wouldn't miss it and put it away with the other remnants. It sure didn't want to spend the rest of its days hidden and in the dark. Just then the artist, who had been staring in the box for a long, long time trying to find just the right final piece for his stained glass window, picked up the little piece of glass. "PERFECT!" he exclaimed, "Absolutely PERFECT!"

As the artist carefully placed the little piece of glass in the last spot, the artist stood back and admired the most beautiful depiction of Jesus the world would ever see. All the church members came to the revealing ceremony for the stained glass window, and from there on, for hundreds of years, everyone who saw it noticed the little piece of glass said, "Look at the SPARKLE in Jesus's eye...look at it shine! GORGEOUS, ABSOLUTELY GORGEOUS!"

And so the little piece of glass found its way into the stained glass window as the most important piece in the entire window. It shined every day, and all throughout time, with pride and joy. Although ever so small and different from all the rest, it found its niche and made a difference in the world!

THE SPARROW
by Someone at Camp

Before there were people on the earth, there were animals walking around being greedy and not treating each other with kindness or respect. God saw this and was angry. He said, "You're not following the golden rule: Do unto others as you would have others do unto you." The animals heard what God had to say and replied, "So? We're going to do whatever we darn well please!" Well, then God placed a black cloak between the earth and the sky so that there was no more light on earth. The animals were very upset: They didn't think God had the power to do such a thing. They cried to each other, "What are we going to do? We can't see! Someone has to go and talk to God and tell him we're sorry". They tried to find God to tell him they were sorry, but it was too dark, and they couldn't see to look for him. They gave up all hope of ever apologizing to God for their transgressions and having light back on the earth. The animals reconciled themselves to living out the rest of their days in the dark. Except for one little sparrow, who said, "I'm not giving up. I'm going to fly up and see if I can reach God and tell him we're sorry and get us our darn light back!" The next day, the little sparrow took off and flew as high as he possibly could. Each day he tried again, his little beak poking further through the darkness with each attempt before he got tired and came back down. The little sparrow refused to give up. He spent many days flying up attempting to reach God. This last time, he tried so hard and flew so high, that, exhausted, he fell back down to earth and died. All the other animals felt bad for the little sparrow.

God was touched by the sparrow's dedication and tenacity. He said to the animals, "Because your little sparrow was so determined to let me know you were sorry and ready to change your ways for the better, I will give you another chance and give you your light back. But it's only going to be light half the time. The other half of the time, you will have darkness. That way, you will always remember to follow the Golden Rule and be kind to one another." And that's why we have stars. When you look up at the sky at night after dark, you can see all the little poke marks the sparrow made each time he tried to reach God.

CHAPTER 26

LET'S REVIEW

you cannot overload a kid . . .
if they feel loved and supported

You're probably wondering, "How can a kid do so much and never get overloaded?" I honestly feel you cannot overload a kid – as long as they feel loved. Because they're so in the moment. If they feel loved and happy and not pressured to be any way or do any certain activity, and not criticized, but rather appreciated, acknowledged, validated, encouraged, and complimented, they're going to live each moment in the moment. And then nothing can overwhelm them. They will never feel overwhelmed because they're not thinking about the past; they're not thinking about the future; they're in the moment, enjoying life.

If you keep all that I have written in mind and give your child the opportunities, and if they feel loved and wanted and supported, they can handle anything. They will live in the moment and never feel overwhelmed or weighted down. And that's really the key to happiness: living each moment in the moment and not dredging up your past or worrying about the future.

keep your child busy with
constructive and fun activities

If you keep your child busy with constructive, creative, and fun activities, that will keep their mind occupied. It'll keep their energy channeled, and then they won't have a single chance to think about or contemplate doing anything other than constructive, creative, and fun activities. They'll just be in the moment creating projects, swinging on the swings, singing, dancing, and playing sports.

Children are an endless source of energy. For parents, it's just a matter of steering that energy – offering their children constructive pathways for that energy, giving their boundless energy an outlet – somewhere to go – enveloped by positive and expansive parenting.

Children have boundless energy because they are as close to pure spirit as any light being can get. Spirit has boundless energy. If you don't cover over your child's spirit with doubts, fears, criticisms, and judgments, they will have boundless energy all their life. You'll raise an "ascended master". An ascended master: an enlightened being. Just happy and light and expanded and in the moment in each moment! Honor their spirit by encouraging them to excel in whatever it is that they want to excel in. Do your best never to make them wrong. Constantly be praising the heck out of them. Praise them and compliment them and encourage them and support them. Pretend you're their happiness coach – their expansion coach – their spiritual awakening coach.

You may be wondering, "How busy should my child be?" Leave that up to your child. Give them options. Like I have said, children are not a piece of clay; they're a frozen pizza! They already know what they love and what they want to excel at. Ask them, "Would you like to go to the park right now?" "Would you like to do some crafts?" "Would you like to take some dance classes?" "Wanna sing with me?" Give them choices, and they'll pick something, I promise.

Interaction is a big key. It's not only about taking your child to dance classes and signing them up for baseball. It's about you singing with them and making crafts with them and swinging with them on the swings with them. It's about doing fun, interactive things together: the fun times that you have together. It's both. Giving them music lessons and baton lessons and sending them to martial arts classes is a big part of helping them get good at something and experience what the world has to offer. It is equally beneficial for you to spend time with your child doing things that don't necessarily cost money. I mean, maybe you have a ton of money, or maybe you are just barely squeezing by. Either way – it doesn't matter: It's the quality of time you spend with your child that matters. If you have plenty of money and want to enroll your child in dance lessons and singing lessons and Karate, by all means, do it! Those things are wonderful for children! But if those kinds of things are not in your budget, then teach your child what *you* know – teach them what *you* are good at, and have fun doing it. They will remember those times with great fondness their whole life. Every time they do an activity you taught them or introduced them to, they'll look back and remember that; a smile will come over their face, and they will feel a fondness for that time. It will remind them of your special times together.

Spend plenty of time together with your child – reading, telling stories, singing, dancing, laughing, and going to the park. If it's doable, say to them, "Are there some classes you would like me to enroll you in?" Maybe go watch one together. After you've watched for a while, ask, "Is this something you would like to learn?" "Yes, it is." "Okay." Defer to your child constantly. They know what they want. They know what they need.

When you provide your child with fun, creative, and fulfilling things to do, you are not only channeling their energy in a positive direction, you are exposing them to the different activities in life. You are giving them options – trying on different outfits, sampling the different flavors of ice cream, letting them do as much as they want. Children have boundless energy, and a week chock-full of a variety of different activities will keep them focused, occupied, and busy with constructive, fun, and challenging projects and activities.

but don't show them *Bambi* until they're eighteen!

Definitely don't show them *Bambi*. They can watch *Bambi* when they're eighteen. On their eighteenth birthday, you can tell them, "Well, now that you're eighteen, you can watch *Bambi*. But you don't have to. You don't *ever* have to."

why are these pillars so important
to your child's development?

All these skills that I have given you: the gift of pets, making your child laugh, sharing music with them, dancing together, showering them with compliments, quality time spent together, keeping your mouth shut. These pillars are important because they will allow your child to feel relaxed as they try all the different flavors of life. Crafts, sports, the park, writing, reading. Like you're taking them wine tasting – non-alcoholic, of course. Or like you're going to the bakery to sample wedding cake. You get to take them to sample everything. Every time you introduce something to them, your child's memory of that activity and their feelings towards it will be infused with joy and love, because they're with you, they're feeling loved, they're feeling safe, they're feeling acknowledged, and they're feeling empowered. Every memory they have of their sampling of the different activities is going to be infused with fun and good feelings. That will give them the opportunity to see what kinds of things they want to focus on in their life. It gives them a frame of reference for what's out there in the world. It trains them. It develops their mind in positive and challenging ways. It gives them the ability to pick and choose what they want to do on a larger scale. When you expose them to the different activities, they can evaluate whether they like them or not. It's not that, "Oh, well, now that I've signed you up for this, you gotta do it for the rest of your life." Rather, it gives them the ability to re-evaluate and be open at different points in their life to the fact that different things will be a good fit at different times.

honor your child's choices

If your child tells you, "I want to take dancing lessons." "Okay, what kind?" "Ballet." So you enroll them. Then a few months later they say, "Mmmm, I don't really want to take ballet lessons any more." You just say, "Okay." If you force them – if you try to force them to participate in or stay with any particular activity or interest that they no longer want to do, it's going to turn them the other way. Let your child take the lead.

You simply introduce them to things. It's like you're their tour guide, and you're letting them decide what cities they want to see. Honor and have full respect for their wants, needs, desires, and opinions as human beings. Give them credence for everything they say, think, and feel. That way, you'll have a blast being a parent. And your child will have a blast being a kid.

making your role as a parent easier

Treating your child with respect and giving their ideas credence will make your role as a parent a whole lot easier than if you don't. You will also be given the added benefit of watching your child develop into a person who treats others with respect. In addition to them being happy and fulfilled, they also will treat others with kindness and caring, because that's the way you treated them. That's what you modeled for them. That's what you taught them was the right way to be. You will have in your home a human being who creates healthy relationships, one who treats others, including you, with respect, and one who expects that they, themselves, will be treated with respect, and acts accordingly.

the benefits of keeping this book handy
and on the bottom shelf

This was not meant to be an "entertaining" book. My goal in writing this book has not been to "entertain" parents or have them rolling on the floor. That's coming in my next book, *"No Soup for You!"*, an expose on how to attract the people you want in your life and create your dreams to come true, by being autonomous, confident, and happy on the inside and keeping your sense of humor about everything.

I know you are looking for information on the best way to parent your child, and I have tried to give you the necessary principles for raising your child into a healthy, happy, confident, and respectful adult. There will be situations that arise in the course of your child-rearing that you will just scratch your head and go, "I have no idea what to do here!" Believe me, that is a normal reaction to almost every situation when parenting a child. You will read a chapter and say, "Huh. That's good information. I've been wondering about that." But then you'll read the book again a year later, and there will be something in another chapter that will jump out at you to use in your current situation. I guarantee that as you look at these principles, one of them will talk right to where you are in your life and your child rearing. What chapter speaks to you and when will depend on where you are in your life and what challenges you are facing at that particular moment. What works when your child is two years old – what skills you will need at that age – will be different from what works and what skills you will need when they are sixteen. Feel free to read this book multiple times and reference whatever chapters apply to where you are in your life and your child's upbringing.

no addicts here!

Aside from helping you raise a healthy, happy, expanded, and creative child who is pleasant to be around, my intention has been to show parents specifically what to do and what not to do so that their child never feels the need to turn to addiction or other self-destructive behaviors in order to survive life's difficulties. By sharing with you what Chris had to say about what got him to the park and what caused him to become an addict, I feel I have given you valuable information. I have shared with you what he feels as he looks back over his life about what caused his malady and what he wishes his grandmother had done differently. You have the benefit of learning, from the work I have done with him, what he figured out at age 30 after living a not-so-healthy, happy, or expanded life for that time. It's not just about not putting your child on drugs – my suggestions come from fifteen years of working with addicts and people with depression and other mental and emotional maladies, seeing what their parents did and didn't do that caused them problems later in life, and figuring out what their parents could have done differently so that they could have avoided those problems.

As they say, "An ounce of prevention is worth a pound of cure." It's true: Listening to suggestions from someone who has worked with countless clients helping them shed their depression, anger, and resentment; their longing for loving, nurturing, and supportive parents;

and their sadness that they never got what they needed is invaluable. Being equipped with valuable knowledge gleaned by one who has gone before you and harnessed what *to* do and *not* to do as a parent to raise a happy child is going to make the difference between a parenting experience filled with angst, frustration, and disappointment and a parenting adventure infused with confidence, enjoyment, love, and fun. So there you are. You're welcome.

CHAPTER 27

....

THE BLINK OF AN EYE

the most empowering thing
my parents ever did for me

Looking back at my childhood, I see that the most empowering thing that my parents ever did for me was to take a hands-on interest in my life. It enabled me to turn out brilliant, happy, and successful. They gave me whatever lessons I asked for and stayed to watch – never a single complaint. They were always absolutely engrossed in whatever it was that I was learning. And they let me decide what I wanted to learn and participate in and when, and they let me learn at my own pace and practice on my own. They trusted me to keep myself safe and always be at my best.

My parents were intimately involved in my performing arts pursuits. They came to every concert, every dance recital, every play I ever performed in. Either my mom or my dad were there at most of my singing lessons, fascinated and interested throughout. When it came to pursuing my performing arts endeavors by myself, I pursued them with panache and an unbridled passion and became a brilliant performer. I LOVED it. Even as an adult, my parents were supportive about whatever I wanted to pursue. They told me how proud they were of me – I mean, yeah, my dad would bug me about professional theatre; yeah, there were glitches, but he came to be proud of me – even though I was "only" brilliant in my "community" theatre productions. My parents were involved, hands-on parents. Like I said, there were some glitches, like when my mom was out to lunch when she and my dad were going through their break-up. But for the most part, they were absolutely involved, hands-on, interested, and patient parents.

the great bonding experience
of clothes shopping with my parents

My mother would take me shopping for clothes. It was clear that she really cared about every aspect of my life. I always felt she wanted to make sure I was taken care of. When we went clothes shopping, we'd go in the dressing room together, and she'd help me try on clothes and then put them back on the hanger when they didn't fit. We just had a ball going clothes shopping. It was clear my mom thoroughly enjoyed our shopping escapades. "Does this look good on me?" "Oh, I don't know, try this one." Or, "I'll go get you a bigger size." It was a total mother-daughter bonding experience just going shopping. Same when we went out for a meal at a restaurant or to the movies or to see a play. And we'd sing on the way there. When I was a teenager, my dad used to take me to "Fred Segal" and buy me hip huggers and other 'hip' outfits. To this day, I remember how much fun I had clothes shopping with my parents. Because they were so happy to be clothes shopping with me.

Parenting is going to be a mixed bag; you're never going to be a perfect parent. Your child is going to grow up, and they're going to find stuff to complain about. But they're mostly going to find stuff to appreciate, because those are the things that led them to become the superior person that they are.

The most important thing – even though you're not going to be a perfect parent – is to, as much as you can, have a hands-on interest in your child's happiness, upbringing, life, development, and learning. Don't just send them to school and never ask them what they're learning. Be involved in...*want* to know what they're learning. Know who they're spending their time with. Be involved, be very involved, in their life, their activities, their relationships, but allow them the space to hang out with their friends and figure out by themselves who they want to be.

one day out of the year they get to do anything they want with you

I have a good friend who raised a daughter who is now accomplished and happy and married with a little boy of her own. One of the things my friend did when his daughter was young was to set aside one day out of the year – I mean, he didn't restrict this to just one day – but one day a year, *in stone,* when he would take off work and the two of them would go and do whatever the daughter wanted.

If she wanted to go to Winnipeg to the zoo, they would do that. Maybe it was the Children's Museum. When she became a teenager, they would go to the theatre. She always knew she could pick one activity that was exciting to her, and her dad would take her to do that activity. On that day, they would give each other their undivided attention – no cell phones were allowed the entire time they were together! And then when she grew up, once a year, she would take a day off from work, and they would go to a baseball game in the afternoon and have lunch at the restaurant on third base. They would eat on the patio together and watch the game. It was pretty far away to see the game, but it was a special time for both of them. One time, her husband wanted to tag along. She told him, "No, this is a special day for just me and my father – you and I can go to a baseball game another time." Those are the times daughters and sons remember all their lives and hold in their hearts forever.

The same friend has a son who, rather than go and eat lunch on third base, wanted his parents to come and watch his baseball games. He *loved* that his parents came to every *single* game he ever played and cheered him on. It didn't matter who won; they were there to show their support for him and how much he meant to them. When he grew up, the son became a professional baseball player. Hmmmm, see any kind of connection there? When the son graduated from college, my friend and his wife looked at each other and said, "What the heck are we going to do with ourselves now that our youngest son has graduated college?!" They were so used to gearing everything around going to watch him play ball – it had become a highlight of their parenting years. I'm assuming some great nachos, too!!

if you travel with your kids when they're young, they'll travel with you when you're old

The things you do with your children when they are young they will do with you when you are old. Oh boy, will you ever appreciate that! When your kids grow up – and they will – you will appreciate them still wanting to spend time with you.

never a question in my mind

I told you my mom took an active interest in every aspect of my life. Towards the end of her life, when she asked me to come and take care of her, there was never any question in my mind whether or not I "wanted" to take care of her – I did not hesitate for a second to say, "Yes, of course." I *wanted* to come and live with her and take care of her. I mean, yeah, it's karma. But more than that, it's like a thank you. Well, part of it is a thank you, and part of it is that your child has grown to the point where that is just who they are. Because you modeled that for them when they were young, they have an innate desire to return the favor. Giving back will just come naturally to them.

be there for them

I want to talk a little bit about "being there" for your child. I know we've established that if you're there for them when they're young, they'll be there for you when you're old. So, yes, be there for them when they're young. If they ever get in trouble, be there for them. Don't do tough love unless you absolutely, absolutely need to. Tough love is a very, very last resort. If they're way off the deep end, and you've exhausted every avenue, yes, do tough love. But if they need you, be there for them. Nobody's perfect. We *all* make mistakes; we *all* get ourselves into jams. When your parents aren't judging or criticizing you for getting yourself into those jams, life goes a whole lot smoother. The bad times smooth themselves out much more quickly if your parents don't give you a hard time about every misstep and allow you to learn the lesson that was there for you to learn. So be there for them when they get into a jam; don't judge; don't criticize. When it's all over, you can laugh about it and poke fun, but in a sweet way, never in a harsh put-down kind of way. Be the kind of family that is *always* there for each other. Even in times of stupid.

setting up the foundation
for a close-knit relationship

If you are there for your child when they are growing up, they will feel much closer to you later in life, and they will be there for you when you're old and *you* need *them*. When you're a parent, you have to be there for your child so you don't go to jail. But if you do it with great love and devotion and unending compassion, your bond with them will never go away. When your child grows up, they will do the things with you in the same loving and patient way that you did them with your child.

perfectly imperfect parenting

There are going to be times when it's not always perfect; you're not going to be the perfect parent; it's not going to always be the perfect situation. But when you spend quality time on your parenting, it always works out better. Your child will feel your love; they will hear your kind words; they will forgive the imperfections. It's just never going to be perfect, so you had better start forgiving yourself now. If you forgive yourself and lead with love, *that* leading with love is what your child will take away from their childhood and remember always.

it will all go by in the blink of an eye,
so cherish each moment

I *promise* those eighteen years will go by in blink of an eye. I'm telling you, if you don't make every effort to spend quality time with your child in each moment, all of a sudden they're all grown up and out of the house. If you spend that quality time with them, you're going to look back and say, "Shoot! I wish I had spent more time with my child!" If you find that you didn't, there's no going back and re-doing those childhood years – those precious, precious childhood years. Nobody has ever had inscribed on their tombstone, "I wish I had spent more time at the office."

Before you know it, your child will be all grown up. You blinked, and they're an adult. Enjoy every baseball game that you can, because the games are over before you know it.

you'll find stuff to do when they move out, don't worry

When your child grows up all happy and ready to face the world – with all the courage, self-confidence, and excitement anyone could ask for, you may have the feeling, "What the heck do I do now?" I mean, your child has become an adult; they're going off to live their own life; they'll probably go and have a family of their own. When they have their own life and their own family, you will want to continue to have a relationship with them. And you will, if you cultivated a loving and attentive relationship with them when they were young. If you did, you're in like Flynn. With your devotion to their upbringing and your anxious anticipation to be involved in every aspect of their life, while at the same time giving them the space to be their own person and learn through trial and error, you will have built the foundation for that continued relationship. You will have built that foundation when they were young – you will have taken the time and the attention to love them, get to know them, genuinely be interested in their trevails and their feelings and their interests. You will have established a relationship with them that will remain in place forever.

Don't neglect this time – don't waste a single second, because your child's childhood years will be over in the blink of an eye. But if you have taken the time to build that strong foundation, your relationship with them will continue on forever. Those first eighteen years are your time to make your contribution. Make your contribution – in the most enthusiastic, generous, and fun ways, and then you will have them forever. Cherish each moment with your child; you will be glad you did. Cherish each precious moment. Make each moment wonderful.

The most important job you will ever have is being a parent to the child sitting in front of you. You are the most cherished gift in the life of that child. Make that gift magnificent!

www.ingramcontent.com/pod-product-compliance
Lightning Source LLC
Chambersburg PA
CBHW051509120626
46551CB00012B/839